IS THERE A HUMAN NATURE?

BOSTON UNIVERSITY STUDIES IN PHILOSOPHY AND RELIGION

General Editor: Leroy S. Rouner

Volume Eighteen

Is There a Human Nature?

Edited by

Leroy S. Rouner

UNIVERSITY OF NOTRE DAME PRESS

Notre Dame, Indiana

Library of Congress Cataloging-in-Publication Data

Is there a human nature? / edited by Leroy S. Rouner.
    p.   cm. — (Boston University studies in philosophy and
religion ; vol. 18)
  Includes bibliographical references and index.
  ISBN 0-268-01181-8 (cloth : alk. paper)
  1. Philosophical anthropology.   I. Rouner, Leroy S.   II. Series:
Boston University studies in philosophy and religion ; v. 18.
BD450.I592   1997
128—dc21   97-20808
                                                     CIP

Contents

Preface

Boston University Studies in Philosophy and Religion is a joint project of the Boston University Institute for Philosophy and Religion and the University of Notre Dame Press. The essays in each annual volume are edited from the previous year's lecture program and invited papers of the Boston University Institute. The Director of the Institute, who is also the General Editor of these Studies, chooses participants to lecture at Boston University in the course of the academic year. The Editor then selects and edits the essays to be included in the volume. Dr. Barbara Darling-Smith, Assistant Director of the Institute, regularly copyedits the essays. In preparation is Volume 19, *Loneliness.*

The Boston University Institute for Philosophy and Religion was begun informally in 1970 under the leadership of Professor Peter Bertocci of the Department of Philosophy, with the cooperation of Dean Walter Mueder of the School of Theology, Professor James Purvis, Chair of the Department of Religion, and Professor Marx Wartofskky, Chair of the Department of Philosophy. Professor Peter Bertocci was concerned to institutionalize one of the most creative features of Boston personalism, its interdisciplinary approach to fundamental issues of human life. When Professor Leroy S. Rouner became Director in 1975, and the Institute became a formal center of the Boston University Graduate School, every effort was made to continue that vision of an ecumenical and interdisciplinary forum.

Within the University the Institute is committed to open interchange on fundamental issues in philosophy and religious study which transcend the narrow specializations of academic curricula. We seek to counter those trends in higher education which emphasize technical expertise in a "multi-versity" and gradually transform undergraduate liberal arts education into preprofessional training.

Our programs are open to the general public and are regularly broadcast on WBUR-FM, Boston University's National Public Radio affiliate. Outside the University we seek to recover the public tradition of philosophical discourse which was a lively part of American intellectual life in the early years of this century before the professionalization of both philosophy and religious reflection made these two disciplines topics virtually unavailable even to an educated public. We note, for example, that much of William James's work was presented originally as public lectures, and we are grateful to James's present-day successors for the significant public papers which we have been honored to publish. This commitment to a public tradition in American intellectual life has important stylistic implications. At a time when too much academic writing is incomprehensible, or irrelevant, or both, our goal is to present readable essays by acknowledged authorities on critical human issues.

Acknowledgments

Our first debt, as always, is to our authors, who make these volumes possible. I am especially grateful to my colleagues at Boston University who participate in the Institute's programs without honoraria. But my major debt is always to my colleague and dear friend Barbara Darling-Smith, the Institute's Assistant Director, who does the hard work of manuscript preparation with awesome expertise, indefatigable good cheer, and a sunny optimism which will not down. She is a joy to work with; each year is more fun than the last.

This year she has been greatly helped by Charity Rouse who now knows things about our scanner which Barbara and I can scarcely imagine. Charity has skillfully balanced her graduate work in music and theology with her work at the Institute, and has been an invaluable contributor to the preparation of this volume. Syd Smith and Alicia Jones also provided last-minute assistance.

Ann Rice, our Editor at the University of Notre Dame Press, shepherds our manuscripts through the publication process. Her calm in the midst of crisis, and her quiet efficiency, are as legendary as her warm good will, and I am delighted to have this annual occasion to thank her.

Finally, another tip of my Chicago Cubs baseball cap in the direction of Jim Langford, Director of the University of Notre Dame Press. He is our fast friend and a fellow philosopher as well as our publisher. He has lectured in our Institute program, has coedited one of our volumes, and continues to be a source of insight and inspiration in planning our programs.

The Institute is supported by the Graduate School of Arts and Sciences at Boston University. Major funding for our program comes from the Lilly Endowment, Inc., through the good offices of Craig Dykstra and Jeanne Knoerle. To all these friends and colleagues, our grateful thanks.

Contributors

SISSELA BOK was born in Sweden, was educated in Switzerland and France, and received her Ph.D. from Harvard University. A Distinguished Fellow at the Harvard Center for Population and Development Studies, Bok has written a number of books, including *Lying: Moral Choice in Private and Public Life; Secrets: On the Ethics of Concealment and Revelation; A Strategy for Peace: Human Values and the Threat of War; Alva Myrdal: A Daughter's Memoir;* and *Common Values.*

LISA SOWLE CAHILL is Professor of Theology at Boston College and was a Visiting Scholar at the Kennedy Institute of Ethics at Georgetown University. Her Ph.D. is from the University of Chicago. An editor and member of the Board of Directors of *Concilium,* she is the author of *Between the Sexes: Toward a Christian Ethics of Sexuality; Women and Sexuality; "Love Your Enemies": Discipleship, Pacifism, and Just War Theory;* and *Sex, Gender, and Christian Ethics.*

DANIEL O. DAHLSTROM is Professor of Philosophy at Boston University and was previously Professor of Philosophy at the Catholic University of America. He has been the recipient of various awards, including two Fulbrights, a Mellon Grant, and a grant from the National Endowment for the Humanities. He received the Ph.D. from St. Louis University and is the author of *Das logische Vorurteil: Untersuchungen zur Wahrheitstheorie des frühen Heidegger,* as well as a number of articles and reviews.

KNUD HAAKONSSEN was born in Denmark and is an Australian citizen. He studied at the University of Copenhagen before going to the University of Edinburgh, where he received the Ph.D. He is Professor of Philosophy and Director of Graduate Studies in the Department of Philosophy at Boston University. He has written *The Science of a Legislator: The Natural Jurisprudence of David Hume and Adam Smith* and *Moral Philosophy and Natural Law: From Hugo Grotius to the Scottish Enlightenment,* and has edited a number of volumes.

RAY L. HART's Ph.D. is from Yale. He is Professor of Religion and Theology at Boston University and chairs the Department of Religion there. He has served as President of the American Academy of Religion. The author of numerous monographs and articles, he has written *Unfinished Man and the Imagination,* has cowritten (with Julian N. Hartt and Robert P. Scharlemann) *The Critique of Modernity,* and has edited *Trajectories in the Study of Religion.*

GLENN C. LOURY is University Professor and Professor of Economics at Boston University and was most recently Professor of Political Economy at Harvard University's John F. Kennedy School of Government. His Ph.D. is from the Massachusetts Institute of Technology. He was named a Fellow of the Econometric Society and was winner of a John Simon Guggenheim Fellowship. He has written *One by One, From the Inside Out: Essays and Reviews on Race and Responsibility in America,* as well as a number of essays.

ROBERT CUMMINGS NEVILLE received the Ph.D. from Yale and has also received honorary doctorates. A former President of the American Academy of Religion, he is Professor of Philosophy, Religion, and Theology and Dean of the School of Theology at Boston University. Among his many books are *God the Creator, The Cosmology of Freedom, Reconstruction of Thinking, The Tao and the Daimon, The Puritan Smile, Behind the Masks of God, Eternity and Time's Flow, Normative Cultures,* and *The Truth of Broken Symbols.*

BHIKHU PAREKH obtained his Ph.D. from the London School of Economics and is Professor of Political Theory at the University of Hull. He has taught at a number of universities, including, most recently, serving as Visiting Professor of Government at Harvard University. His books include *Hannah Arendt and the*

Search for a New Political Philosophy, Karl Marx's Theory of Ideology, and *Gandhi's Political Philosophy.* He was elected the British Asian of the Year in 1992.

GRAHAM PARKES is Professor of Philosophy at the University of Hawaii at Manoa and has also been a Visiting Scholar at Harvard's Reischauer Institute of Japanese Studies and a Senior Fellow at the Center for the Study of World Religions at Harvard. He was born in Scotland, studied in England, and received his Ph.D. from the University of California at Berkeley. He has written *Composing the Soul: Reaches of Nietzsche's Psychology* and has written, translated, and edited a number of other volumes.

STANLEY H. ROSEN received his Ph.D. from the University of Chicago and is Borden Parker Bowne Professor of Philosophy at Boston University. He has written numerous books, including *Nihilism, The Limits of Analysis, Plato's Sophist, Plato's Symposium, Hermeneutics as Politics* (which was named an Outstanding Academic Book of 1987 by *Choice*); *The Quarrel between Philosophy and Poetry, The Ancients and the Moderns, The Question of Being, The Mask of Enlightenment: Nietzsche's Zarathustra,* and several others.

LEROY S. ROUNER is Professor of Philosophy, Religion, and Philosophical Theology and Director of the Institute for Philosophy and Religion at Boston University. His Ph.D. is from Columbia University. Author of *Within Human Experience: The Philosophy of William Ernest Hocking; The Long Way Home* (a memoir); and *To Be at Home: Christianity, Civil Religion, and World Community.* He has also edited fifteen of the volumes in Boston University Studies in Philosophy and Religion, as General Editor of that series.

TU WEI-MING is a Fellow of the American Academy of Arts and Sciences. He is Professor of Chinese History and Philosophy at Harvard University and has also taught at Princeton University and the University of California at Berkeley. His books include *Neo-Confucian Thought: Wang-ming's Youth; Centrality and Commonality; Humanity and Self-Cultivation; Confucian Thought: Selfhood as Creative Transformation;* and *Way, Learning, and Politics: Essays on the Confucian Intellectual.*

Introduction

LEROY S. ROUNER

WE HUMANS ARE DEEPLY CONVINCED that there is something distinctive about us as a species. We are different from those others—plants, animals, rocks, gasses, galaxies, whatever—who also make up our world. This instinctive common sense has long been presupposed in most philosophical and religious thinking, although some traditions show little interest in exploring it.

Admittedly, philosophers and religious thinkers have historically had different interpretations of what makes human beings distinctively human. The major argument in Western culture is between the religion of Israel and the philosophies of the Greeks. The religion of Israel put much emphasis on the will as the fundamental vehicle of our relation to God and therefore the determining characteristic of our humanity. To obey God by doing God's will was the human vocation, and the sinful temptation to substitute our own will for the will of God was the great human problem. So, for Israel, both good and evil were fundamentally a question of will.

For the Greeks, on the other hand, the distinctive characteristic of humankind was our capacity for reason. This was less a question of the human mind's ability to make logical enquiry than it was an awareness of the mind's expansive and instinctive self-transcendence. We are the animal who goes to school; the one who can stand apart from himself or herself and know that she or he doesn't know some things that need to be known. It is reason which makes us "little lower than the angels." It is this transcendent, almost God's-eye view of reality which tempts us to *hubris,* subjecting us to tragic irony, and making us "human, all too human." So, for the Greeks, the distinctive mark of humankind was this capacity for self-transcending knowledge.

1

In our day, however, serious questions have been raised about the legitimacy of the idea, no matter how human nature is interpreted. The questions arise from the pluralism of contemporary American culture and the rapidly increasing interdependence of various world cultures. We are now mindful, in a new way, of how peoples in different cultural situations deal with their lives on the basis of different foundational values. If their values can be so different, what common ground makes it possible to claim a universal human nature?

The new questions are sociological, psychological, and pragmatic. The key question is one beloved of deconstructionists: Who states these "commonly accepted" cultural views? Is it possible that these views are strongly influenced by the social, cultural, and economic status of the viewers? And if so, does that qualify the common wisdom regarding the idea of a human nature? The new questions are also philosophical in challenging the validity of any universal view on the grounds that universal judgments are nothing but instruments of power in the hands of the cultural ruling class. On this view there can be no objective universal statements of rational truth on human nature or anything else.

Among our authors there is occasional, qualified sympathy for that point of view. Mostly, however, there is a chastened reaffirmation of universal human ethics, based on the intuitive commonsense instinct which I noted at the outset. But the tradition of both Israel and the Greeks continues in our authors' struggle with the personal, immediate, and concrete issue of human moral pretensions being mocked by human moral performance. So what follows is both a study in the metaphysics of human nature and the ethics of being humane, since we eventually become who we have consistently understood ourselves to be.

Our first section asks "What does it mean to be human?" and we begin with our title essay by Bhikhu Parekh. The author of several books on Gandhi, Parekh is familiar with the uses of power in India during the British Raj, so he approaches the issue in gingerly fashion, noting that while we know what the term *human* refers to, our understandings of *nature* are various. He proposes a minimalist view of the matter, arguing that there are a set of permanent properties that all human beings share in common. These properties must be inherent and distinctive to humankind, have a specific character or content, and operate in a specific manner. He notes, however, that while Western philosophy tends to take the concept for granted, this has not been the case in the great world cultural traditions of India and China.

Parekh's "minimalist" view on the universality of human nature notes that, while we are not prisoners of different cultures, such common properties as humans share are doubly mediated, first by their different cultures, and secondly by their own self-reflection. So he sees three dimensions of our human nature: one universal, one culture-specific, and one self-reflective. This tripartite division of the notion conforms to the emphases of the great world cultural tradtions: one may speak of individual natures as the Hindus do; of cultural communities as the traditional Chinese have done; and of the human species, as most Western thought has done. Parekh's point is salutary. "To equate human nature with only the last is to take too narrow a view of it. Worse, it ontologically and morally privileges our species nature, and marginalizes the other two."

Daniel Dahlstrom puts the problem in a political and cultural context with specific reference to the human need for recognition. We can be confident of our inherent humanity only when that "property" in us, as Parekh would say, is recognized by our fellows. Dahlstrom explores Francis Fukuyama's thesis, in *The End of History and the Last Man,* as to whether or not liberal democracy can provide that recognition. The issue centers on the liberal democratic notion of human equality based on the inherent dignity of each individual. There are three threats to recognition of these qualities or properties in liberal states. The first is the wide economic disparities which exist alongside the doctrine of human equality. Second is the fact that some people desire to be recognized as superior, not equal. And finally, some members of the liberal state have a stronger sense of recognition and identification among their own group than they have with members of the liberal state as a whole. This threat is critical, in Fukuyama's view, because he regards the human desire for recognition as the fundamental property of our human nature.

Dahlstrom's criticism of Fukuyama's thesis centers on Fukuyama's interpretation of human nature, which is based in turn on Plato's view as expressed in the fourth book of the *Republic.* Plato had argued that *sophia*—wisdom—is the fulfillment of the soul's capacity to think. Fukuyama, on the other hand, argues that the sole task of reason is to secure satisfaction of those needs shared with the animals, and the human desire for recognition. For his part, Dahlstrom understands the crisis of recognition as an antinomy, brought to a head by the tensions within liberal democracies outlined by Fukuyama. The resolution does not come naturally but must be fashioned from certain ideals, and that fashioning requires wisdom and not just "technical" reason. The antinomy sets an idealist-technical thesis over against a naturalistic antithesis. The idealistic-technical thesis is that, because each individual has its own identity and dignity, all human beings should be treated in the same way. The naturalistic antithesis is that just because each individual has its own identity and dignity—and is therefore different from each and every other individual—human beings should not all be treated in the same way. Dahlstrom concludes that the measure of success for liberal democracies lies in resolving this standoff through their capacity to promote a "just" harmony of moderation, courage, and wisdom in their people.

Stanley Rosen argues that the founding of philosophy reveals that "doing" philosophy is not some external activity in which one may or may not choose to engage, but rather an expression of our humanity. Philosophy enters our lives unannounced, "like someone who has been present with us from the beginning." At the same time, the stimulus which leads to philosophizing, and which illuminates ordinary life, comes from outside ordinary life. So, he argues, we live in two modes of time, the (ordinary) historical and the (extraordinary) cosmological. In our ordinary historical mode of life we are engaged in particular events. In the extraordinary cosmological mode we are engaged in making sense out of those events.

This philosophical adventure of making sense founds us, so philosophy is to be understood as a "tuning of the soul." It is not a science, a method, or a body of dogma. Rosen uses several examples from ordinary human experience to show how philosophy founds itself. "Philosophy begins in wonder or surprise, in puzzlement or in the experience of a dislocating mood, not in a deductive argument." Its beginning is already always underway. It is not the case that the self-founding of philosophy has specific content and can tell us what to do. It cannot do this because philosophy is not about itself; it is about life in the world. Its self-founding is simply an openness to the human love of wisdom.

Knud Haakonssen shares many of his colleague Stanley Rosen's views, but he differs on the fundamental notion that philosophy is a "tuning of the soul," as Rosen put it. Rosen's philosophical insights often refer to Plato, whereas Haakonssen's views have been strongly influenced by the modern Enlightenment. Haakonssen is concerned with the role which reason and will play in human rationality, and he begins with a critical exploration of postmodern hermeneutics and deconstruction. Especially through the influence of Hans Georg Gadamer, contemporary hermeneutics (interpretation of texts) "'de-privileged' both the interpreter and the author or agent and left text as the subject of the humanities and the substance of human life. With Jacques Derrida the text goes by the board too, and with it the last vestiges of the interpreting self." Deconstruction sees life as a series of incommensurable occurrences of text reading. Anything can be a text, and the interpreter's identity is determined by the text being read.

In rejecting this view Haakonssen offers a modest alternative. Deconstruction argues that since there are no conclusive arguments for views such as a universal human nature there can be no such thing. Haakonssen holds that, while we do not have ultimate certainty on matters of this sort, we do have better and worse hypotheses, as well as rules of grammar and logic with which to explore them. Irrationalism of the deconstructionist sort gives a logical argument for rejecting logic and therefore inevitably contradicts itself. While remaining noncommittal in ontology Haakonssen is nevertheless ready to exercise the spirit of "the Enlightenment project" in experimental attempts to see where promising hypotheses might lead us. Unlike Rosen's interest in the desire which founds philosophy and sets us to philosophizing, Haakonssen's focus is on the object of knowledge.

Lisa Cahill puts the human nature question in the larger context of natural law in the tradition of Catholic moral theology. Acknowledging that feminists have regularly been critical of Catholic natural law theory—she quotes Beverly Harrison as saying it was "every bit as awful as Protestant biblicism on any matter involving human sexuality"—Cahill nevertheless argues that there is an enduring value to natural law approaches to ethics, and that it makes an important contribution to contemporary feminist claims about the rights of women. She finds a meeting ground for feminists and natural law theorists in their common emphasis on practical reason and virtue.

The critical issue is universal judgments. Feminists have been drawn to deconstruction because they also suspect the motivations of those who claim insight into universals. Further, they wish to emphasize the distinctiveness of women's experience, and not have it swallowed up in an abstract judgment controlled by a patriarchal authority. Cahill points out, however, that feminists cannot articulate their claim for particular rights without reference to a universal. Her argument is not unlike Haakonssen's point regarding the deconstructionist rejection of logic by means of a logical argument. Cahill quotes Susan Thistlethwaite arguing that the battering of women is "always and everywhere wrong" and "must be stopped." Her argument is that, for all their different cultural, racial, socio-economic, and political situations, the freeing of women "for the achievement of full humanity" is best understood as an aspect of natural law.

Our final essay in this first section is Robert Neville's reflection on whether or not there is an essence of human nature. He begins with some of those reasons for skepticism with which we are now familiar, such as the imperialistic implications of universal judgments. Especially important for him is the argument which formed half of Dahlstrom's antinomy for a liberal democracy, and which Parekh included in his "three natures" argument: that because each individual is made up of both essential and conditional features, individuals differ in nature from one another. "Because people are differently connected causally and live in different contexts, their natures are different, even if one might say that their essential features are similar: the essential features have to integrate the conditional features at hand."

Neville's concern is to do justice to the variety of individual lives and human cultures. This is a concern he shares with several of our authors, perhaps especially Bhikhu Parekh, and his resolution of the issue is not unlike Parekh's. As individuals we require orientation to ourselves, to our culture, and to the history and cosmic order in which we are engaged. Like Stanley Rosen, Neville believes that the task of philosophy is to make sense of our history. "The closest thing to an essence of human nature is having the obligation to take responsibility for being part of the history in which we ourselves are engaged, and including that in one's orientation to the orientation points of reality."

Our second group of essays is more concerned with practice than with theory; or, perhaps better, initially with practice, in order to see how theory operates. As Cahill noted in her essay on natural law, human practice often clarifies theoretical concepts because we can observe them working close at hand. Most Americans have at least a little pragmatism in their souls, and would probably agree with Ernest Hocking's "negative pragmatism"—if an idea does no real work in the world then it can't be true.

We begin this section with Glenn Loury's critical evaluation of how the ideas in Murray and Herrnstein's *The Bell Curve* actually work. The thesis of the book is that the twentieth century has seen the emergence of a "cognitive elite"; that poverty, unemployment, illegitimacy, and crime are determined significantly by low intelligence; and that racial and ethnic groups differ, on the average, in intellectual abilities. While the book has some eight hundred pages of text, appendices, notes, and references, Loury argues that it is not legitimate science, but a work of advocacy for a particular vision of human nature and social inequality. For Loury, the critical issue is the moral one: "Can we sensibly aspire to a more complete social integration than has yet been achieved of those who now languish at the bottom of American society?"

Murray and Herrnstein have argued that Americans must be realistic in formulating social policy, and Loury agrees. His point is that *The Bell Curve* claims to have achieved a scientific understanding of people's moral performance which can serve as the basis for formulating policy, and this claim he calls "breathtakingly audacious." He responds, "Access to morality is not contingent on mental ability. God is not finished with us when he deals us our genetic hand. . . . Of course, we are constrained in various ways by biological and environmental realities. But with effort we can make ourselves morally fit members of our political communities."

Loury's essay is followed by Ray Hart's exploration of human nature as inherently faulty. While the Christian tradition is the context of his reflection, and the theological doctrine of original sin its background, his point of departure is philosophical. Noting that "fault" is a crack, breach, or rupture, he argues that fault in human nature is marked by acute self-consciousness of ontological instability. We do not coincide with ourselves. At any given moment we are one thing but intuitively sense that we should be other or more than what we are. Hart notes that an analysis of the problem is to be found in much Western philosophy. In further elaboration of his view he turns to William James's argument that we all have an uneasiness about ourselves, "a sense that there is *something wrong about us* as we naturally stand." Hart agrees and asks: What then do we hope for? He answers his own question: "The human person yearns, longs for the finishing of her unfinished selfhood."

Hart then turns to the question of *fall* as an explanation for how human nature becomes faulty. In keeping with the traditions of Israel and Christianity he argues that "it is by reason of *will* that we are two-in-one." A classical exposition of the ambivalent will is in Augustine's *Confessions,* and Hart recalls how Augustine ruthlessly confronts his motivation in the now-famous pear-stealing incident. He wasn't hungry; he did it just because he wanted to. But, Hart notes, "all taking of liberties merely in the service of what I want is at the cost of freedom," since this "taking" eventually reduces the range of possibilities for the exercise of freedom. The fallenness of human nature is recognized in the cry of any addict, or indeed anyone at all, since we have all struggled with the ambivalence of our willful desires. The cry is this: "Who or what can deliver us from what we want?" To be human is to know that we are not who we should be.

John Calvin would have liked Ray Hart's essay. While Graham Parkes is no Calvinist, his essay nevertheless has a good deal in common with Hart's. He, too, presupposes the ambivalence of the human will, offers a clear condemnation of human *hubris,* and recognizes our present need to be delivered from what we want. But Parkes is concerned with our present environmental crisis, and is persuaded that "a major factor in our having reduced nature to such a state is a prevalent conception of the human being's relations to the natural world." Here his difference from Hart begins to be clear. Hart sees human nature in terms of its dualities, especially the distinction between essence and existence. Parkes leans toward a nondualistic view in which various parts are understood in relation to the whole. For Parkes, therefore, human nature is to be understood from within the context of the natural world, and not as some exempted and privileged reality which transcends nature as a whole.

The thrust of his paper, however, is a recovery of those views— both ancient and modern, Eastern and Western—which express more salutary attitudes toward the environment. He acknowledges an ancient worldview tradition in the West from Orphism through Plato's *Phaedo,* Cartesian philosophy, Newtonian science, and Christianity in which "the *separateness* of humans from natural phenomena, as well as our putative superiority to them . . . combine to sanction a condescending attitude toward nature as 'other' and inferior, and ulti-mately suited for domination and exploitation by humans." But Parkes shows that there is a countercurrent from the Pre-Socratics through Stoicism, the Italian Renaissance, Goethe, Nietzsche, Emerson, and Thoreau, which are in harmony with the salutary East Asian under-standing of humankind's integration into the natural order. The mes-sage of this tradition, which Parkes endorses, is that we will stop our present rape of nature only when we recognize that we are all fellow creatures of the natural world.

Parkes's essay is followed by Tu Wei-ming's exploration of the Confucian idea of filial piety in a global ethical perspective. Tu's Con-fucian project wants to make classical Chinese Confucianism rele-vant to a modern world philosophy. He acknowledges the long period in which Confucian ideas have been derided, both in the West and in China, but explores the Confucian spiritual resources which have nevertheless made filial piety a cardinal virtue in East Asia. In articu-lating what makes for human flourishing, he begins with the Con-fucian view of concentric circles encompassing the self, family, com-munity, society, nation, world, and cosmos. Each set of relationships enhances the next. Filial piety as embodied love is both a principle of differentiation and a principle of communication.

His Confucian project counters the Enlightenment project which Knud Haakonssen represented. Tu acknowledges that the Enlightenment project has been the source of much that we value in the modern world. Tu, however, proposes that Confucian values can deepen and broaden the Enlightenment project. Like Parkes, he is concerned for "a new vision of humanity which transcends anthropo-centrism and locates the meaning of being human not only in an anthropological but also in a cosmological sense." While Tu is even less of a Calvinist than Parkes, his argument—like Parkes's—focuses on "human arrogance" and the rape of nature. Tu sees the ecological crisis as a crisis in Enlightenment mentality. Confucianism, he argues, can deepen Enlightenment values by grounding them in the particu-larities of the human condition.

My essay on "Why Good People Do Bad Things" explores the question of human arrogance or *hubris* in terms which Ray Hart's essay has already made familiar. While the topic is the classical Chris-tian doctrine of original sin, the approach is not theological, since that requires language and intellectual presuppositions which are internal to the Christian faith community. I agree with Stanley Rosen that philosophy is about ordinary human experience, and I am persuaded that for every authoritative theological doctrine there can and should be a good philosophical argument. This exploration of Kierkegaard's views on how the fault in human nature functions is therefore an essay in philosophical psychology.

Since Kierkegaard was, in many ways, an Augustinian, my analysis has much in common with Hart's exploration of Augustine, particularly in centering on the idea of freedom. It is in the exercise of freedom, Kierkegaard argues, that we suffer a "fall" and become "faulty." The vehicle of that fall is our experience of dread while we are still in a condition of "dreaming innocence." Dread is dread of the possibility of freedom, or "the dizziness of freedom." In choosing freedom we grasp at a finite possibility, in order to sustain ourselves. "And because that 'grasp' at a specific, finite possibility was done in the dizziness of freedom, and 'in order to sustain ourselves', we are now an actualized self, no longer mere potential; we are spirited and free; but we are now also guilty because we chose egoistically, in order to sustain ourselves. It was not an 'act of love.' It was an act of self-establishment and, at the same time, an act of self-preservation. So we are no longer innocent."

We conclude with Sissela Bok's exploration of "Lifeboat Ethics." She finds the lifeboat metaphor helpful as a thought experiment, and asks, "What becomes of fellow-feeling, of what the ancients called *humanitas,* and of the respect for human rights when survival itself is threatened?" She begins with an analysis of Alfred Hitchcock's film *Lifeboat,* centering on the moral dilemma faced by survivors of a German U-boat attack when they rescue a man who turns out to be the captain of the U-boat. They eventually throw him overboard. Later, however, they rescue another German soldier whom they treat humanely as a prisoner of war. Regarding the earlier incident one character seems to speak for them all in shame and regret for their lack of humanity. He says, "My only regret is that I joined a mob."

Bok then goes on to consider several works of art in which the lifeboat situation appears. In her conclusion she begins by cautioning that the lifeboat metaphor is limited, and that the comparison of humanity as a whole to the few occupants of a lifeboat is probably not helpful. She further cautions that, even within narrow limits, discussions of issues like who deserves and does not deserve to be rescued can readily overlook the near impossibility of making that judgment on a sound, humane basis. Nevertheless she notes that "films such as Hitchcock's and paintings and novels and plays can help ward off such shortchanging and make us see more deeply into all that a metaphor can convey."

So we come back to our question "Is there a Human Nature?" Our authors seem to think so, for all their cautioning. There also seems to be some tacit agreement that any viable definition must now be more varied than in the past. Parekh and Neville probably speak for many in suggesting that we have individual and cultural natures as well as a "cosmic" human nature. Two other characteristics of these essays also seem notable as I reread and reflect on them. One is that our dreadful century has shaken the optimism about human nature of even hopeful Western liberals and kindly affectioned Eastern non-dualists. Whether the crisis is related to the environment, race, or some other issue, human arrogance and *hubris* are widely acknowledged. The other characteristic is that there seems to be less concern to argue whether reason or will most accurately characterizes the universal in human nature, and more concern for "genuine humanity" as an achievement.

In spite of arrogance, *hubris,* and perhaps even sin, this sometimes glimpsed and always hoped-for humaneness is both classical and modern, both Enlightened and Confucian. It is characterized by a generous rationality and a controlled will which is attentive to the particulars of everyday experience and unafraid of that cosmic perspective on ourselves and our world which makes humankind "little lower than the angels."

PART I

What Does It Mean to Be Human?

Is There a Human Nature?

BHIKHU PAREKH

JUST AS THE QUESTION WHETHER GOD exists cannot be discussed, let alone answered, unless we are clear about what we mean by *God* and *exist,* the question whether there is a human nature cannot be discussed unless we are agreed on what we mean by human nature. In the history of philosophy there has been little consensus on the meaning of the term, and not surprisingly the discussion has often lacked focus and clarity. Although there is a broad agreement on what the term *human* refers to, there is considerable disagreement on the meaning of the term *nature*. Some use it in a descriptive sense to refer to what all human beings can be shown to share in common. For others it refers to what human beings are ideally capable of becoming. Some, again, take a mechanical (whereas others take a teleological) view of nature. For some what is natural must be unchanging; others think that it can be modified within certain limits. For some, again, to say that a particular tendency is natural to human beings is to say that it determines them to behave in a relevant way. Others take a weaker view of nature and think that the tendency in question only disposes or inclines them to behave in a certain manner.

Depending on how we define human nature, we arrive at different views on whether or not human beings have a nature. For the purpose of this paper I shall take a minimalist view of it, and define it as a set of permanent properties that all human beings, and only they, share in common by virtue of being human. The definition is neither arbitrary nor eccentric, for many influential past and present writers have subscribed to it. Even those who take a stronger view of human nature should have no difficulty accepting it as a useful starting point. If we can show that the concept of human nature is problematic even when defined in such thin or minimalist terms, it becomes even more problematic when defined in stronger or thicker terms.

15

As I have defined it, the term *human nature* implies the following.

(1) It refers to certain properties, a term I use widely to include capacities, desires, dispositions, or tendencies to act in specific ways, and so on.

(2) The properties are shared by all human beings. This does not mean that there might be no exceptions, but rather that those who lack some of these properties are to that extent defective and not fully human.

(3) Only the humans share these properties. Humans do, of course, possess several other properties as well that they share in common with other sentient beings, especially the animals, and these too form part of their nature. However, since they are not unique to human beings, they belong to their animal and not *human* nature.

(4) The properties in question are not socially or culturally derived; they belong to human beings "by nature" or "from birth," and constitute their species heritage. Although society might modify them and regulate their expression, it can do so only within strict limits and can never entirely eliminate them.

(5) The properties in question inhere in each human being. They form part of his or her physical and psychological constitution, and each alike possesses them in a broadly equal measure. Human beings share these properties not in a way that those sitting around a table share it in common, but rather in a way that they share their eyes and ears in common.

(6) The properties are not abstract and indeterminate but have a specific character or content, and operate in a specific manner. To say that all human beings seek to preserve themselves is to say that they do all they can to avoid death, including eschew suicide. And similarly to say that they seek to realize themselves, possess an inherent love of God, strive for happiness, have an inclination to do evil, are naturally curious and seek knowledge, and so on, is to give these tendencies and capacities a specific content and to point to their mode of functioning.

Since the concept of human nature is one of the oldest and most influential concepts in Western philosophy, there is an understandable tendency to think that it is self-evidently indispensable to systematic reflection on human beings and is to be found in all philosophical traditions. This is not the case. Traditional Chinese thought devoted little attention to it. It was primarily concerned with how people should live and answered the question in terms of specific cultural norms, rituals, and so forth. The concept has not played an important role in much of classical Islamic thought either. Several Indian philosophical traditions considered the boundary between humans and nonhumans porous and took only a passing interest in what was unique to humans. Thanks to the theories of *karma* and rebirth, some of them thought that each individual had a unique psychological and spiritual constitution or nature fashioned by him or her over a series of rebirths, and saw little need to explore the common features of the species.

There is nothing surprising about this, for the concept of human nature rests on certain assumptions and arises and acquires dominance within a worldview that shares them. First, it assumes that humans and nonhumans can and ought to be unambiguously distinguished. Second, it assumes that only what all humans share in common is ontologically significant, or at least that it is far more significant than what separates them. Third, the concept of human nature assumes a fairly clear distinction between nature and culture, between what is inherent in humans and what is created by them, and it assumes that only the former represents their "truth" or "true identity," the latter being contingent, subject to change, and of marginal importance. Fourth, to talk about human nature is to assume that it is possible for us to know it wholly or at least substantially. Without such an assumption, an inquiry into it is pointless. Fifth, to inquire into human nature is to assume that the inquiry is valuable, that the concept of human nature serves purposes no other concept can. Broadly speaking, philosophers have used it to serve three purposes: to identify or demarcate human beings; to explain human behavior; and to prescribe how human beings should live and conduct themselves.

Many cultural and philosophical traditions do not share some or all of these assumptions or consider them central to their understanding of the world. They have therefore no theoretical space or practical use for the concept of human nature, and either ignore it altogether or make do with ad hoc and tentative generalizations about it. Many Indian thinkers did not share the first and the fifth assumption; classical Chinese thought did not share the second and the third. For various reasons which I cannot here consider, all five assumptions underlay Western philosophy almost from its very beginning. Over the centuries it has devoted much agonized attention to theorizing about human nature and has built up a rich and varied tradition of discourse on it. In recent years, however, many writers in the West have expressed varying degrees of dissatisfaction with the concept of human nature. They have argued that it denies human freedom, that such self-creating beings as humans cannot have a nature, that human beings are too embedded in it to take an objective view of it or to know it fully, that the concept is too ahistorical to be satisfactory, that it rests on too simplistic a view of the human, and that the neat disjunction between humans and nonhumans is too crude to be acceptable in the modern ecologically self-conscious age.

I share this unease and intend to press the point further. I shall argue that although the concept of human nature has some value, it is too problematic to be accepted without a radical redefinition. For analytical convenience I shall state my objections in a schematic fashion.

First, as we saw earlier the concept of human nature implies two things, namely that human beings uniquely share certain properties in common, and that they do so by nature or as their species heritage. Each of these assertions creates problems. Not much reflection is needed to see that human beings do uniquely share several properties in common. However, the latter are too many and too complex to be listed. Human beings can think, will, judge, fantasize, dream dreams, formulate concepts, worship all manner of gods, build theories, use language, build myths, remember their past, anticipate future events, make plans, and so on and on. At a different level they are capable of such a vast range of moral and nonmoral emotions as love, hate, anger, rage, sadness, sorrow, pity, compassion, meanness, generosity, self-hatred, self-esteem, and vanity, and of such dispositions as the tendency to explore new areas of experience, to seek human company, to ask questions, and to seek justification of their own and others' actions. Although these capacities, emotions, and dispositions are distinct and have their unique modes of operation, they are interrelated and both partially presuppose and contradict each other. Human nature therefore is not made up of a set of discrete, readily specifiable, and mutually compatible properties but represents a complex world of related but often dissonant capacities and dispositions, each capable of generating many more and of taking several different forms. Faced with this vast array of human capacities and dispositions, philosophers of human nature have often sought to reduce them all to a single master capacity, often reason or conceptual thinking. However, this is too crude, for it is difficult to see how such a reduction is possible, and no philosopher, including Hobbes (one of the few to attempt such an exercise), has succeeded in demonstrating it. Reason itself takes several different forms, of which theoretical and practical reason are but two, and they are not all reducible to so many different expressions of an allegedly generic and neutral reason. And the fact that humans can reason does not by itself explain why they can also construct myths, dream dreams, and imagine wholly new experiences and entities.

The assertion that human beings possess these properties by nature is even more difficult to establish. Thanks to centuries of social existence, human nature has been so deeply informed and shaped by organized social life and so profoundly mediated culturally that we have no access to it in its raw or pristine form, and cannot detach what is natural from what may loosely be called manmade or social. Many writers did, of course, appreciate this fact, but thought that it was nevertheless possible to uncover human nature either by imaginatively abstracting away the influence of culture or by looking at the behavior of primitive peoples, children, or civilized people in times of social disintegration. None of these, however, helped them or helps us much.

One can't abstract away the influence of culture without some conception of what culture is and how, and how much, it influences human beings. That in turn presupposes some conception of human nature and how it is to be distinguished from culture. Far from arriving at human nature by abstracting away culture, we in fact begin the very process of abstraction by assuming a conception of human nature. As for the so-called primitive societies, they are by definition social organizations and cannot give us access to presocial human nature. Besides, there is no reason why such societies, in which the natural forces wield enormous power and do not let humans come into their own, should be considered authentic repositories of human nature unless we already begin with a fairly definite notion of what human nature is like. As for children, they are subject to deep social influence from the very moment of their birth or even perhaps conception. And when societies disintegrate, their members' behavior does not reveal raw human nature but the influence of their residual cultural beliefs and practices in a climate of chaos and uncertainty. In short, human nature is not a brute and empirically verifiable fact which we may hope to discover, but an inference or a theory which we have no reliable means of corroborating.

Second, human beings are culturally embedded in the sense that they are born into, reared in, and deeply shaped by, specific cultural communities. Depending on their traditions, temperament, changing forms of self-understanding, and geographical circumstances, different communities organize their collective lives differently. They conceptualize human life and one's place in the world in their own different ways; emphasize and develop different human capacities, emotions, and dispositions; relate them differently; cherish different ideals of excellence; follow different practices, and so on. Such human capacities and dispositions that human beings universally share therefore undergo deep and important changes and come to be reconstituted in very different ways. For example, although all human beings have the capacity to reason, they reason differently. The Platonic *nous*, the Christian *ratio*, the Cartesian *cogito*, and the Hobbesian reckoning with consequences represent very different modes of reasoning and thinking. Again, different cultures differently map out and individuate human faculties. Some disjoin reason and feelings; others cannot see how the two can be separated. Some distinguish between theoretical and practical reason or between thinking and willing, whereas others hold that reason has both theoretical and practical impulses built into its very structure. Different cultures, again, encourage different emotions and feelings. Some develop a privatized conception of conscience and know what guilt and remorse mean; others find these emotions incomprehensible. Some cultures have a poorly developed sense of history and cannot make sense of the desire to gain historical immortality or to leave a footnote in history. Some others lack a sense of tradition and cannot make sense of the desire to be worthy of one's ancestors, to be loyal to their memories, or to cherish their heritage.

Human beings, however, are not prisoners of their culture. Although the space for critical reflection and diversity varies from culture to culture, no culture can be so monolithic as to deny it altogether. Drawing upon the resources of their own culture and those of others, human beings reflect on their experiences; dream different dreams; try out different experiments; develop different capacities, feelings, and dispositions; and reconstitute themselves in their own unique ways, albeit some more successfully than others.

This means that such shared properties as humans have are doubly mediated, first by their culture and second by their self-reflection. Different cultural communities and, within them, different individuals appropriate and reconstitute the shared human properties in different ways and give them novel forms. Additionally they also

develop capacities and dispositions that are wholly new, entirely un-
predictable, and go far beyond the universally shared properties.
Cultures are not superstructures built on an identical foundation or
merely veneers on a self-same substance, but represent new modes of
reconstituting and going beyond the shared human properties. Given
that the capacities for critical self-reflection and self-transformation
are an integral part of human nature, human beings cannot share a
nature and belong to their species in the same way that the animals do.

We might press the point further. As members of a specific
cultural community, we acquire certain tendencies and dispositions.
In some cases they are as deep and powerful as those we are deemed
to possess by nature. For example, as human beings we seek to preserve ourselves. Yet as members of a specific community we might
develop such a strong religious commitment that we might be prepared to die for our religion or in the cause of God. We have now
acquired a "second" nature, which overrides the "natural" nature. The
tendency to die for one's religion or community is not universally
shared, and in that sense it is not a part of universal human nature.
However, it is a part of our culturally derived nature, that is, of our
nature as members of a specific community. There is no obvious reason why we cannot talk of specific natures, of *our* nature as different
from *theirs,* when it displays all the obvious properties of nature.

The same thing also happens at the individual level. We might so
shape ourselves that a fierce sense of independence, an uncompro-
mising commitment to integrity, a passionate love of God or of our
fellow humans, or an absolute concern for justice might get woven
into our being and become an integral part of our nature. We then not
only instinctively and effortlessly act on these inclinations but even
feel helplessly driven by them. These dispositions have the same force
as the tendencies deemed to be inherent in our shared human nature,
and are just as inseparable and ineradicable from our being. We often
call them part of our *character* to show that they are our achievements. However, character is not external to who we are, and constitutes our *nature*.

This means that our nature is articulated on (at least) three
different though interrelated levels: first, the nature that we share as
members of a common species; second, the nature we derive from
and share as members of a specific cultural community; and third,
the nature we succeed in giving ourselves as reflective individuals. All
three are parts of our nature and relate to three different dimensions

of our being. What is more, since they are distinctive to us as human beings they are all part of our *human* nature. It therefore makes perfect sense to talk of our distinct *individual* natures (as the Hindus do), of our nature as members of specific *cultural communities* (as traditional Chinese thought did), and of our nature as members of the *human species* (as much Western thought has emphasized over the centuries). To equate human nature with only the last is to take too narrow a view of it. Worse, it ontologically and morally privileges our species nature and marginalizes the other two.

Third, the concept of human nature is profoundly ahistorical. It implies that human beings begin their history endowed with a specific set of properties, which no doubt undergo some but not much modification in the course of their historical development. As to how they came to acquire these properties or their species nature in the first instance, the usual nonreligious answer is to appeal to natural evolution. The traditional view postulates a fairly neat division between evolution and history. In the former, nature holds sway, creates humans as we more or less know them today, and brings them to the threshold of history, which they are then at liberty to make within the constraints imposed by their nature.

This is a highly misleading account of human nature. It takes an arbitrary cut-off point in evolution and defines as humans only those who broadly resemble us. In other words it begins with a specific conception of human nature and uses it to define humans. Furthermore, human evolution does not occur behind their backs; they are active participants in it. As human beings acquire a posture broadly resembling their current one and some capacity to understand themselves and their world, they increasingly begin to engage in a creative interaction with their environment and to change it in harmony with their needs. As their environment is humanized, it provides a relatively safe island of stability within which they can develop at their own pace and from which they can strive to further humanize nature. In the course of this dialectic with nature, they change both themselves and their world, develop new forms of social organization, and acquire new capacities and dispositions. These historically acquired capacities and dispositions become institutionalized, form the bases of new demands and ideals, are reproduced during the successive generations, get consolidated, and both acquire the force of a "second" nature and transform the "first" often beyond recognition.

Almost all the distinctive human capacities and dispositions are products of such a dialectic. Our primitive ancestors possessed little of what we call reason. They had some capacity for a largely instrumental understanding of their environment, which gave them some advantage over the animals. More sophisticated forms of reason developed later, and theoretical reason came much later, and both are products of a semiconscious dialectic between society and nature. What is true of reason is true also of such capacities as willing, judging, formulating ideals, audacious dreams of differently constituted societies, and courageous attempts to realize these dreams. This is equally true of such motivations as greed, striving for domination, and the desire for self-respect and social preeminence. Take greed. As John Locke suggested and as Marx more fully explored, greed is inseparable from money and is unthinkable in a society in which different kinds of use-values are not all reducible to a universally accepted measure. Almost all that is distinctive to humans is a result of their conscious and unconscious, planned and unplanned struggles. It is not an inexorable unfolding of, nor inherent in, nor entailed by, such primitive cognitive equipment as humans acquired through their natural evolution. The equipment did start them off on their historical journey, but all that developed later was largely a semiconscious human achievement. Most of what is human in human nature is not a product of nature but of human struggle.

Fourth and finally, the concept of human nature as it has been traditionally defined is centered on those properties that inhere in or are internal to human beings. Such distinctive human capacities as reason, will, self-reflection, and judgment; such distinctively human desires as desires for self-preservation, liberty, happiness, and property; and such distinctive human dispositions as intellectual curiosity, pride, aggressiveness, and love of God, which form the substance of much of the traditional exploration of human nature, are all internal to each human being. They are their individual or subjective properties, possessed by them in their unique isolation. It is not the case that these properties are all self-centered and do not draw human beings out of themselves into the world of nature and society where alone many of them are satisfied, but rather that they are all located within each individual. Although they point beyond the individual, their basis is within.

Since it concentrates on the internal constitution of human beings, the concept of human nature excludes what lies outside or between them. It excludes such *objective conditions of human existence* as that they are born in a specific historical epoch, within a specific cultural community, and with a particular color, gender, and shape; speak a specific language; must find ways of living together in peace; carry throughout their lives a large and only dimly grasped unconscious; and must work to stay alive. It also excludes such *conditions of human development* as that human beings require a prolonged period of nurture with all that this entails, a secure and stable environment in which to grow up at their own pace, access to the resources of a rich culture, and a more or less coherent conception of themselves and the world to act as a cognitive and moral compass. It also excludes such *basic life experiences* as falling in and out of love, growing old, suffering loss of memory, anticipating their own death, seeing their loved ones die, deep disappointments and frustrations, inability to realize all their dreams and desires, being bonded to specific individuals in a special way, growing up in a specific social milieu, and building up certain traits of temperament, attachments, affections, and loyalties that define their personal and social identity, and so on.

These and many other features of human existence are not internal to human beings but either external or interpersonal. As such they are not part of human nature but of the human condition or human predicament. Not surprisingly they get ignored in almost all discussions of human nature. Since they profoundly shape the context and content of human conduct, theories of human nature remain incapable of giving an even remotely adequate explanatory or normative account of it. And since human nature and the human condition are inextricably tied up together and unintelligible in isolation from each other, such theories cannot offer a satisfactory account of human nature either.

It should be clear that the concept of human nature is of limited value. That value is threefold. First, it highlights certain basic properties that all human beings come to share in common after reaching a particular stage in their evolutionary development, and it captures an important aspect of human life. Second, it stresses the fact that despite all our diversities and differences we belong to a common species with all that this implies. And third, it emphasizes the fact that however great our differences and inequalities, none of us is so different as to be wholly unintelligible or so superior as to belong to and to feel entitled to claim the rights and privileges of an entirely different and superior species. Thanks to all this, the concept of human nature embodies a specific conception of how beings are and should be related to each other and provides a regulative moral principle. In other words human nature is not just a concept but a moral practice.

While these and other insights embodied in the concept of human nature are most valuable, that concept is inadequate and even misleading in crucial respects. As we saw, it is atomistic and simplistic, and naively defines human nature in terms of a set of abstract and isolated capacities and desires. It implies an ahistorical view of humankind and obscures the fact that all human capacities and dispositions beyond the most primitive are not natural species endowments but human achievements. It ignores the cultural embeddedness of human beings, privileges nature over culture, and ignores the countless different ways in which human beings reconstitute and enrich their shared nature. It looks inside human beings to identify their distinctiveness and ignores their no less important and universally shared life experiences, conditions of development, and objective conditions of human existence.

If we are adequately to conceptualize human beings, we need to replace the concept of human nature with one that both preserves its insights and value and is free of its limitations. The term *human essence* basically belongs to the same family, shares all the limitations and associations of the term *human nature*, and cannot serve the purpose. The term *human condition* is not atomistic and inward-looking, and is in that respect better. However, it too is ahistorical, acultural, highlights only the external conditions of human existence, and is therefore unsatisfactory. It would seem that although the term *human identity* too has its obvious limitations, it is perhaps less misleading than its rivals. Unlike the terms *nature, essence,* and *condition, identity* is not static and is constantly recreated. Unlike them it accommodates the obvious fact that different human beings give themselves different identities, and thus it stresses the role of culture, leaves space for internal variation, and admits of the several levels of human nature referred to earlier. Unlike them again identity points both inward and outward, and is inherently relational. Rather than ask what human nature, human essence, or human condition consists of, we might more profitably ask how human identity is constituted and developed or, what comes to the same thing, what central and necessarily interrelated features characterize human existence and both condition and aid in the construction of human identity.

Humanism

When formulated in this way, the exploration of human identity entails an inquiry into the universal constants of human existence, and the ways in which they are creatively interpreted and incorporated into the process of human self-articulation and self-understanding. The universal constants include both basic human capacities, dispositions, etc., and the objective conditions of human life, inescapable life experiences, and so on. We can now ask how human beings endowed with certain common basic capacities and dispositions respond to their common conditions of existence. Since they are creative and reflective beings and prone to making mistakes, they respond to these conditions in their own different ways, develop different cultures and forms of social organization, and cultivate different capacities and dispositions. However, since they also share common capacities and conditions of existence, such identities as they develop have common features. Their differences are embedded in and grow out of their shared similarities. They are never therefore totally different from or wholly unintelligible to outsiders, and remain capable of engaging in a mutually enriching dialogue. Since the constants of human existence are articulated differently and undergo important changes, no human society or human being is either exactly like another or wholly different. In short, human similarities and differences interpenetrate, are both equally important in constituting human identity, and reveal to us human beings who are at once both alike and different.

When confronted with others we do not therefore act on the assumption either that they are basically like us as the concept of human nature encourages us to do, or that they are basically different and largely unintelligible, as the concept of radical pluralism urges us to do. As opposed to both these views, we approach others on the assumption that they share with us the universal constants of human existence which they articulate and respond to differently, and that therefore they are unlikely to be either wholly like us or totally different. We therefore neither assimilate them to our conception of human nature and deny their individuality or particularity, nor place them in a world of their own and deny the universality they share with us. Instead we acknowledge *both* their universality and particularity, and accept the obligation both to respect them for what they are and to understand them in their own terms.

To conclude: what then is my answer to the question we started with, namely, "Is there a human nature?" The answer is fivefold. First, there is a human nature in the sense that human beings do share certain basic capacities, desires, and dispositions which collectively individuate them as a species and distinguish it from others. Second, human nature is only a small part of what individuates and distinguishes humans. Third, human nature is so overlaid with culture that we have no direct access to it, and our description of it is necessarily inferential, a little speculative, and never wholly free of our conception of what we would like it to be. Fourth, since self-reflection, self-determination, and creativity are all part of human identity, such nature as we have does not wholly determine us and is largely a resource which we can tap and mobilize in formulating and realizing our ideals of self-development. And finally, human beings are capable of giving themselves, and have indeed given and continue to give themselves, new natures with the power to rival the force of such nature as they inherit.

The Human Need for Recognition and the Crisis of Liberal Democracy

DANIEL DAHLSTROM

THE VERY EXISTENCE OF THE United States in the world at the present time, Alexandre Kojève observed in 1968, prefigures the future, the eternal present of humanity as a whole. The American way of life is, in his words, the genre of life proper to "the posthistorical period," signaling nothing less than the end of history as we know it, the consummation of the human, all-too-human struggle for recognition, on the one hand, and a return to the world of animals, on the other.[1] In his book, *The End of History and the Last Man,* Francis Fukuyama takes pains to point out certain tensions within liberal democracies that have been ignored or underestimated by Kojève, yet have the potential to wreak havoc on these governments and the American way of life they are meant to protect and shepherd. *The End of History* concludes with an impressive litany of doubts about the sustainability and desirability of liberal democracy or "political liberalism," defined by Fukuyama "simply as a rule of law that recognizes certain individual rights or freedoms from government control."[2]

Nevertheless, the greater part of Fukuyama's deliberations is devoted to showing how Kojève's general thesis has in essence been corroborated by events on the world stage in the second half of the twentieth century.[3] "Kojève identified an important truth," Fukuyama observes, "when he asserted that postwar America or the members of the European Community constituted the embodiment of Hegel's state of universal recognition," a state synonymous with the end of history as we know it.[4] According to the argument appropriated by Fukuyama from Kojève, modern liberal democracies present the best possible solution to the human dilemma because they best satisfy the preeminently human need for respect. To the extent that they satisfy this need, liberal democracies mark the end to the human struggle for recognition, which is the very matter and form of history.[5]

28

"Universal recognition" in modern liberal democracies obviously does not mean—and neither Kojève nor Fukuyama understand it to mean—that all social inequities have been eliminated. Nature and culture see to it that gifts and talents, training and expertise remain unequally—indeed, unjustly—distributed. The division of labor inevitably leads to class and economic disparities.[6] Fukuyama himself observes that, rather than universal recognition, an "ultimately irrational" recognition within a particular group "growing out of preliberal traditions" often provides a necessary foundation for the stability of liberal democracies.[7]

In liberal democracies such natural, cultural, and economic inequalities exist side by side with the universal recognition that is the hallmark of those democracies and the centerpiece of the "end of history" (or "posthistorical") thesis. "Universal recognition," as it is understood by Kojève and Fukuyama in regard to liberal democracies, primarily signifies a form of equality which ultimately is based upon the alleged moral equality of all human beings.

Because people recognize each other as, by nature, rational and free and thereby worthy persons, they relate to one another politically as citizens with the same fundamental responsibilities and the same fundamental claims on the protection of the law.[8] Moreover, they strive for a further ordering of their society in which the only remaining barriers to social equality are the nature of things and not people's caprice and prejudice.[9] If one assumes with Kojève that the struggle for recognition of this sort has been the engine of history, then history in an important, political sense of the term does, indeed, come to a close with the attainment of universal recognition.

Fukuyama insists, to be sure, on distinguishing two broadly conceived traditions of liberalism, each with its own understanding of the principle of equality. For Hobbes and Locke *equality* means one thing, for Kant and Hegel something else. Hobbes roots equality in a mutual fear based upon a mutual capacity to kill one another, while Locke roots it in the shared desire for happiness, which he finds principally in the acquisition of property. So construed, the principle of equal recognition amounts to a means of survival and/or of unrestrained accumulation. By contrast, the liberal tradition of Kant and Hegel takes its bearings from the originally Christian view of equality, namely, that God recognizes all human beings as equals because every human being has the capacity either to accept or to reject the divine call to the demands of moral goodness.[10] On this view, the principle of equal recognition is no mere means, but far more an absolute value.

The difference between the two liberal traditions is summed up by Fukuyama as follows: "If Hobbesian or Lockean liberalism can be interpreted as the pursuit of rational self-interest, Hegelian 'liberalism' can be seen as the pursuit of *rational recognition,* that is, recognition on a universal basis in which the dignity of each person as a free and autonomous human being is recognized by all."[11] According to the Hegelian version of liberalism, the primary sense of equality consists not so much in a capacity of human beings to kill one another, or to pursue an individual conception of happiness, as in the capacity of each person to determine and to maintain himself or herself. The liberal state is superior to other forms of government precisely because it is founded on a recognition of this basic human dignity.

The Hegelian vision of liberalism is, Fukuyama argues further, not only the nobler but also the more accurate and telling vision of the course of world history over the last two centuries. The language used by people in contemporary America to describe their society and form of government, Fukuyama contends, is "more Hegelian than Lockean."[12] For all their debt to Locke, the authors of the *Federalist Papers* themselves, Fukuyama observes, appreciated the importance of the desire for recognition, something that is today taken for granted in democratic countries and inscribed in their constitutions. Indeed, while Hegel, in contrast to Hobbes and Locke, may be credited with having clearly stated this view, the American founding fathers deserve accolades for having successfully steered "the desire for recognition in a positive or at least harmless direction" within the democratic political process.[13]

Despite his enthusiasm for the power of the principle of recognition over the last two centuries, Fukuyama concludes with an exploration of three tensions within liberal democracies that threaten the survivability of these democracies.[14] There is, first of all, the fact that wide economic disparities exist side-by-side with the so-called political equality of the liberal state. Secondly, there is the fact that some people desire to be recognized, not as equal, but as superior to others. Finally, some members of the liberal state have a stronger sense of recognition and identification among themselves (for example, through cultural, ethnic, or nationalistic bonds) than they have with members of the liberal state as a whole.

The identification of these tensions, like the "end-of-history" thesis itself, is based upon a conception of human nature that Fukuyama largely takes over from Kojève. Kojève's thesis that the victory of the principle of recognition coincides with the end of history rests, it bears recalling, on the claim that the desire for recognition is not only the human being's most important, but also the human being's most distinctive, desire. In contrast to the other basic need, namely, the need shared with animals for self-preservation, the desire for recognition is a distinctively human desire, distinguishing the human being as such.[15] But does the reciprocal recognition of the sort practiced in a liberal democracy in fact satisfy the need for recognition? Is it not more likely that some people will only be genuinely satisfied by the realization of economic equality or with the establishment of their political and/or economic superiority?

Removing those conditions in the economy which systematically hold back certain groups in society is, for the most part, considered a staple of a fair and secure domestic policy in liberal democracies. For this reason Fukuyama thinks that the disparity between political equality and economic inequality is far less ominous than the need of specific individuals and groups for recognition that is different from or even superior to the sort of equal recognition guaranteed by a liberal democracy. In connection with this threat Fukuyama points to the many possibilities that liberal democratic societies afford their members—for example, in business, science, politics, sport, and art—"to be recognized as better than others."[16] Yet, despite these outlets, the possibility of political relationships falling back into a struggle for political domination can by no means be dismissed.

By raising these questions about the prospects of liberal democracies in view of the tensions mentioned, Fukuyama demonstrates his agreement with a significant part of Strauss's criticism of Kojève. In all likelihood there will be no "last human beings," no return to the animal world, because the struggle for recognition of one sort or another will make itself felt unmistakenly even in the liberal epoch of so-called political equality. Yet Fukuyama's warnings about precipitously accepting Kojève's sanguine vision of a liberal and democratic, posthistorical world are grounded in the conception of human nature underlying that vision itself.

The following reflections aim at complementing Fukuyama's investigations by way of criticizing them. The criticism is, however, not based upon the familiar reproaches that Fukuyama merely dresses up Kojève's fundamental misunderstanding—or, put more kindly, his free reading—of Hegel's political philosophy in new garb,[17] or that Fukuyama's reading of contemporary events is a gross oversimplification.[18] There is much to be said for both of these objections. For example, in Hegel's analysis of the master-slave dialectic he attaches major significance to the slave's *greater* awareness of death, an awareness that more than compensates for what might otherwise appear to be the slave's lesser need for recognition. Yet this central insight is strangely missing from Fukuyama's interpretation of Hegel, a neglect that weakens not only the presentation but the very substance and force of his argument regarding the reasons for the historical ascendancy of liberal democracies. Nor can there be any doubt that Fukuyama's attempt to write a "philosophical world history" of the past century or more is guilty of overgeneralizations (for example, labeling the U.S., Romania, Turkey, and Lebanon in 1990 all "liberal democracies") and of many a philosopher's penchant for overlooking the power of contingencies (such as Chernobyl or Gorbachov's persona). Nor, finally, given capitalism's track record, its relatively brief appearance on the world stage as a dominant economic form, and its own technological and political dynamics, is there any reason to share Fukuyama's sanguinity about the capacity of contemporary political economies to keep economic disparities within acceptable social limitations. More importantly, what about their capacity to ward off depression, an environmental catastrophe, a disastrous lack of opportunity and employment, egregious global imbalances of production and consumption, and a general despair on the part of the citizenry regarding the economic and social prospects of their families?

Nevertheless, there is every danger that, by concentrating too much on these negatives, critics may fail to appreciate Kojève's and Fukuyama's genuine contributions. Included among those contributions is the outline for a powerful hypothesis regarding the causes of major political events in the past half-century. Perhaps even more importantly, the argument is based upon a conviction that an adequate interpretation of political events depends on a suitable understanding of human nature.

My criticism is directed at the understanding of human nature that underlies Fukuyama's interpretation of the contemporary state of liberal democracies. Fukuyama's argument involves a conception of human nature that in one vital respect stands in stark contrast to the classical (or "Platonic") view of human nature, a view which he otherwise endeavors to appropriate.[19] In the evaluation of the events of world history, Fukuyama takes into serious consideration only two of those three parts of the human soul—*thymos* and *epithymetikon*—elaborated by Plato in the fourth book of the *Republic* (439d, 440e). Instead of discussing the meaning of wisdom—*sophia*—as the perfection of the human soul's capacity to think, Fukuyama presents the third part of the soul—*logiston*—in such a way that its sole task, the task of reason, consists in securing satisfaction of both those needs shared with animals and the human desire for recognition. In this respect, Fukuyama's analysis and his liberalism remain quintessentially "modern."

Fukuyama's neglect of the traditional role assigned to reason by classical political philosophy is far from idiosyncratic. That neglect is symptomatic of an entire culture of political thinking within contemporary liberal democracies. The consequences of such neglect for this political culture are neither merely academic nor benign. Rather they present contemporary liberal democracies with a genuine crisis. The crisis at issue can, to be sure, take many forms. Nevertheless, at bottom it is the crisis that emerges whenever two parties make claims that are contradictory and yet apparently equally justified. When, for example, some members of disadvantaged groups or minorities—some women in a patriarchal society, some Afro-Americans in the United States, some Québécois in Canada, some Sinti and Roma in Germany, and so forth—demand special treatment from society, they often justify that claim on the basis of a right to equality, the fundamental principle of liberalism.[20] When adversaries declare these demands illegal, they also appeal to the principle of equal recognition before the law. As a result, within liberal democracies two contrasting types of politics typically emerge, "the politics of difference" and "the politics of equal dignity," as Charles Taylor characterizes them, each of which corresponds to a competing conception of liberalism.[21]

In what follows the crisis of recognition is presented as an antinomy, although its ultimate import is to point to alternatives not only within liberalism but also to liberalism itself. The antinomy is designed to bring to a head the tensions within liberal democracies mentioned by Fukuyama and to do so in a way that makes patent the necessary but neglected role that classical political philosophy assigns to wisdom. Accordingly, in the course of pursuing this objective it will also be evident that the antinomy revives in a certain sense *la querelle des anciens et des modernes* on the foundations of an adequate political philosophy.

THE CRISIS OF RECOGNITION AS AN ANTINOMY

The antinomy of recognition consists of an "idealistic technical" thesis and a "naturalistic" antithesis. The thesis involves the assumption that the appropriate sort of political recognition does not come naturally, but must be fashioned or constructed on the basis of certain ideals. The antithesis assumes that the only legitimate sort of political recognition is that grounded in human nature and its natural affiliations. In the course of the presentation of the antinomy the rationale behind these labels will hopefully become clearer. Both thesis and antithesis proceed from the same principle that every human being has an identity and dignity which entail specific obligations and responsibilities and secure certain rights.

The idealistic-technical thesis

Because each human being has its own identity and dignity, all human beings ought to be treated in the same way. If a human being or a specific group demand a special status in society, that could only take place through neglect, discrimination, and even violation of the identity and dignity of others. For this reason, the only sort of identity and dignity that is relevant is the individual's capacity or potential for autonomous or responsible action. This capacity is not immediately overt. Nevertheless, in spite of whatever ostensible and ideological dis-

The naturalistic antithesis

Because each human being has its own identity and dignity, all human beings may not be treated in the same way. If all human beings were treated in the same manner, then the identity and dignity proper to each individual would be disregarded. However, the principle of equality is negated as soon as the identity and dignity of a single human being is not respected. How can it be right to treat people in vastly inequitable circumstances (for example, poor and rich) or of quite different character (for example, honorable and without honor) as

tinctions are dominant in a society, each human being, insofar as he or she is rational and thus can deliberate, has the capacity to make choices. The highest political value consists neither in what a person is or does as a "child of nature," nor in the degree to which a person's existence and accomplishments contribute to the well-being of the society or the state. The supreme political value lies rather in the autonomy of every human being.[22] The principle of equality signifies that each human being has its own identity and dignity and for this reason possesses the right to the respect of fellow citizens as well as the duty to respect this dignity in others. Accordingly, the principle of equality can only be in force when there is universal, fully reciprocal recognition. There may not be any legally privileged people or groups and, by the same token, no conception of the so-called "good life" may be privileged.[23] Under this interpretation of the principle of equality, it would be unjust to take into consideration any properties and capabilities or accomplishments other than a person's inherent autonomy.

though they were fundamentally the same? On what basis and in what way is it permissible to exclude from the identity and dignity of human beings the natural differences of gender or of origin on a particular part of the globe, with its own ethnic tradition and history? Indeed, when such dissimilarities are not taken into account, one cannot help wondering whether a particular (for example, patriarchal or sectarian) conception of identity and dignity, proper to those with the most power in the society, has not been forcibly generalized. In other words, how can one be sure that what a specific part of society allegedly regards as an expression of universal recognition is not in fact merely the cunning, pragmatic imposition of particular, cultural prejudices? This criticism of the idealistic-technical thesis mirrors the problematic character of the so-called "golden rule": "Love your neighbor as yourself!" The problem is, it can be quite unjust and even injurious to a person's neighbor if that person behaves toward that neighbor in precisely the way that person would like to have others behave towards him or her. Is there any reason to think that one person's conception of what it means to be loved corresponds to someone else's conception?

The arguments of both the thesis and the antithesis are based upon genuine insights. On the one hand, in the practical execution of the idealistic-technical thesis there is a genuine danger of repressive hegemony, precisely because a conception of identity and dignity in terms of autonomy alone is purely formal and, hence, unworkable without the addition of other principles that are in fact based upon a conception of human *nature*. It would be naive to think that such principles would not reflect and cement those very relationships of power and influence on the basis of which the society presently functions. On the other hand, the defenders of the idealistic-technical thesis regard the practical implications of the naturalistic antithesis as nothing less than a recipe for regressing into the old power politics that typically defined feudal governmental and economic relations. Hence, the appropriateness of the word *regress* from the perspective of those who embrace the idealistic-technical thesis. For them political society is primarily something to be *constructed* and its construction on the basis of a theory of reciprocal recognition is the severe and violent accomplishment of modernity.

Despite these weighty considerations on both sides, the antinomy of recognition itself is due to diverse interpretations of the principle of equality, that "every human being has its own identity and dignity." Thus, on the one hand, the thesis is persuasive as long as emphasis is put on the word *every* and as long as it is possible to determine the identity and dignity that "every" human being has coming to them. For example, the libertarians, who by some accounts might be considered the purest liberals, ascribe to each human being an autonomy, the right to make free choices, quite apart from what is chosen. On the other hand, the antithesis is convincing if the term *own* is singled out for emphasis. Instead of being able to consist in some universally shared property such as autonomy, each human being has his or her "own" identity and dignity, rooted in natural and cultural determinations of what the human being is and chooses.

From a logical point of view, the antinomy is thus resolvable. No contradiction ensues as long as the two conflicting interpretations of the principle of equality are distinguished. Yet there remains a real problem underlying these two different construals of the principle of equality. That problem concerns the connection or integration of the contrasting understandings of equality. For the necessity of some such integration is patent. On the one hand, the understanding of equality to which the thesis appeals is far too formal, presenting no content for ethical, political decision making. When an actual decision of this sort is made, the content of the choice is paramount. That is to say, who or what is being recognized and not merely that or how the recognition takes place must be the focus of attention. In political terms, concern must be for what is being legislated and not merely for the fact or manner of the legislating. On the other hand, by providing no basis for recognition of the human being as a human being (rather than merely as a male, a Swede, or a Lutheran, and so on), the antithesis seems to lack a foundation for a genuinely moral, political common life.

The reciprocal recognition touted in the idealistic-technical thesis can be realized only by appealing to the sort of good life that befits a human being as such. In order to judge whether, as the antithesis asserts, a particular (nonuniversal) but natural conception of identity and dignity on the part of individuals or groups deserves the recognition claimed for it, members of society have no recourse but to some account of the identity of the human being as such. In short, each interpretation of the principle of equality is incomplete. In order to be complete and rendered sufficiently workable each of these interpretations requires a determination of the good life, the life that is proper to the human being as such. The crisis of recognition can only be resolved through a determination of the content, not of a pure or particular will, but of a good will. What is required, in other words, is nothing less than the accomplishment of the task set by classical ethical and political philosophy, an accomplishment impossible without wisdom, the virtue corresponding to that part of the human soul that thinks and reasons. That this requirement must be met confirms at the same time the unsuitability of the approach of those modern political thinkers who—much like Fukuyama—construe the possibility of the modern state solely or chiefly on the basis of principles of recognition and equality. The crisis of recognition consists in opposed claims either between the part of the soul seeking satisfaction of animal needs and the recognition-seeking part, or demands for recognition as an equal and as a superior to others. The crisis expressed in the antinomy is not resolvable as long as there is no third part of the soul, which occupies a position not simply next to the other parts, but, as it were, *over* them, with the responsibility of ordering them.

THE ANTINOMY OF RECOGNITION AND
THE END OF HISTORY

In his articulation of how liberalism might be construed as the "end of history," Fukuyama remains within the all too confining framework of the antinomy of recognition sketched in the preceding section. The allegedly most dangerous tension, that between the demand for universal, reciprocal recognition (*isothymia*) and "the desire for glory," "to be recognized as *superior* to other people" (*megalothymia*) presents one particular version of the antinomy.[24] In this version *isothymia* is the moral-psychological expression of the thesis; *megalothymia* a corresponding expression of the antithesis. The tension between political and economic equality represents another form of the same antinomy.

The triumph of liberalism is explained by Fukuyama as a combination of two things. Liberalism's success is due, on the one hand, to "the economization of life," the "blossoming of the desiring part of the soul" (that part seeking satisfaction of animal needs), and, on the other, to the replacement of the *megalothymia* of the nobility with "an all-pervasive *isothymia,* that is, the desire to be recognized as the equal of other people."[25] The tensions that continue to be a danger to liberal democracies stem from the conflicts between the desirous and the thymotic parts of the soul or between a measured and excessive expression of the thymotic part of the soul. What is clearly missing in this analysis is the classical role of the third part of the soul and, even more importantly, the role of the virtue corresponding to it: wisdom.[26]

At the beginning of the fourth part of *The End of History and the Last Man* the poles of the antinomy of recognition surface unmistakably in regard to the third tension mentioned by Fukuyama. Fukuyama attempts to explain why it is often so difficult for nations that endorse democratic principles to make the practical transition to democracy. For the most part, the answer lies for him in the distinction between state and society. "The success and the stability of liberal democracy . . . never depends simply on the mechanical application of a certain set of universal principles and laws, but requires a degree of conformity between peoples and states."[27] While the founding of a liberal state is supposed to be "a rational act," the existence of a people with its common notions of good and evil, of the holy and the profane, and so on, precedes the state; while politics is "the sphere of self-conscious choice about the proper mode of governance," the rules of culture and society are "seldom explicit or self-consciously recognized even by those who participate in them."[28] Fukuyama identifies the following cultural factors as the most significant sources of resistance to the march of liberalism: nationalism, religion, enormous social inequality (as, for example, when there is no thriving middle class, the *sine qua non* of a healthy civil society), and lack of experience or capacity of self-governance and self-confirmation on local levels.

This tension between the principles of liberal democracy and the elements of a culture presents yet another version of the antinomy of recognition. The idealistic-technical thesis revolves around the alleged necessity of reciprocal recognition which is embodied in the liberal state alone. Such a state is *created* and, indeed, "at a certain point, it must arise out of a deliberate political decision to establish democracy."[29] By contrast, many of the different features and capabilities of human beings underlying the argument of the naturalistic antithesis are not consciously chosen and created, but rather are rooted in the culture and the society—and indeed, if not prior to, then at least in some important sense independent of the grounding of, the state.

Fukuyama is not completely consistent in his account of this third tension within liberal democracies. Though at one point he insists that the realm of politics is "autonomous" in relation to culture, at another point he concedes "that the dividing line between culture and politics, between peoples and states, is not all that clear."[30] However, it is to Fukuyama's credit that he falls into this inconsistency, for it further testifies to the inadequacy of the conception of human nature with which he is working. If, for example, the liberal democratic form of governance in the United States did in fact fulfill the dreams of its people at any point in the last two hundred years, then the success is based, not upon the expression of some abstract or even concrete *volonté générale*, bent only on satisfying animal desires and a wish to be recognized, but rather on the wise—and extremely fortunate— direction by a predominantly European, Protestant community within the framework of a capitalist economic system.[31] In other words, if liberal democracies manage to contribute to bringing about the good life of a political society, the measure of that contribution can be traced to the extent to which liberal democracies make it possible for reason, spirit, and desire to work effectively together in the soul of each individual and, thereby, in the society. In other words, the measure of the success of liberal democracies lies in their capacity to promote the right, that is to say, the "just" harmony of moderation, courage, and wisdom in its people.[32]

NOTES

I would like to thank Antonio Cua and Thomas Sheehy for their criticisms of an earlier version of this paper.

1. Alexandre Kojève, *Introduction à la lecture de Hegel,* ed. Raymond Queneau, 2nd ed. (Paris: Gallimard, 1968), p. 437, note to the second edition.

2. Francis Fukuyama, *The End of History and the Last Man* (New York: Avon Books, 1992), pp. 42f, 289, 302–3, 314–15, 324–25, 328, 338–39. (Hereafter referred to as EH.)

3. Ibid., pp. 206, 288, 291, 338.

4. Ibid., p. 203; Fukuyama suggests that the liberal democracy is "the most just regime," constituting "the best possible solution to the human problem" (EH, pp. 337–38); see also Charles Taylor, "The Politics of Recognition," in *Multiculturalism and "The Politics of Recognition,"* ed. Amy Gutman, Steven C. Rockefeller, Michael Walzer, Susan Wolf (Princeton, N.J.: Princeton University Press, 1993).

5. See Victor Gourevitch, "The End of History?" *Interpretation* 21, no. 2 (Winter 1993–94): 215.

6. Fukuyama, EH, p. 291: "Middle-class societies will remain highly inegalitarian in certain respects, but the sources of inequality will increasingly be attributable to the natural inequality of talents, the economically necessary division of labor, and to culture."

7. Ibid., pp. 326f, 334f.

8. G. W. F. Hegel, *Vorlesungen über die Philosophie der Geschichte* (Stuttgart: Reclam, 1961), p. 588.

9. See Fukuyama, EH, p. 291; see also Ronald Dworkin, *A Matter of Principle* (Cambridge, Mass.: Harvard University Press, 1985): pp. 187, 192–93, 196, 207–8.

10. Ibid., pp. 196, 199.

11. Ibid., p. 200.

12. Ibid., p. 203.

13. Ibid., pp. 186–88, 199–200, 203.

14. Fukuyama refers to "a continuing tension between the twin principles of liberty and equality" (EH, p. 292), and rational liberalism existing "in some tension" with a preexisting culture (EH, p. 327).

15. Kojève, *Introduction à la lecture de Hegel*, pp. 13–15; Fukuyama, EH, pp. 146–47. It is by no means clear to me to what extent and/or in what sense the desire for recognition is not, in fact, present in some animals. Also, the reduction of courage to the fulfillment of the need for recognition seems to be a perversion of the traditional sense of this virtue.

16. Fukuyama, EH, p. 315; he continues: "Indeed, democracy's long-run health and stability can be seen to rest on the quality and number of outlets for *megalothymia* that are available to its citizens." See also Fukuyama, EH, p. 304.

17. See, for example, Philip T. Grier, "The End of History, and the Return of History," *Owl of Minerva* 21, no. 2 (Spring 1990): 131–44. On the point that Kojève never construed his interpretation of Hegel as an exegesis of the *mens auctoris*, see Michael Roth, "A Problem of Recognition: Alexandre Kojève and the End of History," *History and Theory* 24, no. 3 (1985): 293–306.

18. Endre Kiss, "Gorbatschow als legitimer oder illegitimer Vollender Hegels (Das Ende der Geschichte als eine Theorie der Gegenwart)," *Studien zur Problematik des Endes der Geschichte* (Budapest, 1992): pp. 9, 13, 16.

19. Fukuyama, EH, p. 337.

20. Dworkin, *A Matter of Principle*, p. 190.

21. Taylor, "The Politics of Recognition," pp. 37–44, 60.

22. Dworkin, *A Matter of Principle*, p. 190.

23. Ibid., pp. 191f: ". . . government must be neutral on what might be called the question of the good life"; Taylor, "The Politics of Recognition," p. 57: "Dignity is associated less with any particular understanding of the good life, such that someone's departure from this would detract from his or her dignity, than with the power to consider and espouse for oneself some view or other."

24. Fukuyama, EH, pp. 182f; see also EH, p. 186: "In one society after another, Hobbes's deal has been offered to the old class of aristocrats: namely, that they trade in their thymotic pride for the prospect of a peaceful life of unlimited material acquisition."

25. Ibid., p. 190; see Gourevitch, "The End of History?": pp. 216, 228 n. 5 for a good account of the sources of Fukuyama's reading of Plato's political psychology.

26. Strauss, *On Tyranny*, p. 225: "Modern man, dissatisfied with utopias and scorning them, has tried to find a guarantee for the actualization of the best social order. In order to succeed, or rather in order to be able to believe that he could succeed, he had to lower the goal of man. One form in which this was done was to replace moral virtue by universal recognition, or to replace happiness by the satisfaction deriving from universal recognition." As this text might suggest, Fukuyama is doubtless influenced by Strauss's

analysis. Nevertheless, when Fukuyama discusses reason as the third part of the soul and even when he occasionally mentions wisdom, he subordinates its role to that of serving the other two parts (in the classical tripartite theory of Plato); see Fukuyama, EH, pp. 176–77, 204–5, 220; a similar criticism has been advanced by Gourevitch in his article "The End of History?" pp. 224, 221.

27. Fukuyama, EH, p. 213.

28. Ibid., pp. 212–13.

29. Ibid., p. 220.

30. Ibid., pp. 220–31.

31. See Aristotle *Nichomachean Ethics* 1.10, 1.13 (1100b23–30, 1102a17–24).

32. Walter Bröcker, *Platos Gespräche*, 2. Aufl. (Frankfurt am Main: Klostermann, 1967) p. 268.

Human Nature and
the Founding of Philosophy
STANLEY H. ROSEN

I

PHILOSOPHY ENTERS INTO OUR LIVES unannounced and with no particular preparation. It does not so much enter as call attention to itself,
like someone who has been present within us from the beginning, but
without speaking. In this sense, philosophy is our second and better
self. At the same time, however, the stimulus that leads this better self
to speak comes from outside everyday life. It both disrupts and founds
the ordinary persona. This fundamental dichotomy can also be described as our entrance into two modes of temporality, which I shall
call historical and cosmological.

In the first mode of temporality, we are situated, engaged, absorbed, and directed by events. The structures that shape our thoughts
and actions are themselves defined by previous events. We do not
detach ourselves from these structures or call them into question; they
are "ordinary" in the literal sense that they order us. They come to us
from history and they lead us into history. In an entirely unmelodra-
matic sense, as living, we are "making history." In the second mode of
temporality, we are like rootless travelers, somehow immune to historical time, yet oddly attracted to it as a problem. History requires an
explanation; we have to give an account of it, "make sense," not just
more history.

No doubt there are very few persons who live entirely within one
or the other of these two modes of temporality. But each of us is defined by one or the other; how we accommodate the two dimensions
of this joint residency to one another determines who we are. Some
will object that I have engaged in poetic or mythical language rather
than in the sober discourse of philosophy. I would not deny this. I

have employed poetical language because I am speaking about the human soul. Our theme is not psychology, sociology, or linguistics, but the origin of philosophy. Philosophy is not a science, a method, or a body of dogmas, although it may issue in any or all of these. It is a state of the soul, a psychic activity, a way of seeing historical existence that is itself situated outside history or in what I am calling cosmological time. Cosmological time is the temporality within which we entertain rival interpretations of historical existence.

In Plato's *Phaedrus,* cosmological time is represented as the erotic flight upward to the roof of the cosmos, from which vantage point the soul gazes upon the Hyperuranian beings. In Nietzsche's *Zarathustra,* it is represented by the ship that takes Zarathustra from the blessed isles to the great city from which he will return over another sea to the City of the Motley Cow and from thence by foot once more to his mountaintop cave. The crew of this ship are explorers, sustained by courage, who reside neither on the roof of the cosmos nor on the blessed isles, but certainly not in cities or on mountaintops. They are in perpetual motion, but their motion is circular. This is because they are always looking for the same thing, a land that they cannot discover without negating themselves. Thus their circularity is not that of the eternal return, which is itself one of the sights that they discover on their journey, in this case a sight that is described to them by Zarathustra as a vision and a riddle. The eternal return is an interpretation of the circularity of historical time. We see or discover it within cosmological time.

Socrates is a citizen of Athens who is also a lover of the Ideas. He lives in two residences, two modes of temporality; he is stepping out of ordinary experience but nevertheless has one foot firmly planted within it. Zarathustra is a citizen of no city; his home is in a mountaintop cave from which he periodically descends, no doubt in eternal recurrence, but therefore as the exemplification of the perpetual motion, the unending search for an explanation of history. Zarathustra does not step through the gateway of the moment into historical time. He is thus related to the explorers on whose ship he travels away from the blessed isles. The blessed isles are no blessing for Zarathustra; that is his anti-Platonism. In more prosaic terms, Zarathustra does not live in the dwelling called ordinary experience.

Socrates and Zarathustra are alike in that they see the dualism of human existence. Socrates acknowledges an eternity that Zarathustra denies; or rather, when Zarathustra says "I love you, eternity," he is referring to eternal time. Despite his citizenship within Athens, Socrates is obviously a transpolitical person. Despite his isolation and perpetual motion, Zarathustra longs for a political expression of his perception of spiritual excellence. Socrates, despite such strange doctrines as that of the Ideas, respects ordinary experience and common sense and invariably begins his explorations from situatedness within the everyday, even the historical or the typically Athenian. Zarathustra, despite or because of his desire for political fulfillment, despises the everyday and the ordinary and attempts to uproot us from its grip. This should suffice to indicate the sameness and the difference of our two heroes. The sameness is the root of the difference; it is their perception of the doubled nature of human existence that launches them on their journeys. But Zarathustra repudiates ordinary experience whereas Socrates begins and ends with it.

I believe that Zarathustra is much more difficult to understand than Socrates, if by understanding we mean the ability to see the inner coherence of his enterprise. I will illustrate this greater difficulty as follows. The acknowledgment of eternity, as Zarathustra regularly points out, leads to a diminution in the status of history. But the doctrine of the eternal return serves to render history circular and thus finite. The structure of time thus seems to take the place of, and to serve the same role as, the Socratic Ideas. In my opinion, the similarity between Nietzsche's hero and Plato's Socrates is an inevitable consequence of philosophy. If philosophy is possible at all, it is always as a comprehensive view of life, and so of history with respect to its fundamental possibilities. But please note the following crucial point. To see human existence as a whole is not the same as to explain it in a philosophical doctrine or system. As residents of cosmological time, we are free to reject both the doctrine of Ideas and the myth of the eternal return. What we cannot do is to insist upon the impossibility of viewing human existence as a whole; otherwise stated, as soon as we insist upon this, we claim to have seen it as a whole. Once we enter into cosmological time, there is no escape in the sense of a complete immersion back into history.

The purpose of these preliminary remarks is to illustrate what I mean by saying that philosophy is a state of the soul, not a doctrine. This is not to deny that philosophers promulgate doctrines. But they are not themselves their doctrines. Socrates is not an Idea, and not the Ideas, just as Zarathustra is not the eternal return. All this is essential for what follows. I have argued that philosophy originates in ordinary experience, that it is an extraordinary disruption that nevertheless retains its affiliation with, and is in a fundamental sense about, ordinary experience. I have also noted that philosophy can begin anywhere within everyday life, and that in a real sense it never begins but is coeval with humanity. All this being so, there is no question of seeking for a foundation or *punctum inconcussum* outside of philosophy itself, on or in which philosophy may ground itself. There is no foundation for philosophy other than itself. But this does not mean that philosophy is vitiated by relativism, or that we cannot say what is philosophy and what is not. That problem arises only for those who confuse philosophy with its doctrines.

When I speak of the doubled nature of human existence, and so of the relation between the ordinary and the extraordinary, I intend to be offering not an interpretation but rather a description of the psychic structure that allows philosophy to occur. When psychologists, neurophysiologists, or philosophers offer interpretations of perception, they begin with the fact that we perceive things. This fact is not part of the interpretation but what requires a theoretical explanation. In a similar manner, I have begun with the fact of philosophy as it originates in our everyday life. There is, however, a crucial difference between philosophy and sense perception. The latter is itself an ingredient in ordinary experience, whereas philosophy participates in ordinary experience as a disruption. In thinking about this disruption, we instantiate it. We are ourselves the existential embodiment of this disruption, which must accordingly be approached from both directions, the ordinary and the extraordinary.

I chose Socrates and Zarathustra as illustrations of my thesis because they are in a way the beginning and the end of the Western philosophical tradition. Certainly they have become paradigmatic of a fundamental difference between two modes of philosophizing. At the same time, it has to be said that illustrations of this sort are useful only to those who are already aware of the disruption. All accounts of philosophy are circular or, as Socrates calls them, recollective. They do not speak to those who are outside the circle, any more than a description of perception would speak to a nonsentient being. We must be brought into the presence of philosophy by our own words. This is one of the reasons why Plato wrote dialogues; it is why Socrates insists upon the necessity of agreement with his interlocutor. And this is also why Nietzsche shifts from the monologues of his other writings to the quasi-dialogue of *Thus Spoke Zarathustra*.

Philosophical dialectic is thus neither a Hegelian speculative logic nor an open-ended conversation in which we describe to each other our respective points of view and grant their incommensurability. The former is the discourse of gods; the latter is a sacrifice of our humanity. I have argued what I believe to be incontrovertible, namely, that our common experience directs us toward the satisfaction of individual desires, the resolution of puzzles, the expression of preferences, recognition of beauty or nobility as well as of ugliness or baseness, and so finally, by a series to which you may add whatever steps I have omitted, to the understanding that all these partial desires, puzzles, and preferences require some coherent account of the totality of our experience. In particular we require some coherent account of the unity of our individual lives if we are to retain the particular triumphs of satisfaction and overcome the individual losses that make up the fabric of quotidian existence. In short, no argument is required to demonstrate the actuality of philosophy. Philosophy is its own demonstration. It compels us even as we speak against it.

Paradoxical as it may sound, the extraordinary is ordinary in its reiterated appearance. Otherwise we would never recognize or understand it. But the force of persuasion comes from outside and above us, like what the Greeks called a *theia dosis,* a gift from the gods. Perhaps it will cause no irreparable misunderstanding if I say that the appreciation of the extraordinary is an act of the piety of thinking. This expression, which sounds Heideggerian, is anticipated by Socrates in the *Philebus* (28c6–9), when he says that the wise make *nous* their god, thereby exalting themselves.

If all this is so, the extraordinary event of philosophical origination is not a new and outlandish thesis or a baffling first principle, but the spiritual act by which we disrupt the common opinions that blunt our wonder or prevent us from arranging the fragments of our lives into a rational totality that we have thought out for ourselves. This is what I mean when I say that philosophy founds itself. I want to defend this assertion in some detail. And I do so, not by attempting to provide you with an extraordinary description of the extraordinary, but by starting just where we all do: in the midst of the everyday.

II

The English word *foundation* is derived from the Latin verb *fundo, fundare*: "to set up or to establish." We may found a city by deciding to build it in a certain geographical location; the building is subsequent to the decision. To found by decision is to set the mind in a certain way, to take something—say, a plot of land—as something else, the future home of our people. We assert an intention, and so hold ourselves in readiness to act in such and such a way. Buildings are artifacts that we produce as a result of the founding decision. The founder first sanctifies the ground and calls the city into being without thereby producing any artifacts distinct from the founding pronouncement.

One could easily imagine a case in which a city is founded but never built. The site is selected and sanctified, but the founder and the followers may be destroyed by an unexpected enemy before they are able to erect a single structure. The act of founding is here almost but not quite a phantom, waiting, perhaps forever, for some descendants of the slaughtered troops. Their children, or the children of their children, may someday, having heard of the original founding, arrive at the site in order to bring the city into physical existence. Or consider the case of a soldier who decides that from this moment forward, he will face the exigencies of battle with resolute courage, come what may, no matter how desperate his situation. His acts are at this moment founded in this decision, yet he builds nothing. In the extreme case he may never do anything but die in the instant following his resolution. Can we say that such a man died bravely or resolutely? If the decision was genuinely taken, then I believe that we must. The act of dying has been sanctified by the foundation of courage.

Unbuilt cities and unfulfilled decisions are of course extreme examples of the act of founding. I do not present them as foundations for an elaborate theory of founding, but as evidence of the ambiguity of the concept *foundation*. One can found without building or producing anything external to the act of deciding to hold oneself in a certain way, on the basis of a definite intention to act henceforward. We found ourselves by taking a stand in preparation for building, producing, or acting. Although the etymology is entirely spurious, we may nevertheless say that the meanings of the concepts provide a poetical justification for the claim that we "find" ourselves by founding ourselves. It is in no way melodramatic, but a simple description of how we behave, to say that the foundation for our actions is the ground we stand on, whether we are gazing at the stars on a clear night or looking into our souls in order to determine who we are.

These decisions are not made on the basis of scientific evidence, say from psychology and sociology, and certainly not from the study of biology or neuroscience. The decision to investigate oneself scientifically is itself a nonscientific act of foundation. And not even neuroscientists turn to their own textbooks in order to justify their contents, but instead to speeches founded in everyday decisions about truth, rationality, and the rhetoric of persuasion. It would be absurd to attempt to decide how to live one's life by reading a sociological treatise on lifestyles, although we might very well decide to become sociologists as a result of the illumination we find that such treatises shed on our everyday concerns about the choice of a future profession. But these concerns were not learned from reading technical books. One does not fall in love by reading a marriage manual, not even by reading novels and poems. It is by living that we understand books. No doubt the process is reciprocally enriching, once it has reached a certain point. But the origination or founding comes from within us; it is our own wonder and desire that opens the book, not just literally but in the deeper sense of the expression.

It might be objected that the founding acts to which I refer are themselves inarticulate assertions of first principles. In a sense the objection is well-taken. By holding myself ready to act in such-and-such a manner, I make myself the foundation of my future acts, for which I assume responsibility regardless of what psychologists, sociologists, or postmodern hermeneuticists tell me to the contrary. But this amounts merely to the tautology that there is no human action (as opposed to random motion) without intentionality. To go directly to the crucial case, if I hold myself open to investigation of the unity, totality, and value of my life, or in more pedestrian terms, to the investigation of the principle of the satisfaction of desire, this is not the same as to enunciate a principle by which the investigation, whether in its exalted or pedestrian sense, is to be conducted. One does not become a philosopher by enunciating one's allegiance to Platonism, Cartesianism, or postmodernism. The philosopher is ready for anything, including failure.

Let me interpolate a word here about the apparent similarity between this account of self-foundation and the Heideggerian doctrine of resolution (*Entschlossenheit*) and authenticity (*Eigentlichkeit*). The problem with the Heideggerian doctrine, as I understand it, is that it is on the one hand lacking in all content and on the other too dependent upon the contingencies of the concrete historical situation. This apparent contradiction arises in the following way. To be resolute is to take a stand from within the tradition that has produced us, but as modified by the authentic possibilities that emerge from the future. Resolution thus comes perilously close to stubbornness, that is, to the stubborn affirmation of who we are; and this in turn is defined by the race, religion, nationality, class, family, and autobiographical experience that constitute our historical existence. What counts as a genuine or authentic possibility in each case is accordingly contingent upon who we have come to be at the moment. But this might be anything at all, depending upon the individual case.

Philosophical foundation, on the other hand, as a disruption from above, is, if not a transcendence of contingent history, certainly a detachment from it. The philosopher is detached from historical or autobiographical time and enters into what Plato called the Hyperuranian and Nietzsche the Hyperborean realm of philosophical or cosmological time. To say this in another way, there are no authentic alternatives to philosophy for the recipient of the divine Eros. The disruption of the traditional mode of existence is the same in all cases, even if the common philosophical activity requires quite different historical actions in different individual contexts. There is a fundamental difference between founding philosophy and making a political decision. To confuse the two, as did Heidegger, is to make it impossible for philosophy to illuminate politics. Instead, philosophy is politicized, even if that politicizing is disguised by ontological rhetoric.

If it is true to say that Heidegger must be judged as a thinker on philosophical rather than on moral or personal grounds, then one must say that he is philosophically defective because his ontology of human existence produces an abstract structure that functions to restrict our self-defining decisions to the possibilities that are furnished by the contingent local situation. The philosopher, on the other hand, must be free to reject the local situation, free to choose a mode of conduct that is not a genuine possibility for those who are bound by locally resolute expressions of the contingent historical past, and so by an antecedently defined future.

The previous interpolation was necessary in order to distinguish between stubbornness and the act of philosophical founding. Let us now return to the main line of the argument. What would it mean to be a person without foundations? Consider again the example of the soldier; only now imagine that he has failed to establish his mental or spiritual attitude toward danger and death. This soldier is neither brave nor cowardly, nor does he respond in accord with any other principle, for example, expediency. He has not found himself; he cannot find what has not been established, nor can he even begin to look without deciding that there is something to be found. Our soldier is not a skeptic, because he lacks the impetus to look for himself. *Skepticism* means literally the process of looking for something, and not, as it has come to be used, the position that suspends belief. In fact, there is no such position. It is not a position to say on every occasion, "I do not know." Not even Socrates' assertion that he knows that he does not know is such a universal suspension. In fact, the soldier in our example has not suspended any beliefs because we have imagined him as never having had any. As entirely without foundations, he is the radically contingent being of antifoundationalist postmodernism. He is neither here nor there. In the midst of battle, the soldier does not act; he merely reacts, as for example by falling to the ground when he is shot.

The radically contingent man cannot be said to die; he is "terminated" or, still more brutally, "put down." This is of course the technical vocabulary of the contemporary adventure film, in which the agents detach themselves from their own founding decisions by the temporary adoption of a phenomenological bracketing of values that permits them to dehumanize their victims. I suppose that the surgeon has to perform the same bracketing, not in order to put down but instead to raise up the patient. The underlying motives of the bracketing are in each case different. Sometimes they can be deduced from the detached acts and sometimes not, but the main point is that the motives are external to the detached acts and constitute their foundation. Bracketing makes no sense except to those who are outside the brackets.

Where is the radically contingent man, the hypothetical soldier who lacks all foundations? In our imagination, but not in actual life. There are no such persons; it is impossible to be a person without any foundations whatsoever. Human beings may be treated like brutes or inanimate objects, as when they are "put down" like a sick dog or, in another sense of the term, like a pair of shoes. But unless their humanity has been destroyed, they protest against such treatment, and whether or not they can articulate the content of this protest, it is the expression of their foundation. The imaginary soldier or radically contingent man has no foundation; hence his remaining erect or falling to the ground has no significance. He was already dissolving, already a decentered subject, a trace of difference, before the bullet took his life. The work of the bullet may be the consequence of a founding act; the undergoing of its impact is not.

I conclude from my examples first, that the act of founding is independent of the production of technical artifacts; and second, that there are no radically contingent persons or that in other words, life is foundational. What then does it mean to speak of philosophy without foundations? Is the term being used in a completely different sense from the one conveyed by my examples? One could certainly distinguish between the act of founding philosophy as a decision to look for first principles, and the consequent act of discovering or producing them. And this is precisely the distinction I have in mind. There can be philosophy without first principles, whether for better or worse remaining to be determined; but there can be no unfounded philosophy, because philosophy is founding, albeit of an extraordinary kind when contrasted with the foundings of my examples. Philosophy is not a profession or a set of technical acts that we perform for no reason connected with our "pretheoretical" lives. It is the transformation of our lives in such a way as to allow us to devise technical procedures that receive their sense and value from those whom we have become through self-understanding.

These very simple reflections lead to the following thesis. For those who are not frightened by poetical imagery, it is possible to compare the philosophical life to a voyage on strange seas, in a search for new races of humankind and monuments to those long since dead. Something very much like this image is in fact employed by Nietzsche's Zarathustra, as I noted previously. It has the disadvantage of evoking a discontinuity between the ordinary and the extraordinary, and so of suggesting that philosophy is a radical departure from the everyday. I on the other hand am attempting to bring out the sense in which philosophy is a disruption of the ordinary that comes in response to ordinary needs but with an extraordinary remedy. This is the sense of the Platonic doctrine of Eros, which comes to us from above like a god or a daimon, but in response to the human desire for beauty. One does not need to be divinely mad in order to fall in love;

but the ordinary forms of love will not by themselves raise us to the level of philosophical madness.

Allow me to repeat the reason why I insist upon this point, since it is of crucial importance. If philosophy is altogether extraordinary and transpires entirely outside everyday life, then it is something akin to poetical fantasy on the one hand and the construction of abstract scientific models on the other. But this is not the whole story; poems and models are constructed on the basis of our experience within everyday life. A thoroughly extraordinary philosophy would have no such connection to ordinary experience. It would be a poetical assertion, exactly on a par with other such assertions, among which we could choose only on the basis of taste. On the other hand, it is phenomenologically false to say that philosophy is altogether ordinary, or that it arises naturally by a kind of thickening of experience analogous to the legendary "gathering of the data" that according to old-fashioned textbooks is supposed to turn into a scientific theory.

My adoption of a Platonic teaching should not be taken as a blanket endorsement of the wisdom of the ancients or a repudiation of modern thought. One can restate the doctrine of Eros in a partly modern idiom: the human being is fundamentally desire for what it lacks. This thesis can be found in Hegel, who seems to have derived it from Hobbes. But Hegel is something much more complex than a Hobbesian. One could say that his absolute spirit is a synthesis of Eros and Agape. In somewhat less metaphorical terms, Hegel objects to the Platonic thesis that human beings may love but never possess wisdom. He asserts that it is impossible to love what one does not know. In this case the founding of philosophy is entirely arbitrary until it has been verified by wisdom. This objection, if it were sound, would lead not to Hegelianism but to the impossibility of philosophy. It is therefore worth considering more closely.

A reply to Hegel could be stated abstractly as follows. According to Hegel, it is necessary to rise to the level of the absolute by an arbitrary act of the will. This is tantamount to the admission that philosophy begins as a disruption within the everyday. The conceptual gears of the system, whether phenomenological or logical, do not begin to engage for us until we have rejected common sense and external reflection, as Hegel refers to traditional rationalism. Within the act of will itself, understood as an initiation, wisdom is at best potential. How then explain the force that sustains us at the level of the absolute? And still more sharply, how explain our recognition of the absolute *as* absolute before we have completed the conceptual articulation of totality?

This is not the place to explore the technical details of Hegelianism. I believe that the force of his point is accessible, together with my reply to it, on the basis of our ordinary experience. In order to make it accessible, I reclaim for ordinary experience what Bertrand Russell called the distinction between knowledge and acquaintance. It is impossible to fall in love with someone with whom one is not acquainted (and this is true even of fantasies), but knowledge of the beloved is certainly not a prerequisite. And as we know from our own experience, when knowledge comes, it is often disastrous. We may learn that we have fallen in love with the wrong person, or that knowledge of the person's character has evaporated our love.

The act of falling in love is itself contingent in the precise sense that it may never happen to us, even though the circumstances are prepared by our very humanity. On the other hand, we are usually surprised by love, and this is why we speak of "falling" into it. Love as a human phenomenon is ordinary, but here and now, for me or you, it is extraordinary. This fall founds us; it gives a basis and order to our subsequent actions. Love "opens the horizon" for us. But this is not a construction, a choice of first principles or the discovery of a method for satisfying our erotic desire. It is rather the tuning of the soul. And the conductor who tunes us is not ourself but a god or a daimon, Eros, who has come from outside and above our lives yet in response to the conditions and needs of those lives. And this helps us to understand the crucial function of the Platonic Ideas. Philosophical Eros is the love of the Ideas; when these are repudiated, there is nothing to love but historical contingency.

Let us now shift our attention slightly to the experience captured in the words "love at first sight." We may fall madly in love with someone about whom we know nothing, and whom we have never seen before. I mention this to remind you that the most minimal acquaintance is sufficient for being surprised by love, and that knowledge of any particular sort is altogether unnecessary. I will not enter into the pathological; let us grant that in order to fall in love, we must know, or believe ourselves to know, that the beloved is a human being. This knowledge and its modalities is furnished to us by nature, not science. The scientific study of Eros comes into being only because humans experience love by their very natures. No one can learn what it is to love by reading books. At the same time, whatever the future may hold in store for me, I cannot be mistaken about the fact of love. There is something incorrigible about desire.

So far so good with respect to the comparison between the origin of philosophy and falling in love. The comparison enables us to explain, not by elaborate theories but on the basis of our own everyday experience, how our lives can be founded without recourse to arbitrary principles or methods. The act of founding is both extraordinary because it comes from outside unexpectedly and takes us into very deep waters, and ordinary because it is the sort of thing that happens quite naturally to human beings. No one can persuade us by rational argumentation or scientific instruction to fall either into or out of love. There is no doubt that love has seized us, but the certitude comes from within ourselves, not from others, not even from other lovers. And more could be said to buttress the analogy, but it would be otiose to proceed further in this direction.

In fact it would be dangerous, since there are also serious disanalogies between philosophy and love in the usual sense. To mention only the most important of these, at no time does love fall under the sway of knowledge. I mean by this that knowledge is not what we are driven to pursue when we fall in love. We may wish not to know the true nature of our beloved, and our love may continue even if we learn unpleasant truths about its object. In a sense, the latter (but not the former) is true of philosophy as well, but there is a crucial difference. The unpleasantness of certain truths is mitigated if not eliminated by the pleasure derived from the illumination of knowledge. One might suggest an analogy with the jealous lover who derives a perverse joy in "knowing the truth at last" about the infidelity of the beloved. I think that there is something in this suggestion to the extent that it shows the pleasure intrinsic to knowledge of any sort. But the end of love is not knowledge of this or any other sort.

We can get at this point from a slightly different angle. Once again let us distinguish between what we call "true love" and undifferentiated desire or lechery. True love has nothing to do with truth in the philosophical sense because it is directed toward absorption in a single beloved rather than in every lovable thing. Socrates seems to contradict this assertion when he says in the *Republic* that Glaucon is an erotic man because he is attracted to all boys, handsome or ugly.

In fact, there is an implicit equivocation here between desire (*epithumia*) and Eros. If human love is the model here, then philosophy is closer to desire than to Eros, because the philosopher desires to know every truth or at the very least a wide variety of truths, rather than to be entirely absorbed in one unique truth.

The ambiguity inherent in the Platonic portrait of philosophy is compounded by the multiplicity of the Ideas or pure forms that are the ostensible end of the philosophical Eros. The Ideas are multiple because each is a paradigm of some family or set of spatio-temporal entities. But as Ideas, they are all alike; to be absorbed in the love of the Ideas, as has often been objected to Platonism, is to be detached from, or to ignore, everyday human existence. Yet it is clearly an exaggeration even of the Platonic conception of philosophy to say of it, as does Socrates in the *Theaetetus*, that it is a preparation for dying, or that it consists entirely in the pure intellectual apprehension of formal structure.

Human love both separates us from others by absorption in the beloved and binds us to ordinary experience because it is a fulfilment and a modification of our nature. The love of Platonic Ideas separates us from ordinary experience, and so too from our historical or spatio-temporal selves. The philosopher's concern with everyday life then sinks to the level of a surrogate for genuine *theoria:* to a largely vain attempt to prepare for the departure from ordinary experience. Please note: my point here is not to offer a sound interpretation of the Platonic dialogues but to bring out a problem in the Platonic presentation of Eros. The divine madness that strikes us down from above must be supplemented by the secular desire that comes as it were from below. Only the two together allow us to stand on our own two feet, for, in order to stand, we require the services of the body. It is too paradoxical and simply unacceptable to be told that philosophy is entirely or fundamentally a flight from this world. I do not mean by this to rule out such a flight altogether. But we cannot fly except with reference to the earth. Without such a reference, appeals to transcendence, the *Jenseits,* or a Hyperuranian *topos* are invitations to leap into the dark.

So much for a general statement of the sense in which philosophy founds itself. I turn now to an obvious objection that could be raised against that statement. It is all very well to say that philosophy founds itself, but such a disruption of the ordinary seems to be lacking in all content. How is it to be distinguished from a mystical seizure or a sudden shift in mood? In what direction does the founding point us? What happens next, and how do we know that we are heading into philosophy rather than into ideology or rhetoric? These questions are not unreasonable. They are similar to questions I would myself address to the Heideggerian doctrine of authenticity. As a kind of preface to my reply, I want to warn against the implication of the questions just raised that there is some determinate answer to them. If there were, of course, it would serve exactly the same function as a first principle or *punctum inconcussum* from which to move the world; we should have returned to the foundationalism that is under contemporary attack, and which I myself reject.

Let me now say why I reject foundationalist appeals to first principles, axioms, methodologies, and so on. Every first principle must itself emerge from a horizon of ordinary or pretheoretical experience in order to be intelligible. To take a simple example, if I state as my first principle that everything is matter in the void, I take it as a presupposition that my audience is familiar with the ordinary experience in which not everything is matter in the void, and particularly not myself and my audience as made up of conscious, discursive human beings. Either there is a relatively detailed chain of reasoning by which I believe myself to have reduced mind to matter, or the first principle is entirely arbitrary. In the former case, the first principle is not a ground but a conclusion, and we are thrown back upon the inspection of ordinary experience in order to determine the validity of that conclusion. In the latter case, the first principle is a mere interjection, and carries no founding weight whatsoever.

I need to emphasize that I am not appealing here to the thesis that all so-called first principles are arbitrary perspectives that are incapable of verification. On the contrary, there is a sense in which I hold that first principles may be verified, but not as first principles. The main point is that philosophy does not get started like a deductive science. In fact, even deductive sciences themselves do not originate as deductions. Everything begins with ordinary experience, which does not itself begin except at some unascertainable moment in our individual lives. We always find ourselves in the midst of things, as already underway in our lives, and so as already looking for answers to questions that do not so much emerge from as they constitute our existence. On this point, Heidegger is entirely correct, which is not surprising, since he borrowed his argument from Aristotle, who derived it from Plato. Unfortunately, Heidegger rejects the Greek notion of nature in favor of historicity, and so empties his account of authenticity of any stability.

The appeal to first principles with respect to the origin of philosophy is an appeal to the wrong model. A first principle defines, or is the first step in the definition of, a narrow expanse of inquiry as a deductive structure. If the first principle consists entirely of symbols from some artificial or mathematical language, it cannot possibly have any empirical content, and so is not genuinely philosophical. But if it has such empirical content ("everything is matter"), then it cannot be genuinely first; we have to know what is meant by matter, and this entails a juxtaposition with mind, or in other words a recognition of ordinary experience as the sense-bestowing context of the formulation of first principles.

The error implicit in foundationalism is without doubt the view that philosophy requires certitude of a deductive nature in order to begin at all. But this is entirely unwarranted; philosophy begins in wonder or surprise, in puzzlement or in the experience of a dislocating mood, not in a deductive argument. To say this, however, is not to accept the antifoundationalist position as traditionally formulated, since that position is merely the mirror image of foundationalism. I mean by this that it either denies the possibility of philosophy at all, or else it asserts antifoundationalism as the foundation of a genuine philosophy. On the latter alternative, philosophy is held to require the absence of all foundations, and so to be equivalent to disruption without a stabilizing context; that is, it is equivalent to sheer difference. In my terminology, antifoundationalism attributes to philosophy the status of an extraordinary beginning outside of ordinary experience, which does not exist at all unless we invent it, in Proust's great image, as the excrement secreted by each individual attempt to create a private world.

As the inescapable beginning, a beginning that is always already underway, ordinary experience is secure in a sense that goes entirely beyond the security of deductive certitude. Even the Cartesian *cogito,* assuming it for the moment to be an argument, requires that we know what it means to think as an I, and so to exist. But this understanding comes from ordinary experience, not from a prior transcendental deduction. Exactly the same considerations apply with respect to the attempt to begin with a certified method for solving philosophical problems. The method has been derived from success in the resolution of problems of a particular kind, and so through a narrowing of the range of experience held to be definitive of philosophy. The outstanding example of such a narrowing is the appeal to mathematics as the paradigm of rationality. Let me say a few words about this paradigm.

I am not aware of any serious claims to the effect that philosophy and mathematics are identical. The claim is rather that only those problems are amenable to resolution that can be mathematicized. But there are two difficulties with this claim, one so obvious that it needs only to be mentioned here. When we mathematicize, we abstract from the problems of ordinary experience; we do not resolve them. But this abstraction, or what comes to the same thing, this reduction, requires a philosophical argument to justify it. The argument usually appeals to the success of mathematics in its own domain, to the precision and verifiability of its methods in contrast to the endless and quite fruitless disputes of traditional philosophers, and so to the need for elaborate formalism in order to clarify the imprecise language of ordinary experience, and thereby to avoid the meaningless language of metaphysics.

It is evident that the appeal to mathematics is closely related to the apparently opposite appeal to ordinary language. In both cases, the assumption is made that we can purify philosophy by regulating our discourse. The appeal to ordinary language is in fact an illusion, since the standard for proper discourse is invariably a technical dialect of ordinary language. Even in cases of considerable subtlety with respect to the nuances of everyday speech, the underlying paradigm of meaning or propriety tends to be a derivative of the mathematical paradigm of rationality.

I do not mean to say that this appeal is entirely mistaken; no one can go very far in philosophy without the ability to analyze speeches, investigate inferences, and establish as well as distinguish relations or orders. But none of this can be accomplished by recourse to artificial standards of precision or a narrowing of linguistic horizons in accord with a priori conceptions of discursive legitimacy. To do so is once again to appeal to the wrong paradigm, namely, that of the certainty of deductive formalisms. Grammatical correctness is an admirable virtue, but one must also say something interesting and pertinent to the issue of the inquiry.

Equally significant in the appeal to the mathematical paradigm is the tacit assumption that success is the same in philosophy as in mathematics. But this assumption would require a long philosophical argument rooted in a comparison of ways of succeeding, an argument that could hardly be provided in mathematical terms. We would have to explain why success in one linguistic domain is transitive to others. But such an explanation obviously begins with the diversity of linguistic registers as exemplified by ordinary experience. The great defect of ordinary-language philosophy is that it has little to do with ordinary language.

The pure language of mathematics is not "about" anything outside itself. In order to connect mathematics to human experience, an interpretation is required. And these interpretations all require the mastery of other languages, most obviously the languages of the particular sciences that are employing mathematical models. But the interpretation of the models via the technical scientific language is itself embedded in ordinary language and experience. We have to state the reasons for the adoption of a particular model, and, more generally, for the adoption of a mathematical model of any kind. This leads to fundamental debates in the philosophy of science. The problem is clear from the very success of mathematical and scientific techniques. This success does not eliminate discursive philosophy but multiplies it. We now have the philosophy of mathematics, the philosophy of physics, the philosophy of biology, and so on. In each case, the traditional philosophical problems, prominent among them the ostensibly meaningless or nonrational metaphysical disputes, are reincarnated; it is they that give significance to the extraordinary display of technical virtuosity.

It is no doubt impossible to philosophize entirely without technical terminology. Every investigation of ordinary experience is a modification of it, and in particular of the language we employ to explain it. But one cannot understand that experience by disregarding it. No single method can do justice to the diversity of the phenomena, and it is from this diversity that we start in our effort to determine which procedures to employ with respect to the particular question we are attempting to answer. If success is the criterion, then recourse to formalization is demonstrably a failure. I dare say that every fundamental human problem remains today much the same, and exactly as problematical, as it was twenty-five hundred years ago. The formalists are right when they say that no progress has been made by philosophy, because they mean by progress the removal of problems. But the removal of philosophical problems would amount to the removal of human existence.

The serious threat to philosophy today is not universal formalization but rather the more insidious influence of the paradigm of mathematics. Even those who would repudiate foundationalism in the vulgar form that is given it by its fashionable contemporary critics, and those who would admit the persistence of traditional philosophical problems in theoretical debates about the nature of mathematics, physics, and so on, have been influenced, positively and negatively, by the extraordinary prestige of mathematical or technical thinking. On the one hand, it is assumed that whereas mathematics is clearly incapable of resolving philosophical questions, it remains the paradigm of rationality; accordingly, what cannot be formalized is undoubtedly irrational or meaningless. The so-called "limits of reason" thus lead inevitably to the denaturing or abandonment of philosophy, which is replaced by rhetoric. On the other hand, unresolvable problems are replaced by "puzzles," or scaled-down surrogates of problems, which have been constructed in accord with presuppositions that render them amenable to solution. Philosophy is then replaced by technical games. And where the questions are technical, there we find progress.

It is a simple matter to dismiss criticism of this sort with charges of obscurantism, fear of analytical precision, technical incompetence, and even worse. But it is equally simple to point to the theoretical incoherence of the various procedures of the puzzle solvers, as well as to the persistence of the unresolvable at the heart of analytical rigor. Nothing is accomplished by the exchange of ideological bavardage; the only sound method, if that is the right term, is to return to that from which we cannot escape without destroying ourselves. Analytical precision is of course a prerequisite for philosophical investigation. But "precision" requires a fine distinction of the heterogeneous, not an ultimately clumsy because intrinsically mindless manipulation of exquisitely refined tools.

To summarize this series of remarks, every attempt to assign to a technical language or a first principle the role of philosophical foundation or indubitable starting point inevitably raises questions of its own foundation. All acts of technical founding occur as disruptions of our ordinary experience. It is therefore correct to say that the self-founding of philosophy does not by itself tell us what to do next. It cannot do so because philosophy is not about itself. Philosophy is not self-referential because it is not a language but an openness to the linguistic modalities of the love of wisdom. This is why it is a mistake to spend too much time brooding about the nature of philosophy. But neither can one "do" philosophy, as though it were an external activity in which one may engage or not, as the mood strikes us or our professional obligations require. One can do it only as an expression of our humanity.

Reason and Will in the Humanities
KNUD HAAKONSSEN

IS HUMAN RATIONALITY A MATTER of choice, an act of will—a commitment, as the relentlessly moralistic language of our public debate has it? The question is old, as old as the skeptical questioning of rationality, and it has generally been put in order to show that rationality is inherently limited, that it does not rest in itself, that it cannot be without foundation in something other than reason. In contemporary debate, this line of argument has developed into a wholesale rejection of the philosophical tradition as the essence of rationalist hubris and, especially, of philosophy in the modern period from Descartes and Bacon onwards. It is this postmodernist refashioning of the old question of reason versus will in a historical perspective that is my concern. I shall try to show that the dispute between postmodernism and the modern philosophical tradition paradoxically arises from the fact that the two parties share the same ideal of knowledge and rationality and that this is an untenable ideal. Indirectly this will provide an argument for a different, critical notion of rationality which is well able to keep the will in its place.

I. HERMENEUTICS

In order to understand the postmodernist attack on rationality, we have to appreciate the underlying transformation of the central epistemic situation. Instead of the traditional confrontation of mind and world, postmodernism sees knowledge in terms of the conduct of discourse or rather, and in a sense to be explained, the occurrences of text. This elevation of text as the paradigmatic vehicle for the human spirit, and of reading as the model for all cultural understanding, is certainly one of the apparent paradoxes of modern humanities. After

generations of immersion in living pictures and mechanically reproduced sound, it is still the written word that provides the starting point
for the dominant ideas of both the subject matter and the method of
the humanities—although sui generis studies of the "new" media of
course have made significant inroads in recent years. One explanation
of the tenacity of the literary model is, of course, that the concept
of *text* has been constantly broadened to the point where one now
virtually has to specify whether one means the word literally or metaphorically. Still, it is to theories of text interpretation proper, or hermeneutics, that we have to go for the roots of many more general
ideas of how to study our humanness. I shall therefore begin with a
few remarks about hermeneutics as presented by its most influential
proponent, Hans Georg Gadamer.

The central point in hermeneutics is that the humanities are
radically different from the theoretical sciences, including the social sciences to which some hermeneuticists allow a certain limited
role. The aim of the sciences is explanation, that is, the establishment
of theories which will account for the occurrence of particular phenomena and types of phenomena. The aim of the humanities is understanding, that is, to capture the meaning of human behavior of which
linguistic behavior is the most telling. In this form the idea goes back
at least to the nineteenth century and especially to Wilhelm Dilthey's
attempt to establish a basis for the *Geisteswissenschaften*. As has often
been pointed out, also by Gadamer, the idea in this form was force-
fully presented in the English-speaking world by R. G. Collingwood.[1]
While standing in this tradition, Gadamer develops it by radicalizing
an idea which was already central to Collingwood, namely, the idea of
the interpreter's reenactment of his or her subject's behavior.

The problem with classical hermeneutics, on this view, is that it
maintains a separation and opposition between the interpreter and
the object of interpretation, typically a text. All interpretation is in
danger of being entirely external. The virtue of traditional hermeneutics is that it goes to great lengths to establish the meaning of a text by
a combination of textual and contextual means. But in practice this
amounts to recreating some kind of "original" meaning—in effect, the
author's meaning. The result is a purely external relationship, an existence side by side, of the respective worlds of the author's meaning
and that of the interpreter. One of the central concerns of Gadamer
and his followers is to break down this barrier between interpreter

and the object of interpretation and to achieve what he calls a fusion of their horizons (*eine Horizontverschmelzung*).[2] This can only succeed if the interpretation takes place neither on the premises of the interpreter, nor on those of the author, but purely on those of the text itself.

Classical hermeneutics had already got rid of the privileged status of the interpreter. Gadamer's mission is to take away the privilege of the author. Authorial intention is not qualitatively different from any other understanding of the meaning of the text. It is in the text itself that all readers and the author meet and where their horizons, under fortunate circumstances, fuse. The challenge, or guiding ideal, for an interpreter is therefore to take part in the text to the extent that this is possible. For Gadamer, ancient tragedy is the paradigm of a text which can so capture the interpreting audience that interpretation here becomes identification in all but overt movement. Even this limitation will disappear once we have got rid of the privileged status of a preexisting text or work, as well as that of author and interpreter: write your own, play your own, paint your own! That, however, is very far from Gadamer's heart. For him the central notion is a text that transcends individual readers and authors, and with which they have to come to grips as with all other aspects of life. For in the end it is not only books and works of art that have to be understood as texts; life itself has to be understood as a text. Anything whatsoever that involves human activity invokes meaning and meaning is a linguistic category. Unless and until we grasp the meaning of a phenomenon in the same way as we grasp the meaning of a text, we cannot see it as part of the human world: we cannot understand it at all.

II. DECONSTRUCTION

There is a certain classical serenity in Gadamer's work. While there are a number of Nietzschean moments of despair at the difficulties of overcoming the mere being-for-oneself and finding a sustainable meaning in the texts of life, there is at any rate always the ideal and the measure of ancient tragedy. Turning from Gadamer to Derrida and deconstruction, Nietzschean despair has become accepted and so much a matter of course that it has lost its demonic power. Meaning is out of the question and the message is not to ask for it.

We have seen how hermeneutics—as the jargon has it—"deprivileged" both the interpreter and the author or agent and left text as the subject of the humanities and the substance of human life. With Jacques Derrida the text goes by the board too, and with it the last vestiges of the interpreting self. Derrida takes the hermeneutic idea of the interdependence of interpreter and text to the limit along something like the following route.[3] The person in the act of interpretation is defined by the text, or, in old-fashioned but deconstructionally illegitimate language, the interpreter's identity is determined by the text being read. Further, every aspect of life is a "text," in the sense that it can only be understood through textual means, and everyone is constantly in the process of interpretation, or in search of meaning. To the extent that the texts change or fluctuate, the interpreting individuals are in a process—or, rather, *are* a process—of redefinition. There is no other self than the text-reading self. The concept of personhood is accordingly seen as an historical formation.

Against this background it is with some anxiety that one turns to the notion of a text. The apprehension is not unwarranted. What counts as a text depends on what is singled out for interpretation by an interpreter. A text is not a given entity with an objective or transcendent meaning; a text does not exist except in the act of being interpreted. The famous deconstructionist method—or, rather, anti-method—is to show that there are no objective or even arguable criteria for singling out what can count as a text. What for one interpreter is literal description is for another high allegory; what for the same interpreter is at one time unambiguous is at other times fundamentally ambiguous; what for some is a coherent pattern of meaningful behavior is to others, or at other times, disjointed events. Indeed, what, according to the traditional canon of criticism, is counted as one work or, according to the author, one chapter or, according to conventional grammar, one sentence may, for other interpreters, be more or less than either of these. Neither the canon of criticism, nor authorial intention, nor traditional grammar has any privileged status or authority in the access to texts. In fact, rather than guides to meaning, they are themselves nothing but "texts" to be deconstructed. What we call a text is up to us; whether we take a book or a single word, it is radically undecipherable; or, in the case of *text* in the metaphorical sense, whether we take a whole culture or a single gesture, they have no inherent meaning that we either get or not.

We must take it, then, that ultimately there is no stable, coherent self that interprets, nor is there any objectively given text, or unit of meaning, to be interpreted. If—as the joke goes—psychiatry is the study of the id by the odd, surely deconstruction is the study of the odd, but without any id. Life is but a profusion of acts of interpretation in which both the interpreting self and the interpreted text are being momentarily defined. Furthermore, such acts of interpretation are themselves objects of interpretation—except that one cannot legitimately talk of them as "objects" but only as components in an act of meta-interpretation, as it were.

Within both hermeneutics and deconstruction a constant theme is the death of philosophy or of metaphysics. What principally is meant is the disposal of the idea of a coherent self as a knowing subject and hence of the opposition of subject and object, as previously sketched. An element in this is yet another death, that of humanism. By this is meant the tendency in the philosophical tradition to see the individual human being as the focus of all meaning—a tendency allegedly so strong that it even corrupted the radical mind of Sartre. In fact, the existentialist affirmation of individual being in the face of nothingness can be seen as the ultimate desperate step of humanist arrogance.[4]

In an attempt to keep the philosophical undertakers in business, deconstruction disposes of one more *topos* in traditional philosophy, namely, the idea that linguistically formulated knowledge could be said to have meaning—or even truth value—because of its referential function, that is, because it refers to some kind of object or reality beyond itself. Many texts may appear to have such referents, but this is a dangerous and dogmatic illusion. Whatever is offered as a referent must be put into a linguistic context in order to have any meaning. Even the most "naked" physical fact must be formulated in language if it is to be understood, and every language is infinitely ambiguous and deconstructable. Every apparently extralinguistic referent is in fact inescapably linguistic or textual. It is thus a senseless dispute whether the Song of Solomon is to be read in the orthodox way as an allegory for God's dealings with the Church or the individual soul, or in the literal manner of the Anabaptists and of modern scholarship as an erotic work. On the one hand, for the Talmudists and Saint Bernard it invoked a "text" called "God" and a "text" called "the Church" or "the congregation of Israel"; that is, it invoked meanings out of other texts, such as the Talmud or Bernard's eighty-six homilies on the Canticles or the behavioral "text" called a church. On the other hand, for those giving a literal interpretation of the Song of Songs, it invokes the behavioral "text" of erotic conduct. A deconstruction of this text would aim at showing that, while the two readings at one level are in conflict, they yet presuppose each other if they are to be conceptualized at all. All texts are thus interlocked with other texts, and with nothing else, in an indeterminate chain of "intertextuality." The world—if one could use such a word—is nothing but text, in the sense that one only has access to any of "it" through text, and all so-called interpretation is nothing but invocation of further text. In so far as one can talk of the meaning of a text, it consists of the use of further texts, *ad infinitum*. We can never get "beyond" or "behind" the textuality of our world. In other words, there is no meaning to a text beyond the deconstructionist experience of the moment.

The deconstructionist idea of life as a series of discrete, indeed incommensurable, acts—or, rather, occurrences—of text reading is the closest we come to a coherent theory of postmodernism. It is a true philosophy of bits and pieces. It also has some extraordinary implications, which often seem to be inferred with disconcertingly gay abandon. The most publicized consequence of deconstruction is to reject all ideas of a canon of great, paradigmatic works of literature or art. No aspect of tradition has special authority in the interpretation of text, whether in the literal or the metaphorical sense; nor does the author, artist, or agent. Consequently literary and cultural history is not inherently more relevant to an understanding of the artifacts of human life than the invocation of any other material which might be suggestive in the deconstructive business of disclosing hidden meanings, ambiguities, and other points of what is called undecidability. Hence the mixing of genres, the use of advertising slogans in the analysis of a novel, the fascination with separating parts of a text from the rest, the deliberate confusion of artistic styles, and so forth. The basic principle is that there is no authoritatively established, or establishable, organization of knowledge. Periodization, styles, genres, traditions, and criteria for assessment of artistic, moral, or other values are nothing but inventions. When they become entrenched, as they tend to do, in institutional settings of teaching and publishing, they assume an authoritarian character, and the mission of deconstruction is to break such establishments and free the spirit to go its own deconstructive ways. More particularly, since the so-called self is nothing but a mouthpiece for the social and institutional structures that surround it, an especially important task for deconstruction is to lay bare such structures. Hence such phenomena as Marxist and feminist deconstruction; hence also the deconstructionist attempts to revise existing curricula and university structures.

III. AN ASSESSMENT

I shall leave this here, for I have ranged sufficiently widely to lend credibility to the suggestion that the problem of rationality and the possibility of rational discussion and the associated problem of relativism are at the very heart of a great variety of humanistic inquiry. Some of my comments may have indicated that I am critical of the way these problems are being discussed, especially within deconstruction. So I am. But before I proceed to explain why, let me say that mine is not an unqualified criticism. There is more common ground than I dared hope when I set out on this attempt at a general consideration of the theoretical basis for the humanities. The main virtues I find in hermeneutics and deconstruction may be summarized in the following points.

(1) I am at one with the idea that knowledge cannot fruitfully be characterized exclusively in terms of mental states and that it is much more interesting to consider knowledge in nonsubjectivist ways. (2) Similarly, I find it empirically, conceptually, and methodologically plausible that there are a variety of forms of knowledge, and that it is dubious what might be gained by attempts to reduce understanding to explanation or vice versa. (3) I find particularly valuable the emphasis given to the need for a multiplicity of perspectives in humanistic inquiry, the stress on the open-endedness and ultimate uncertainty, and the consequent virtue of ongoing criticism. At its best, deconstruction is anti-authoritarian, irreverent, and willing to play around imaginatively with received ideas—a feature that often has made it a valuable resource for critics of intellectual and institutional power brokers.

My problems with deconstruction begin with the frequent experience that these virtues seem to change, chameleon-like, into their virtual opposites. To take them in turn, while we may have gotten rid of traditional ideas of knowledge as reducible to products of mental faculties—reason or sense perception—we certainly have not gotten rid of the subject or the ego. Hiding behind the funeral fanfares for the death of the self is an often uninhibited expressionism, and this is in keeping with the deconstructionist idea of knowledge as discrete experiences of deconstructing the text of the moment. Short of keeping one's experiences silent, knowledge can only consist of expressions of such experiences. And since requirements of logical consistency, stylistic coherence, grammatical "correctness," or even typographical conventions have no objective justification, the expressions of one's deconstructive exploits can take any form whatsoever; that is, they can be nothing but pure self-expression. Second, the hermeneutic idea of understanding as the form of knowledge characteristic of the humanities and distinct from explanation as found in the theoretical sciences is more or less deprived of significance once the notion of textual meaning is deconstructed, for the implication is that understanding can amount to no more than discrete experiences of deconstruction. Third, the multiplicity of perspectives end up as disjointed worlds of discourse between which there can be no meaningful discussion and criticism. In fact, apparent criticism is itself nothing but deconstructive experience, and the open-endedness and lack of sure foundations for knowledge simply provide a vacuum for self-expression and self-assertion. As one of the foremost American practitioners of the art has been reported to declare: "I want to be able to walk into any first-rate faculty anywhere and dominate it, shape it to my will. I'm fascinated by my own will." Clearly there is here no will to reason, and whatever the reason to will, it seems unlikely to be of intellectual interest.

The problem with deconstruction is, paradoxically, that it shares too much, rather than too little, with the philosophical tradition which it presumes to end. That is to say, deconstruction and the traditional philosophy that it intends to refute share expectations of what real knowledge would be, but deconstruction rejects the traditional claim that such knowledge can be had and jumps to the conclusion that therefore *no* knowledge can be had. Let me take the most central cases, meaning by "traditional philosophy" the stereotypical disjunction of Gallic Cartesianism, Teutonic Kantianism, and Anglo-Scoto American empiricism which deconstructionists of all stripes seem to operate with. First, then, traditional philosophy is supposed to have operated with the idea of a universal human nature, and especially of universal cognitive powers. Yet it is evident that every aspect of human nature, *qua* human, is malleable by time and circumstance. Consequently there is nothing to be said in universal terms about human nature. Similarly, traditional philosophy assumed that there was an ultimate reality which formed the transcendent object of human cognitive powers. Yet we have no proven access to such ultimate reality. Consequently there is no such reality nor anything to be said about it. Third, traditional philosophy, and especially classical hermeneutics, thought that human behavior, and not least verbal behavior expressed in text, has an objective, ascertainable meaning. Yet all behavior and all texts are fundamentally ambiguous and radically undecidable. Consequently there is no transcendent meaning to be ascertained. Fourth, traditional philosophy posited universal values or criteria for practical decision making. Yet no such values and criteria can be ascertained. Consequently there are no such values or criteria nor anything to be said in general terms about practical matters. Finally, traditional philosophy thought that the rules of argumentative logic enabled people to have rational discussion and criticism in science, humanities, morals, and arts. Yet people are not rational as such. Their so-called rationality is dependent upon their particular context, and the rules of discussion are generally devices for dominating their fellows. Consequently there is no rationality in so-called critical discussion; it is basically power play.

While obviously schematic, these points capture the essence of the deconstructionist starting point in and rejection of what it sees as traditional philosophy. It will be immediately evident that the pattern of argument is the same on every point—and that the same non sequitur is involved in each case. It goes like this: Traditional philosophy maintains that so-and-so is the case; but so-and-so cannot be shown conclusively to be the case; consequently so-and-so is not and cannot be the case. The non sequitur is what philosophers might call an inference from epistemic failure to ontological impossibility, that is, from what we do not know with certainty to what cannot possibly be the case in the world. Let me explain a little further. Deconstruction seems to share with what it calls traditional philosophy the ideal that real knowledge is veridical, that is, gives direct access to and is guaranteed by its object. But from that it jumps to the conclusion that the absence of such knowledge is proof of the nonexistence of the object and of the impossibility of all knowledge proper. Once we have adopted the ideal of knowledge and followed the non sequitur, we are well on our way to the bric-a-brac philosophy of deconstruction. I see no reason for taking either of the initial steps.

IV. RATIONALITY IN THE HUMANITIES

First of all, it is strange that a purportedly antiauthoritarian philosophy like deconstruction so slavishly adopts the traditional notion of epistemic certainty as the ideal to be despaired of. There is no a priori argument why deconstructionists, as well as any other critics of traditional philosophy, should not try to formulate less despair-inducing ideals of knowledge. And argument is precisely what is at stake. Of course it is true that we have no proof or indubitable knowledge that there is a universal human nature or a transcendent reality or a Platonic realm of stable meaning and value, but equally we do not have proof that there is not—and in fact no such proof could be given. The point is that "traditional philosophy"—if there ever was one such thing—is mistaken in thinking that our claims to knowledge imply a commitment to such an ontology. Consequently it is a mistake to think that if you deny the ontology, this will have implications for the claimed knowledge. It is precisely because we do not have proof or certainty either way in this ultimate ontological question that knowledge about the world has the character it does, namely, that it is intrinsically uncertain and hypothetical.

The hypothetical nature of knowledge gives room for a large element of what we may broadly call conventions or—in the moralizing language that I heartily dislike—human commitments. One possible convention is, of course, that knowledge which is less than veridical, that is, which falls short of giving certain access to ultimate reality, should not be considered knowledge at all. But the important point is that this is a convention or a chosen commitment and not something that is subject to proof. This is, as previously indicated, the error made by deconstruction in the argument with traditional philosophy. What deconstruction takes to be traditional philosophy may be dead, but its demise does not *imply* that knowledge about a text-independent reality is impossible. That is a stance *chosen* by deconstructionists. Once this is appreciated, we can ignore all the categorical statements to the effect that texts *cannot* refer to anything but other texts since there *is* nothing but text. All that remains of these prophetic pronouncements is a number of specific, and often very suggestive and imaginative, examples of how texts can be analyzed in the light of other texts. Few would disagree with that.

Although one may choose to commit oneself to the idea that texts do not deal with anything outside texts, it is a difficult choice to defend. For a start, there is something paradoxical about formulating the idea at all. The point in such a formulation seems to be communication with something which apparently is nontextual, namely, other people. Of course, one may—as is not uncommon—take other people to be nothing but figures of speech, that is, as nothing but their linguistic appearance in one's text. But the end of that road is a kind of self-imposed linguistic solipsism that makes itself true by definition.

The problem is that unless we choose to see texts as being about something external to themselves, they do not tell us anything. If there is nothing but text as deconstructed by each of us, then there is nothing in common between us, that is, nothing to talk about. We each have our deconstructive game or discourse. But if we choose to take our respective texts as referring to something else, such as what they purport to refer to, then there is a possibility of engagement. This engagement may, of course, go completely wrong. We may be referring to entirely different things; both of us may be wrong about the matter in question; we may be wrong in thinking that the other person is talking to us at all; what we say may be adopted unconsciously from some other source and hardly be our own thought at all, and so forth. On all such points, methods like those of deconstruction may be—and often have been—very useful. However, the point is that only by sticking to the commitment—or the pretense, if you like—that we are talking about *something*, as opposed to just talking or expressing our own text, will we have a chance of discovering these mistakes.

The procedure indicated here clearly presupposes an acceptance of the rules of logic which make discussion and criticism possible. A deconstructionist will ask what forces these rules on us, and the answer is, once again, our own choice. Even more than in the case of external reference, it is a choice which is difficult to avoid. It is extremely difficult to undertake even a modest piece of deconstruction without implying the rule of noncontradiction or of the excluded middle. And much deconstructive *practice* is in fact to apply such basic rules of logic to passages of text which, despite appearances, do not obey them. Nevertheless, use of the rules of logic is a commitment which one may accept or reject, but it is hardly possible to articulate either without employing those very rules.

As with the rules of logic and objectivism of reference (I am loath to use the term *realism*), so with the other means of formulating and organizing knowledge—grammar, rules of translation, typographical conventions, genres and styles, meters, books, chapters, sections, and so forth. They are all conventions or chosen commitments for which arguments can and sometimes must be given. In some cases the argument is in part that the convention in question is more or less unavoidable if any knowledge is to be formulated at all; in others the arguments for one choice rather than another are bound to be indecisive.

The critics of the rationalism of traditional philosophy, of the "Enlightenment project," and so forth, are therefore right that the commitment to rationality is a choice and that one can make other choices. But they are obviously mistaken in thinking that the will to reason is arbitrary. It is eminently possible to argue for the choice of rationality. To the charge that such argument presupposes the choice that is being argued for, one can only reply that that charge sounds suspiciously like an attempt to argue. To put my point in Kantian language, reason has autonomy to legislate for itself, but that autonomy does not entail arbitrariness, for the very exercise of reason—as in the irrationalist's objection—has reference to the other person. Reason inevitably has reference to a public realm, and that realm can only exist through the observation of certain basic rules. By voicing his or her protest intelligibly, the irrationalist enters into that public realm and thus subjects himself or herself to the rules of reason. Or, as one of the great Kantians of our time, Jürgen Habermas, would put it, the irrationalist enters an implicit contract of rational debate with his or her opponent.

VI. EPILOGUE

I have tried to sketch a broad, general view of knowledge which avoids the dogmatic subjectivism and relativism implied by deconstructionism. Yet it does not commit itself to the equally dogmatic ontological realism and associated ideal of certain knowledge which is *allegedly* to be found in traditional philosophy. To Socrates' question in the *Theaetetus*, "Is it possible, then to reach truth, when one cannot reach being?"[5] I answer, "Let us try—you never know." Inherent in such a view is a noncommittal attitude in ontology: Reality is to be explored according to human ingenuity, and to try to divine the nature of the former—reality—by means of supposed scope of the latter, is the source of most dogmatism.

In my attempt to find a way between foundationalist dogmatism and antifoundationalist deconstructivism, I am far from alone. My colleague Professor Stanley Rosen, for instance, has written a most lucid, elegant, and powerful paper which precedes mine in the present volume, in which he too rejects these alternatives. But in doing so, Professor Rosen offers an idea of how, nevertheless, to "found" philosophy in human nature. I should like to add a few remarks about this suggestion by way of conclusion, for it seems to disagree very interestingly with what I have been proposing. Professor Rosen's argument may be summed up in the following theses.

(1) Philosophy is not a body of doctrine or a method, but a condition of the human soul that may be described as self-reflective love of knowledge. (2) This love comes to us from outside ourselves, as if we were struck from above by Eros. (3) The divine love of knowledge is presupposed in all acquisition of knowledge. It is therefore not itself the object of inquiry; it is the driving force presupposed in all inquiry. (4) At the core of all philosophizing—indeed, of all knowing—is thus a state of insight that is not propositional and hence cannot be learned from either texts or teachers, except that the latter, if sufficiently gifted from above, seem to be able to *show* what love of knowledge might be like. (5) While love of knowledge, when it strikes, takes us outside—or absolves us from—"historical" time and throws us into "cosmological" time, such love nevertheless has to be lived within the time of clocks. It is in our ordinary, sequential lives and times that we have to come to terms with the extraordinary and timeless, namely, the quest for knowledge. Philosophy in the basic sense of love of knowledge thus has to start from the concepts and the language of ordinary life. At the same time, philosophical insight has direct implications for how we should live.

While there is, needless to say, a great deal more to Professor Rosen's standpoint, I have the audacity to suggest that these five points make up the central thesis. It is an attractive thesis, and it is even more attractive in Professor Rosen's "poetic language," as he calls it. Even so, I shall resist its attraction—and for the following reasons.

If we apply Professor Rosen's thesis to what I have been saying about the status of rationality, we will have to conclude that the embrace of reason itself is a matter of being struck from above; it is perhaps the epitome of the "divine madness" of philosophy. For how could reason legislate for itself, as I suggested, without there first being a will, whether divine or otherwise, to do so? The answer to this question is moral—or practical—not metaphysical in character.

The love of knowledge, in the words of Professor Rosen, is "the tuning of the soul"; but I do not trust that we possess tuning forks upon which we can rely when we go abroad from our house into human society, listening to the great melody of humanity. Consequently I do not rely on finding the perfect pitch, that is, on ascertaining the will to reason in the other person; I am happy to settle for a bit of a tune, that is, for signs of an actual argument. In other words, I prefer to see basic philosophy as a public pursuit of reasoning, not as the autobiography of private soul tuning.

This preference is based upon another moral consideration, namely, the fear that philosophy considered as the tuning of the soul may have a tendency to create dependence. The tuning of souls is distinctly knowledge-how, not knowledge-that; and it may be exhibited for imitation but cannot otherwise be taught. When Professor Rosen quite rightly suggests that love cannot be learned from a manual, I, therefore, take this to be an argument against his close analogy between love and philosophy. To be sure, texts cannot teach us philosophy, or anything else, unless we have a desire to learn. As Professor Rosen says, it is not a mechanical process of gathering sense data. But the elementary desire for knowing seems profoundly uninteresting until it has an object of some ascertainable sort; yet about every such object it is possible to reason to and fro. One of the means by which we, in philosophy, argue thus, is through the reading of texts together.

NOTES

1. R. G. Collingwood, *An Autobiography* (London, 1939); cf. *The Idea of History* (Oxford, 1946). Hans-Georg Gadamer, *Wahrheit und Methode: Grundzüge einer philosophischen Hermeneutik,* 6th ed. (Tübingen, 1990), pp. 375–84.

2. Gadamer, *Wahrheit und Methode,* pp. 311ff. The following sketch also draws on Gadamer, *Vernunft im Zeitalter der Wissenschaft* (Frankfurt a.M., 1976).

3. The following outline is mainly drawn from Jacques Derrida, *Marges de la philosophie* (Paris, 1972), and *La Dissémination* (Paris, 1972).

4. Derrida, *Marges,* pp. 135ff.

5. Plato, *Theaetetus,* 186c.

Natural Law:
A Feminist Reassessment
LISA SOWLE CAHILL

THE PROJECT

A FEMINIST REASSESSMENT OF natural law is called for in light of feminists' overwhelming agreement that morality based on supposedly universal "laws of nature" is the mother of all oppression. The judgment of Beverly Harrison is not atypical, and, for that matter, not as strongly stated as some: "Unfortunately . . . all major strands of natural law reflection have been every bit as awful as Protestant biblicism on any matter involving human sexuality, including discussion of women's nature and women's divine vocation in relation to procreative power."[1]

I want to identify what I believe is the enduring value of natural law approaches to ethics, and to distinguish a practical, experiential, and historically sensitive interpretation of natural law from familiar Enlightenment distortions. I also want to show why something like a revised natural law is important to the feminist moral claim that women worldwide are owed certain substantive material goods and protections as essential to our well-being, and not only equal respect in the formal or procedural sense. The sticking point, of course, is how we can identify such goods in any universalizable or generalizable way, given the multiplicity of human goods, the variability of their social interpretation and ordering, and the ways in which particular rankings and distributions of goods have so often reflected cultural bias. Although it would be incautious to claim that the path through these problems is in any sense clear and direct, I will argue that recent emphases on practical reason and virtue as a key to knowledge of the natural law provide access to a more historical and more adequate conception than that which has proved so vulnerable to feminist critiques. An understanding of natural law as discovered within an on-going process of action and reflection converges with the feminist accent on experience, on differences mediated by reciprocity, and on practice as a test of theory.

THE IMPORTANCE OF NATURAL LAW FOR FEMINISTS

Matthew Crowe, a contemporary Roman Catholic interpreter of natural law theory, has written that natural law "has always been a sign of contradiction."[2] Yet the tenuous position of the theory was made even more acute by its assimilation in the eighteenth and nineteenth centuries to an Enlightenment paradigm of knowledge that privileged decontextualized, ahistorical, and autonomous reason, as well as logical, deductive, or empirical models of evidence and argumentation. Jacques Maritain, a Catholic philosopher who in many ways has astutely conveyed natural law in the modern period, was able to assert as recently as 1951, "Since I have not time here to discuss nonsense . . . I am taking it for granted that we admit that there is a human nature, and that this human nature is the same in all men."[3] Moreover, since "man is endowed with intelligence . . . it is up to him to put himself in tune with the ends necessarily demanded by his nature," ends which "necessarily correspond to his essential constitution and which are the same for all." Anything, indeed, which exists "in nature," including humans, is defined by a natural law prescribing "the normality of its functioning," according to a "specific structure" in which it "*should*' achieve fullness of being." In other words, "by the very virtue of human nature," there is "an order . . . which human reason can discover and according to which the human will must act in order to attune itself to the essential and necessary ends of the human being. The unwritten law, or natural law, is nothing more than that."[4]

Even leaving aside for the moment the question of sexist language or of conceptions of the natural order which touch specifically on gender, Maritain's confident allusions to universal, self-evident, essential, necessary, and mandatory features of human being, such as nature, intelligence, reason, ends, and structure, will give most feminists pause. Indeed, it is just such assertions about universal human structures and natural "ends" or purposes prescribing women's behavior and roles which have spun feminist theory off on its decon-structionist and "postmodern" trajectory, along which *nothing* is taken for granted and suppositions of universality are ridiculed.[5]

Matthew Crowe observes, however, that despite the all too evi-dent liabilities of natural law thinking, the method was given renewed importance and vitality in the wake of indictments at the Nuremberg War Crimes Trial, following World War II. Completely vitiating the moral respectability of any positivist conception of law, the world's moral outrage at the activities of the Third Reich, albeit belated and even hypocritical, generated the 1948 United Nations Universal Dec-laration of Human Rights. The consciousness that some deeds and practices are in fact crimes against humanity, and are not adequately judged merely in terms of their coherence with some particular "so-cially constructed" worldview, set before philosophers, as well as po-litical leaders, activists, and governments, the task of understanding, explaining, and in fact advocating generalizable standards of account-ability. The fact that the whole conception of "human rights" has since been criticized as a Western ideal or invention does not obviate this task, but makes it all the more pressing.

Violence against women, certainly not new but newly identi-fied as a human rights issue in our time, is an international crisis of ar-guably equal proportions which raises parallel moral and theoretical challenges. Violence against women, both direct (rape, murder, mu-tilation) and indirect (sickness, injury, and death due to deprivation of clean water and nutrition, health care, or shelter), was recognized as an international problem calling for redress at the recent UN con-ferences on population (1994) and on the status of women (1995) at Cairo and Beijing, respectively. The very possibility of such a devel-opment owes much to modern, international conceptions of human rights. Yet debates at these conferences revealed the vulnerability of any univocal, transcultural understanding of women's roles and inter-ests. The reality and experience of violence against women has mo-tivated feminist suspicion of liberal and postmodern theories and politics. While liberal theories are both too trusting that Western values of privacy and autonomy will be persuasive worldwide, and too limited in their proposals of procedural requirements of respect and free choice, postmodern theories create a moral vacuum by rela-tivizing judgment to enclosed cultural traditions. The need to resist violence impels feminists to seek substantive standards of women's well-being about which there can and must be agreement. Speaking even within the limits of North American experience, Susan Brooks Thistlethwaite can claim,

> Through my work in the battered women's movement I am aware that as many as 50 percent of all women are victims of sexual and domestic abuse by males, often by males with whom they live or work. Rape, incest, battering—all of these crimes of violence claim black women, Hispanic women, Asian women, Native American women, white women—all women every day. It is very important for all women, including white women, to be able to trust the truth of their experience that this violence perpetrated against them is always and everywhere wrong and must be stopped.[6]

"Always and everywhere wrong": Thistlethwaite's absolute and universal judgment is, interestingly and importantly, grounded in the "truth" of practical experience, as is her categorical moral imperative: it *"must be stopped."* Later, I will demonstrate how the feminist turn to experience dovetails with the emergent natural law emphasis on practical wisdom, and on action as a source and not only a consequence of moral knowledge. First, however, it is important to contemplate a related problem in feminist theory: *difference*. When Thistlethwaite calls for unity around the patent immorality of violence against women, she not only begins with experience rather than theory, she appeals to a breadth of experience among women with particular, different racial and ethnic identities. Yet, some women have eloquently resisted the assimilation of culturally different women to a unitary model of women's experience, especially a model devised by white, middle-class feminists.[7]

The issue of difference has become virtually a *topos classicus* for feminist writers, its recognition the *sine qua non* for feminist credibility. Although we white feminists are still often at the level of acknowledging difference rather than dealing with it,[8] the debate about difference is already moving on to the further question of how to establish the reciprocity and common understanding necessary to enable joint action against very concrete moral evils, such as violence.

The black womanist theologian Katie G. Cannon calls the role of "emotional, intuitive knowledge" central in the collective life of the black people. I agree that the emotions and other nondiscursive sources of knowing are a neglected dimension of moral discernment in ethical theory generally, and one which increases in importance as we locate moral perception, reflection, and judgment squarely in the push, press, pull, and heat of practical affairs and personal relationships. Martha Nussbaum, among others, makes the same point.[9] According to Cannon, "black female moral agents' intuitive faculties lead them toward a dynamic sense of moral reasoning," in which it becomes possible both to clarify that "theo-ethical structures are not universal, color-blind, apolitical, or otherwise neutral," and at the same time to prod "society at large" into rescinding its denial of "shared humanity."[10]

Susan Thistlethwaite uses the self-chosen name of the slave woman Sojourner Truth as a metaphor for the process of concrete, experiential discovery which leads to a truth which is highly personal and differentiated yet carries universal appeal. When we meet Sojourner Truth our intellectual apprehension of injustice is profoundly deepened by emotional recognition. Through her story we experience empathy, which reorients our moral dispositions and motivates action. This process is captured in our response to Sojourner Truth's famous and poignant cry, "Ain't I a woman?"

> "Nobody ever helps me into carriages, or over mud-puddles, or gibs me de best places. And ain't I a woman? . . . I have borne thirteen children, and seen 'em mos' all sold all off to slavery, and when I cried out with a mother's grief, none but Jesus heard me! And ain't I a Woman?"[11]

Sojourner Truth's "criterion of truth-in-action mitigates against an abstract, fixed understanding of the nature of truth,"[12] such as that reflected above in the quotations from Jacques Maritain. Yet it mitigates equally against the conclusion that difference prevents common conversation about substantive goods for human beings, goods necessary to human flourishing, goods which can be recognized across differences of sex, race, class, culture, and time. Natural law is a theory of the recognition of such goods. What the feminist debate about difference brings to such a theory, or emphasizes within it, is that mutual understanding and agreement on goods is not achieved in some sphere above or beyond differences, but only from reflection which begins within determinate historical communities with particular experiences of goods and evils, and particular visions or hopes of change. "Particularity and not universality is the condition of being heard and of expressing reciprocity and mutuality in womanist/mu-jerista/feminist work."[13] We shall return shortly to the topic of experience and its particularity as a source for a shared moral vision.

REINTERPRETING NATURAL LAW

This is the point at which to reintroduce the lines of convergence that can be developed between feminist theory and contemporary readings of natural law. As numerous natural law theorists already maintain, its interpretation today must be historically oriented.[14] It would be hard to argue that Thomas Aquinas, whose influence in theologically-based doctrines of natural law is unparalleled, was concerned very centrally or even very visibly with the problem of human historicity and knowledge. Nevertheless, his essentially inductive approach to natural law is more compatible with current concerns about historicity and context than is usually acknowledged.

The defining elements of Aquinas's approach to natural law,[15] still viable today, are his commitment to moral objectivity and his confidence that, as a general proposition, human beings desire and seek to achieve certain goods which are not only fulfilling, but which it is commendable to pursue. Humans are both *reasonable* in their discernment of goods, and *free* to choose them or not, characteristics which together yield the conditions of morality. Morality itself consists in *action* which is consistent with the *goods* reason grasps in its practical functioning. To destroy such goods or to prevent others from enjoying them can be justified only within limits, and in view of serious conflicts. These goods and the means to them will be evident to us if we reflect honestly and seriously on the most fundamental human inclinations. He assumes that these inclinations are basic and shared by all human beings.

Aquinas gives three important examples of inclinations to basic goods and of "precepts of the natural law" which follow from them. Like all living things, humans seek to keep themselves in being, and so it is evident that life is a good to be maintained and protected. Like other animals, humans mate, procreate, and educate their young, and these too are goods to be furthered and protected, both as natural biological processes and as the core of personal and social institutions

like marriage and family. Finally, unique to our species, is the drive
to know "the truth about God" and the need to "live cooperatively in
society." From these higher human inclinations flow social institutions such as religion, economy, and government.

The task of ethics is to specify as clearly and in as detailed a
manner as possible the nature of these goods, what they mean in the
concrete, and what kinds of actions will or will not attain them. This
process of specification produces moral norms, although the more
specific the norm, the more its validity and application will depend on
the contingencies of context. Whatever counts concretely as a good
must be determined by prudence. By consistently acting in favor of
real goods, or denying them, we create in ourselves habits which in-
cline us to act consistently on future occasions. These dispositions are
the virtues and vices. Both virtues and norms are essential to a natural
law ethics. Prudence, the moral virtues, reasonable action, and guiding norms are always intimately connected.[16] In fact, the exercise of
practical wisdom, even in applying rules, always engages a variety of
virtues together, since decision making requires that we assess claims,
weigh risks and goods, and identify alternatives, a process bringing
into play feeling and desire as well as judgment.[17]

Four further points are important to an appreciation of Aquinas's
approach. First, it is strongly social. He has no equivalent to the
modern concept of human rights, relying instead on an organic understanding of right order, within which all parts are interdependent and
hierarchically arranged. His sense of human sociality and interdependence, which developed on too static a model if scrutinized from the
vantage point of modern historical consciousness, nevertheless brings
to social ethics an important corrective to liberalism's excessive stress
on individual autonomy. Second, Aquinas's trust in natural law, especially its objectivity, is founded on a theological premise: creation. God
has imbued all creatures with a tendency to act in ways conducive to
their flourishing. The human difference is the self-conscious, intelligent, and deliberate nature of compliance. Third, while natural law is
founded at its origin by creation, it is completed at its summit by an
orientation to God as the highest good, in which all natural goods are
fulfilled and transformed.

Fourth, because of his religious interpretation of moral evil as
"sin," that is, a culpable refusal of divinely ordained goods to which we
should naturally be attracted, Aquinas believes it vitally important to

rely upon the guidance of scripture, interpreted by the Church, in coming to know what true good is. The degree to which Aquinas would have granted that even sinful humans can naturally seek the good without the benefit of God's self-revelation in Christ is a matter of debate. But I want to maintain strongly that natural law is a viable basis for social ethics, even without a theological context or the remedial assistance of scripture. Ignorance, finitude, and willful perversion of human well-being must be given their due as intransigent parts of the moral scenario. Religious communities and ideals will have a powerful role in providing moral orientation. Nonetheless, the possibility of insight into experiences, opportunities, and things which are goods for humans as such is vital to the creation of conditions of flourishing within and across pluralistic human communities.

SIMILARITIES OF NATURAL LAW AND FEMINIST THEORY

There are affinities between Aquinas's moral theory and that of many feminist writers.[18] His generalizations about natural human inclinations are in essence appeals to human experience, on which basis we are to realize what contributes to human flourishing and what does not. Unlike Kantian approaches to morality, which begin with an abstract principle of respect, and go no further than procedural principles of justice, Aquinas begins "from the ground up," as it were, generalizing from what he observes about human desires, human behavior, and human social institutions. Coming to know the good is an experiential process, even for Aquinas. Some moral truths are known only by way of experience.[19] Moreover, Aquinas's construals of human goods are substantive, and not merely formal or procedural. Certainly respect for the value of other human individuals as such is a basic principle of justice for Aquinas, but he goes beyond this to offer content to the good life for human beings, for example, in matters of politics, economics, family, and marriage. Similarly, feminists begin within different experiences, venture specific construals of goods that women require and harms that must be avoided, and propose that these be refined and enlarged interactively. Moreover, both Aquinas and most feminists see human embodiment as an important factor in defining substantive goods, and want to integrate bodily nature with reason and freedom in a way which enables us to do justice both to our physicality and to our uniquely human capacities for knowledge, morality, love, aesthetic creativity, and pleasure. Finally, both Aquinas and feminists understand action to be the purpose of ethical reflection and of the cultivation of moral virtue. Virtuous, reasonable action, oriented by genuine goods, fulfills the purpose of an individual life and contributes to the common good.[20]

What is novel about contemporary appeals to experience—feminist and otherwise—is not their existence as such, nor the fact that they aim to accomplish social and political goals, but their self-conscious quality and their attentiveness to diversity of experience and to the social location of the one who experiences and interprets. Appeals to experience are used constructively in feminist moral argument to shift the balance within given patterns of interpretation of the human condition. An appeal to "experience" introduces some dimension of women's situation which an existing construct diminishes or leaves out of account. While the reference point of experience does not amount to a universal paradigm or structure, neither is it lacking in normativity, as relevant only to the standpoint of the speaker. Rather, it functions as a testimony to the communal, dialectical, and practical qualities of moral knowledge and judgment.[21]

It is the *dissonance* between Aquinas and feminism, however, that brings us to what is perhaps the most vital and certainly most controverted aspect of natural law theory. Surely no one took in my assertion that both Aquinas and feminists offer substantive proposals about goods to be sought in marriage, family, and political life without silently observing that this is where feminists and Aquinas part company. The inspiration of feminism is precisely an incredulous, justly angry reaction to ideas such as those held by Aquinas about what is "natural" or "good" for male and female persons, and about the role the body should play in defining social roles. It is exactly the determination of *which* bodily capacities, *which* human desires, and *which* social relations constitute authentic goods for persons, as well as how those goods should be ordered in cases of conflict, that constitutes the perennial dilemma of natural law ethics and renders it a "sign of contradiction." On the one hand, natural inclinations, or human experiences themselves, are supposed to mediate insight into moral obligation, into what it is reasonable or good to seek in action. On the other, some sort of value orientation already seems required if we are to make any such evaluation of the many ostensible goods competing for our attention, many of which conflict and some of which turn out to be false.

One preliminary, fairly simple, but quite important observation must be made. While Aquinas in theory prized intelligence and freedom as the crowning traits of our distinctively human nature, the fact is that, in practice, he had a strong tendency to premise moral norms about sex and gender on physical structures and capacities.[22] Not irrelevant in this regard was his uncritical appropriation of Aristotle's biology (attributing the female sex to a mishap at conception), and the understandably strong influence of the patriarchal bias of his and almost every culture.[23] It is only in the modern period that ideals of equality have been extended broadly enough to include women (at least in theory), as well as multiple races, classes, and nationalities.

Thus, intersubjective and social relationships are much more likely to be the controlling values in sexual morality today than in previous eras. My view is that sexuality has moral value in expressing interpersonal goods even more than procreative ones. Surely women's social contribution does not consist exclusively in our biological reproductive function. This view, widely held, has had an immense impact on which human capacities are identified as primary goods for persons. Yet it is true of corrective feminist appeals to goods validated in women's experience that, as Crowe remarks of Aquinas, "it cannot be said that he has solved the central issue of what, in the last resort, constitutes a natural inclination; is an inclination natural because reasonable or reasonable because natural?"[24] In other words, is a desire, good, or value like procreation morally commanding for human choice because it is "natural" to humans—or do we deem it genuinely natural only after we have categorized it as morally choiceworthy on other grounds? Only to mention current debates about the morality of homosexual behavior, monogamous marriage, motherhood, and women's participation in the paid labor force will be sufficient to illustrate my point.

EPISTEMOLOGY REVISITED

It seems then, that for Aquinas and sympathetic feminists alike, problems remain: how to establish basic goods for human persons or for women, how to order such goods, and how even to demonstrate persuasively that goods are in some sense objective and shared, not merely social constructions or the manipulative and self-serving projections of reigning power alliances (Foucault). In the end, the definition and justification of goods to be sought in action may have an inescapably circular character. The circle is both generated and closed by practical experience, with theory as beneficiary and contributor.

Stephen Pope, writing on the use in ethics of scientific descriptions of human nature, affirms that moral evaluation is not given immediately in human experience, whether rendered via personal accounts or scientific description. Thomistic approaches to natural law affirm the intelligibility of the human good, but also admit the difficulty of grasping it. Natural law ethics is, then, best "conceived as an ongoing tradition of moral reflection with plural expressions."[25] Pope confirms Pamela Hall's thesis that knowledge of the natural law has a "narrative nature." Knowledge of human nature and of what conduces to human flourishing "is discovered progressively over time and through a process of reasoning engaged with the material of experience," all within communities of memory, belief, and practice, and not by deduction from abstract principles or ahistorical conceptions of the good.[26]

Hall's proposal is intended to resolve a debate in natural law theory over whether law or practical reason should take precedence. She suggests that they are compatible if one grants (as she believes Aquinas to have done) a large role to "narrative" experience in discovering the natural law and applying it. Natural law can guide reason only with the assistance of prudence; but prudence relies on natural law to furnish the parameters of flourishing.[27] Hall does not, however, subject to radical questioning the essential premise that there are in fact objective and knowable human goods on which flourishing depends. Nor does she press the question of how knowledge and defense of goods can take place across traditions or among a variety of communities of prudential practice. Nor does she resolve the problem of ultimately conflicting goods, an issue Hall poses on the basis of the works of Martha Nussbaum. Nussbaum is an Aristotelian philosopher who likewise identifies prudence or practical wisdom as the way to knowledge of human goods, who expands the notion of reasonableness to include the affections and emotions, and who believes that goods may be objective and shared cross-culturally, without necessarily being clearly ordered or mutually consistent.[28] Sometimes the moral life involves real and not just seeming tragedy, conflict, sacrifice, and compromise. Hall herself simply refers to Aquinas's belief that apparent conflicts could be resolved if it were not for the limits of human decision-makers.

The actual experience of human moral agency, however, even if interpreted theologically in the light of Christ's cross and resurrection, discloses a good deal of radical conflict, despite our hope for the reconciliation of all that we love and hold sacred in the eschatological kingdom of God. Conflicts of values notwithstanding, however, the objectivity of values—of truths which are not "socially constructed" all the way down—are as important to feminist ethics as they are to Hall, Nussbaum, and Thomas Aquinas. And the test of practice bears out this claim. "Difference" does not go all the way down either. For example, a conference of Third World women which met in Mexico in 1986 issued a final document in which participants saw a broadened "understanding of women's situation in our respective socioeconomic, political, and religio-cultural contexts" as part of and not inimical to their "commitment to total liberation and the achievement of full humanity for all, women and men alike."[29] The urgency of understanding dialectically and practically what it means to respect our common humanity is the touchpoint of natural law theory and feminist ethics.

NOTES

1. Beverly Wildung Harrison with Shirley Cloyes, "Theology and Morality of Procreative Choice," in *Feminist Theological Ethics: A Reader*, ed. Lois K. Daly (Louisville, Ky.: Westminster John Knox Press, 1994), p. 214.

2. Matthew B. Crowe, "The Pursuit of Natural Law," in *Natural Law and Theology: Readings in Moral Theology No. 7*, ed. Charles E. Curran and Richard A. McCormick, S.J. (Mahwah, N.J.: Paulist Press, 1991), p. 296. (This article originally appeared in 1977 in *Irish Theological Quarterly*.)

3. Jacques Maritain, "Natural Law in Aquinas," in *Natural Law and Theology*, pp. 114–15.

4. Ibid., p. 115.

5. See, among many possible examples, Judith Butler, *Gender Trouble: Feminism and the Subversion of Identity* (New York and London: Routledge, 1990); Jane Flax, *Thinking Fragments: Psychoanalysis, Feminism, and Post-*

modernism in the Contemporary West (Berkeley: University of California Press, 1990); and Alison Jaggar, *Feminist Politics and Human Nature* (Brighton, Sussex: Harvester Press, 1983).

6. Susan Brooks Thistlethwaite, *Sex, Race, and God: Christian Feminism in Black and White* (New York: Crossroad, 1989), p. 24. See also Karen Lebacqz, "Love Your Enemy: Sex, Power, and Christian Ethics," in *Feminist Theological Ethics*, ed. Daly, pp. 244–61 (originally presented as a Society of Christian Ethics Presidential Address).

7. Audre Lorde, *Sister Outsider: Essays and Speeches* (Trumansburg, N.Y.: Crossing Press, 1984), p. 116; Iris Marion Young, "The Ideal of Community and the Politics of Difference," *Social Theory and Practice* 12, no. 1 (Spring 1986); Maria C. Lugones, "On the Logic of Pluralist Feminism," in *Feminist Ethics*, ed. Claudia Card (Lawrence, Kans.: University of Kansas Press, 1991), pp. 35–44.

8. Ada Maria Isasi-Diaz, "Vive la Diferencía," in *Feminist Theological Ethics*, ed. Daly, p. 94.

9. Martha C. Nussbaum, "Charles Taylor: Explanation and Practical Reason," in *The Quality of Life*, ed. Martha C. Nussbaum and Amartya Sen (Oxford: Clarendon Press, 1993), p. 239. See also Sidney Callahan, *In Good Conscience: Reason and Emotion in Moral Decision-Making* (San Francisco: Harper Collins, 1991); and Jean Porter, *The Recovery of Virtue: The Relevance of Aquinas for Christian Ethics* (Louisville, Ky.: Westminster John Knox Press, 1990)

10. Katie G. Cannon, "Hitting a Straight Lick with a Crooked Stick: The Womanist Dilemma in the Development of a Black Liberation Ethic," in *Feminist Theological Ethics*, ed. Daly, p. 37.

11. As cited in Thistlethwaite, *Sex, Race, and God*, p. 24.

12. Ibid., p. 25.

13. Toinette Eugene, "On 'Difference' and the Dream of Pluralist Feminism," in *Feminist Theological Ethics*, ed. Daly, p. 93.

14. Charles E. Curran, "Natural Law in Moral Theology", in *Natural Law and Theology*, ed. Curran and McCormick, pp. 275–79; Crowe, "The Pursuit of Natural Law," pp. 321–25.

15. The following overview is a rendering of Aquinas's "Treatise on Law," *Summa Theologica* 1.2.90–94.

16. On the connection of prudence, virtue, rules, and action, see Jean Porter, *Moral Action and Christian Ethics* (Cambridge, New York, and Melbourne: Cambridge University Press, 1995), pp. 153–55.

17. Jean Porter, "Virtue and Sin: The Connection of the Virtues and the Case of the Flawed Saint," *Journal of Religion* 75 (1995): 532–33. (See Aquinas *Summa Theologica* 1.2.58.5.)

18. Maureen Dallison Kemeza's Boston College doctoral dissertation on Aquinas and feminism is to be published by Continuum. See also Cristina Traina's University of Chicago dissertation on natural law and feminism.

19. Aquinas *Summa Theologica* 2.2.47.15. On this point, see Stephen J. Pope, "Descriptive and Normative Uses of Evolutionary Theory," in *Christian Ethics: Problems and Prospects,* ed. Lisa Sowle Cahill and James F. Childress (Cincinnati, Ohio: Pilgrim Press, 1996); and "Scientific and Natural Law Analyses of Homosexuality: A Methodological Study," *Journal of Religious Ethics,* forthcoming.

20. See Jean Porter, *The Recovery of Virtue,* pp. 69–70.

21. See George P. Schner, S.J., "The Appeal to Experience," *Theological Studies* 53 (1992): 54; and Pamela Dickey Young, *Feminist Theology/Christian Theology: In Search of Method* (Minneapolis: Fortress Press, 1990), p. 61.

22. "Physicalism" or "biologism" is a constant refrain in criticisms of natural law. See Curran, "Natural Law in Moral Theology," pp. 254–61.

23. See Aquinas *Summa Theologica* 1.92, "On the Production of Woman."

24. Crowe, "The Pursuit of Natural Law," p. 307.

25. Stephen Pope, "Scientific and Natural Law Analyses of Homosexuality," manuscript pp. 32–33.

26. Pamela M. Hall, *Narrative and the Natural Law: An Interpretation of Thomistic Ethics* (Notre Dame and London: University of Notre Dame Press, 1994) pp. 94–95; see also p. 37.

27. Ibid., pp. 21–22.

28. See Martha Nussbaum, "Non–Relative Virtues: An Aristotelian Approach," in *The Quality of Life,* ed. Nussbaum and Sen, pp. 242–69; "Aristotelian Social Democracy," in *Liberalism and the Good,* ed. R. Bruce Douglass, Gerald R. Mara, and Henry S. Richardson (New York: Routledge, 1990); Human Functioning and Social Justice: In Defense of Aristotelian Essentialism," *Political Theory* 210, no. 2 (1992): 203; and "Feminists and Philosophy," *New York Review,* 20 October 1994, pp. 59–61.

29. "Final Document: Intercontinental Women's Conference (Oaxtepec, Mexico, Dec. 1–6, 1986)," in Virginia Fabella, M.M., and Mercy Amba Oduyoye, *With Passion and Compassion: Third World Women Doing Theology* (Maryknoll, N.Y.: Orbis Books, 1989), p. 184.

Is There an Essence
of Human Nature?

ROBERT CUMMINGS NEVILLE

THERE ARE MANY REASONS to say there is no essence of human nature. The first is that to affirm an essence of anything, especially of human nature, is to brand one's own forehead with a big I for "Imperialist." Because I am an unabashed speculative metaphysician and also insist that our philosophical public includes the South and East Asian traditions as well as the West, and therefore have two strikes against me, I want to avoid being an imperialist. That charge is real and not merely ironic. To venture any generalizations about human beings or the human condition is to risk imposing a parochial vision of what constitutes human nature and goodness.[1] There are people who will insist that even in denying an essence of human nature I am committing wicked essentialism by emphasizing human responsibility, as I shall, more than the suffering of the oppressed. Though I shall deny the charge, the ease with which it is made is good cause to be extremely careful about essentialism.

Another reason to deny an essence of human nature is that Plato did, in his argument if not in so many words. Plato, of course, is the one usually blamed for inventing wicked essentialism. I do not find that in Plato's texts myself. Aristotle invented the idea of essences for species and individuals and attributed a deficient version of that to Plato.[2] Some nineteenth- and early twentieth-century philosophers, mainly English men, did believe in abstract defining essences for things, and called them Platonic essences or forms; Bertrand Russell and Alfred North Whitehead believed in them at certain times in their careers and hoped to relate them to mathematical ideas. But those notions are only remotely related to Plato's own ideas. Although Plato discussed the nature of such things as justice, piety, love, and courage, he never discussed human nature as such or said there is a form of it.

In fact, at the end of the *Republic* he said that the most important thing you can do is to find someone to help you balance out all the contingencies in your life—wealth or poverty, talents or ineptitudes, beauty or ugliness—to find the goals and ideals of life that might be unique to yourself.[3] Even in his discussions of justice, piety, and other virtues, Plato's arguments demonstrated that they consist in different things depending on what is included; that is, the ideal patterns defining the virtues are relative to the things that need to be included and the interesting dialectical questions have to do with what ought to be taken as relevant for the virtues under consideration. If even Plato did not believe in an essence of human nature, then surely I should not.[4]

A third, more philosophic, reason to deny an essence of human nature can be drawn from what I take to be an important metaphysical distinction, namely, that between essential and conditional features of things.[5] The best hypothesis about what it is to be a thing, I believe, is that a thing is a harmony of essential and conditional features. To be determinate at all is to be determinate in some respect or respects relative to other things that are determinately different. Therefore things are always to be defined in terms of their conditioning relations with other things. Their essential features are what integrate their conditional features to give them an integrated singular position relative to other things and also their own determinate identities. Both conditional and essential features are necessary, neither more important than the other. The conditional features define a thing's relations according to which it is different from other things, and its essential features define how it turns those potential conditions into its own being.

At the human level, this means that people are always to be defined in terms of their natural and social connections and contexts. Because people are differently connected causally and live in different contexts, their natures are different, even if one might say that their essential features are similar: the essential features have to integrate the conditional features at hand. By their natures, then, people are different, rich from poor, women from men, one culture from another.

These three introductory points—the avoidance of an imperialist description of the human, Plato's avoidance of a definition of human nature, and the metaphysical insistence that things are defined in part relationally and that human beings by nature are related to different important conditions—will play crucial if sometimes unac-

knowledged roles in the following argument. I shall argue that, although there is no such thing as an essence of human nature, there is
something very like that. The first part of the argument will be a discussion of some of the implications of lying under obligation. What is
primarily essential about human beings is that they have obligations.
But human beings may not be the only beings with obligations, and
therefore the second part of the argument will discuss the human condition, or that set of conditions that collectively distinguish and relate
human beings from and to other things, including perhaps other obliged beings. The harmony of essential obligatedness with the conditions that mark off the human sphere comes close to addressing the
interest in whether there is an essence of human nature.

LYING UNDER OBLIGATION

Obligation is the condition that obtains when there is a situation
with various possible outcomes that differ according to better and
worse and over which you have some control.[6] You are obligated to influence things for the better simply because that is the better thing to
do, and your normative or moral identity is built up by how you do the
better or worse from one situation to the next. To the question, Why
be moral and undertake to fulfill your obligations, the first and most
relevant answer is because that is what is good to do and that you make
yourself a better person by doing so, and a worse person by failing to
make the attempt. If you choose to pass when it comes to being moral,
that does not mean you are free of obligations, only that you have de-
liberately chosen a course that might not be the better and might in
fact be the worse; in passing on obligations you fail a special kind of
obligatory norm I shall discuss shortly. You might not be worried about
being a bad person, but you ought to be; that is, it is your obligation
to attend to your obligations even if you choose to disregard both your
obligations and the higher-level obligation to address obligations.

The apparent simplicity of this point about lying under obligation should not be misleading. There are immense complexities involved. It assumes, for instance, that there are real differences in
value among the outcomes of situations, that health is generally better
than disease or trauma, that enjoyment is better than suffering, that
understanding is better than confusion and ignorance, that affection is

better than hatred, and so forth. Of course there might be situations in which the generally worse would be specifically better, but in those situations there would be good reason for the reversal of the customary value, such as the need for sacrifice. I shall not argue here against the philosophers who claim that there are no real differences in the values of possible outcomes.[7]

Whether we can know accurately what is better and worse is even more complicated. Surely we make mistakes and over time sometimes shift our assessments. But the very fact that we change our minds indicates that there are some grounds, however obscure and difficult to discern, to which we appeal in making evaluative distinctions.

But more complicated yet is the fact that we are rarely in situations alone. In fact, most situations are characterized by highly complex social arrangements. Few actions are possible that are not in fact joint actions of several people, actions structured by institutions and social conventions, and nearly always by the meanings conveyed in language. Most situations in which people can exercise some control over outcomes are defined through cultural semiotic constructions, and not just one but several overlapping, competing, and deceptively dissimilar constructions.

Therefore a significant social problem lies in relating individuals' specific responsibilities for the general obligations. *Obligations* refer to what ought to be done by the public; *responsibilities* refer to how individuals diversely bear those obligations. I have argued elsewhere that general public obligations fall upon everyone as personal responsibilities except insofar as social structures channel responsibilities to particular people, relieving the others of those responsibilities.[8] A well-ordered society has developed social structures that assign responsibilities to people equipped to deal with them, granting the others privacy in those matters. Government offices, parents caring for their own children, the division of labor in various economic and domestic jobs, are examples of socially structured responsibilities for obligations in the social situation. Where a society does not have an effective social structure, the obligations remain the personal responsibilities of everyone, as, for instance, all Americans are responsible for overcoming the evils of racism, given the failures of the law and educational system to complete the job.

On top of the complexities of assigning personal responsibilities for obligations in situations is the recursive character of obligation and responsibility. There are situations where possible outcomes differ greatly in value but where we have no control, no capacity to influence the outcome. Nevertheless, if we might have such control, we therefore have an obligation to develop it. Through responsible physicians we have an obligation to cure strep infections, because we have effective antibiotics. We do not have a cure for AIDS; but we do have an obligation to develop one, that is, to attain the capacity to influence the outcome of the disease. There are special problems, rather well understood, for assigning culpability and responsibility for recursive obligations. Although clinicians have the responsibility to cure strep infections, they do not have the responsibility to develop cures for AIDS. That responsibility in American society falls upon scientific researchers, and the higher-level recursive responsibility to fund the research falls on government agencies and drug companies, and beyond that on the electorate to influence the government to structure research well. This illustrates the conjoint character of most actions or potential actions. In the case of personal failures of responsibility, we partially excuse a person who did not know better, but should have. We partially excuse a bumbling social agency or church for inadequacies in welfare, and reserve some criticism for those who should have corrected the bumbling in advance. A painful tension often exists between the stacking up of recursive obligations so that everyone is responsible to make everything perfect, and the humane forgiveness of inattention, unpreparedness, and failure to be able to exercise as much influence on situations as is necessary to bring about the better outcomes. People have many worthwhile things to do other than to prepare themselves for some future responsibility. The stack of recursive obligations carried to an extreme leads to moral and sometimes political totalitarianism. But the admission of incapacity carried to an extreme leads to moral relativism and abrogation of all personal responsibility. American political discourse swings wildly along the spectrum between these two poles in tension.

I want to argue that what is essential in human life is having responsibilities to obligations; this is what is meant by lying under obligation. This is not a human essence in any full sense because the content of the obligations, and the complex assigning of responsibilities, is relative to the nature of the diverse conditions in which we live and to their social structures. But before moving to discuss that conditional diversity, it is important to say more about species of obligations and their norms.

There are at least four kinds or families of norms that are important for defining how we lie under obligation: norms of order, deference, engagement, and identity.[9]

Norms of order have to do with ordering or arranging affairs in
situations so that the better outcome is attained. Sometimes this takes
the form of imposing patterns, as in instances of social justice; other
times it is a subtler form of arranging means and ends. Most of what
we mean by morality—balancing claims, minimizing personal and
social costs, building the institutions of a good society—falls within
the consideration of norms of order.

Norms of deference have to do with acknowledging, and attending and deferring to, the intrinsic and singular values of things.
People, animals, mountains, oceans, works of art, even institutions,
have worthy characters that sometimes resist being assigned roles in a
just order. Part of an appropriate response to things is to acknowledge
them, to defer to them, to take up an attitude of natural piety before
them. Aesthetic apprehension more than moral calculus is involved
in deference.[10] Sometimes the norms of deference are in competition and tension with norms of order. Surely it is morally obligatory
to sacrifice a museum of masterpieces to save a human life; but it is
also deeply wrong to put the art and the person in a balancing order.
Surely it is right to preserve an environment in which natural species
of plants and animals can survive at the price of a human livelihood
based on destruction of the environment; but it is also deeply wrong to
enforce poverty. Surely it is right for a society to condemn blood feuds
and exercise force to prevent them; but it is a deep matter to understand the family loyalties and passions, the biological instincts, that
move human relations blind of the requirements of abstract citizenship. Considerations of deference are more prominent in many
aspects of East and South Asian cultures than they are in Western
European utilitarian cultures. Part of the European Enlightenment's
emphasis on rationality was to suppress the claims of norms of deference in favor of giving things a position in a just order. Immanuel Kant
recognized the beautiful and the sublime as being different from the
moral, but not as having a claim against it.[11] Current philosophical con-
fusions about ecological obligations and the rights of nonhuman
animals, however, indicate that the ordering principles of morality
cannot easily be extended far enough to cover our normative intui-
tions. Norms of deference are at play as well and need to be analyzed.
Even in Kant's moral scheme, the respect for persons as ends in them-

selves is based on deference and is connected with the ordering principles that make the will free only by a sleight of hand.[12]

Both norms of order and those of deference apply to the objective features of situations. The norms of engagement and identity
apply more to the responsible actors within the situation, though like
the objective norms they lay claim to shaping influence on outcomes.

Norms of engagement have to do with how people relate to the
obligations in the situation, with how they take up responsibilities,
especially with their recursive responsibilities to be responsible to
be responsible. Existentialist literature of the twentieth century has
been filled with considerations of norms of engagement. Dostoyevsky's
Raskolnikov tried to be an amoralist; Kafka's K was numbed to insanity
by the perfected banality of bureaucracy; Camus's Meursault laid his
heart open to the benign indifference of the universe. Where disappointment and fear might lead us to back away from our situation, to
disengage as if we were not the ones who might act, or at least enjoy,
the norms of engagement determine how we might take up our lot.

The norms of identity are those that determine how our actions
or nonactions give us normative identity through time. They are concerned with praise and blame, with being able to commit ourselves for
the future and be responsible for past actions. Our own personal normative identity is rarely the only consideration in determining what
to do in a situation. Only egotists think their own virtue is that important. But it does count for something, and that in nearly every situation. The norms of identity include not only moral identity but also
our identity as deferential, engaged, and concerned with our own normative identity.

The norms of identity, deference, engagement, and identity
together mark out important dimensions of value that define the normative weights of possible outcomes to which we might be obliged. To
be under obligation is to have all their kinds of considerations count in
the imperatives that define personal and socially structured responsibilities. However complicated and obscure these considerations are,
they do define dimensions of responsibility for human life.

But they are not limited to the human. Any being that can control behavior to make a difference to the outcome of normatively
freighted situations is under obligation. Some philosophers in the
West have said that obligation adheres in any creature that is rational.
Yet rationality has been defined very narrowly. It is better to say that

obligation defines any creature with a culture that can articulate possibilities, modes of causal action, and patterns of cooperation in the division of responsibility, and exercise control over behavior and its outcomes. To be cultured, or to be possibly cultured, in a world with possible outcomes of different values, is to lie under obligation. Human beings, porpoises, angels, and any beings on a planet of Alpha Centauri who might visit us or throw a party when we finally visit them, all lie under obligation. The radically different conditions of the lives of these beings mean that their cultures barely overlap, if at all. We imagine angelic culture on the analogies of vocal ensembles and the postal service. But what do we know?

THE HUMAN CONDITION

If there is an essence to human nature, it must lie in a definitive group of conditions that mark off human obligations from the obligations of higher, lower, and alien beings. We can consider candidate conditions for the human by asking about common conditions of existence, common goods or rights, and commonality arising from cultural definition.

Human beings share a common nature in at least one clear sense in that they constitute a biological species whose members can interbreed. They do not share all the same genes, but they can reproduce out of a common gene pool. The gene pool is common only potentially, of course, and that potentiality lies in the readiness of genes from any human to join the haploid dance with other genes. Until recently, human beings also enjoyed a common experience of early nurture in a uterine environment, and so far as I know even now test-tube-conceived babies are nurtured for a long while in wombs. Scientifically produced possibilities can easily be imagined, however, for different sorts of incubation.

Human beings also share common constraints on homeostasis with respect to temperature, breathable air, gravity and air pressure, physical metabolism, and such like. In these respects, however, cultures are highly inventive in their adaptation to environing conditions far beyond the naked constraints. Clothing can maintain human body temperature in conditions of killing cold or heat; air can be filtered and artificially mixed so as to be breathable, and modified to humanly acceptable pressures; foods can be cooked and otherwise concocted to serve human metabolism. Astronauts simulate earthly conditions in a pure weightless vacuum, and who knows how the constraints of human homeostasis might be modified by multigenerational trips across the galaxy? Moreover, human beings interact with one another culturally to abide in and modify these empirical conditions, one culture learning from another.[13] Human newborns require families, communities require social roles, and spaceships require decision-making structures. These cultural conditions, of course, are relative to the other empirical conditions, both as causes and effects.

With regard to common physical nature and common environing conditions, nothing but temporary empirical generalizations can be made about a common human nature. As genes are modified and humans adapt to nonearthly environments, that sense of human nature will change. There is nothing sacred or especially dignified about the common conditions that obtain now except in their specific excellences and disadvantages, and in how certain congeries of conditions, often unnoticed by us now, are necessary as a basis for other humanly important things we prize. More important, human obligations are not neatly set off or bounded by these empirical conditions. We have obligations toward nonhuman beings, and it is easy to imagine, as science fiction has done, entering into cooperation with dolphins and aliens, and maybe with angels, to cope with normatively freighted situations.

When we turn to human goods and rights, however, the common empirical elements of human life take on new importance, especially when regarded in connection with their cultural contexts. We can say, generally and tentatively, that the conditions that make human life possible and healthy are good for all human beings, even when they take different forms. So all human beings would prosper with a secure environment, however that is produced; all would prosper with an economy that produces goods for food and the maintenance of domestic life, however diverse the appropriate and effective economies; all would prosper with means for gaining and transmitting knowledge, whatever counts as knowledge. Moreover, human prosperity, like obligation, is recursive. Whatever enables the conditions for prosperity is also a human good, so that culture itself is a good, the richer in service of primary goods and of itself the better.

Beyond the utilitarian functions of culture in securing and improving the lot of human beings, culture brings new dimensions of excellence. Families, for instance, not only make possible the existence and education of human infants but they also make possible human relations of affection, care, and nurture that have nothing to do with infancy. The satisfaction of sexual urges need not be limited to brute bodily passion but can be transformed into profound loving physical, emotional, and intellectual passion. People marry and cohabit in order to attain emotional bonding that was perhaps originally utilitarian for the sake of protecting weak infants but that is clearly excellent and self-justifying on its own. Similarly, utilitarian cooperation can make friendship possible that is more important than mere cooperation. Public life arises out of the need for social decision-making and control of force, but gives rise to a human excellence of broad vision, compassion, and the institution of public roles to channel general obligations to personal responsibilities. East Asian traditions of philosophy have been more articulate about this than the Western.[14]

Some human goods are the fulfillments of antecedently given needs for the maintenance of life. Others arise as civilizations create new possibilities such as family love, friendship, and public life that are immensely attractive and good on their own. The civilizational goods are cultural and exist only in the exercise of the culture. But they too are recursive so that their ideals are taken as signs of ultimacy. Family love is so good that love is the way we symbolize how we should relate to God and God to us. Friendship is so good that the gods are our friends. Public life is so good that the cosmos can be conceived as a divine city or kingdom. Part of human nature is that we are drawn to possible excellences, and where the excellences define possible outcomes of situations, they become obligatory in some way.[15] Nevertheless, cultures are so different that we risk imperialism in characterizing any one kind of family life as normative for all, or one kind of friendship, or one form of public life.

Furthermore, crucial questions need to be brought to attention about how human beings symbolize these human goods to themselves. We symbolize them differently. Charles Taylor, in *Sources of the Self*, has argued that cultures are mightily affected by how they conceive the human good, a conception that orders many if not most of the lesser goods that make up human life.[16] He claims that in mythopoeic Greece the human good had to do with the nobility of pursuing glory, and other occupations were subordinated to the warrior's. With Plato and his peers the human good was transformed to a kind of heroism of rational self-control and organization of social life.

With Christianity that was modified or supplemented with the ideal of the heroic saint. And in the modern period all forms of heroism were subordinated, Taylor argues, to the human good of ordinary life, life as accessible to anyone. These civilization-defining conceptions of the human good that Taylor discusses are diverse, and are only characteristic of the West. Other civilizational traditions have other conceptions. Perhaps some civilizations have no overall defining model of human excellence.

Let us now recall the point of this discussion, namely, to determine whether there are any special conditions that define human nature. There is a potentially common gene pool, although it is not clear what the capacity for interbreeding has to do with the fairly high-flown questions about human nature that deal with its ideals. With regard to the gene pool, we are developing capacities to improve it, and also risky techniques that might introduce new harms. There are physiological characteristics of human beings set within limits of toleration. Yet culture allows us to alter those limits and there is no telling how broad those alterations might be. Human beings do have being cultured in common; we could not have developed smart creatures requiring prolonged infancy without that. But the cultures are different in specifics, and cultures in general can be shared with other animals, aliens, and angels—at least in some cultures' self-conceptions. As to human values, we have noted two kinds. Things are valuable for fulfilling needs, and the needs are defined by the various conditions and cultures of people. And things are valuable as leading us on to higher and better excellences, not just needful fulfillments but satisfactions of high civilized life. These too differ from culture to culture, although perhaps any might come to be appreciated by those who learn its resident culture.

Two more candidate sets of conditions need to be considered, history and orientation. In many simple groups the tribe-name is the word for human being—simply "the people." That seems quaint to us who are anciently multicultural. But suppose we say that human beings are defined by the natural history of the evolution of people on the Earth, diversifying into tribes and coalescing into nations, a complex singular history in which all peoples in all cultures have distinguished themselves from other animals, divine beings, and aliens. For us now, aliens would have to come from other planets, and if those visitors turn out to be the Lost Tribe of Israel or the parent race who seeded Earth with our ancestors, they are not so alien after all. This historical identity of the human is cumbersome in its complexity; one large problem is the difficulty of making a story out of history. But it does offer a way for us now, with historical consciousness, to do some justice to the complexities of human existence and also to its boundaries. With specific history, we do not have to say what human nature is in general but what these people are and did in relation to those people, and these animals, and just who it is we encounter that seem to be angels or aliens. History is not merely human history but the history of us in relation to anything specific whatsoever.

The final consideration of potential common conditions for the human that I want to raise, which I call "orientation," is hard to explain in Western terms although it is a familiar idea in East Asia. Western thinkers such as the idealists and existentialists have been concerned to define the "centered" self, the self with interiority that looks out on the world and struggles to interact with the world with integrity.[17] Many have come to criticize that as supposing too sharp and arbitrary a distinction between self and world, led to exaggeration perhaps by Descartes's distinction between mind and body, which everyone agrees is more wicked even than cultural imperialism. My suggestion is that instead we treat those problems of selfhood and integrity as matters of subtle and appropriate orientation to reality rather than the construction of a self-substance. Let us look to the world and develop ways of behaving properly and keeping our balance, existing in harmony with the dao.

The Chinese were quick to point out that orientation is a complex matter because the movements of reality are so diverse and complex. Xunzi, for instance, a third-century B.C.E. thinker, distinguished three levels of the operation of nature.[18] Some things, such as the rotation of the heavens, are remote and regular and there is nothing we can do about them except note them and perhaps admire. Other things, such as the conditions for farming, are understandable and manipulable. We know how to plant, irrigate, and harvest, as well as how to cook, make clothing, build houses, and the like. We relate to these things with ordinary learning and traditional ways. In between, however, are irregular and often cataclysmic actions of the dao, such as earthquakes, floods, and famines. They cannot be neatly predicted nor controlled, Xunzi thought, but we know that they happen. The excellence of a human civilization consists in part, he said, in how it organizes, through government, to respond to these lurches in the dao in the middle distance. A good government is prepared for disaster relief, for sandbagging swollen streams, and for laying away grain for the years of drought. The Chinese allowed that barbarian cultures could cope with everyday nature, but only a civilized society, with its high levels of integration, science, and control for planning ahead and for action over long distances, could make a properly human response to events in that middle distance. The large events of history, such as an invasion by neighbors or the discovery of another high civilization, are on the scale of those matters of the middle distance. Thus there are three scales of orientation here: settling into the cosmic rhythms, learning the regular coping customs of one's culture, and organizing to act singularly as individuals and as a people.

The Chinese pointed out even more distinctions of scales of orientation than these. On the metaphysical level, the stars are but a distant approximation of the cosmic dao, and that dao which is named in nature is not the most basic dao.[19] More proximately, there are rhythms of the seasons that structure much of peasant culture, and different rhythms of the city, of the family, of one's aging and that of family and friends, of one's profession, special interests, and so forth. To be properly oriented in life is not to define oneself by any one of these scales of orientation to natural or social processes, but to all of them together, harmonizing their diversities, responding to their different demands and needs. Orientation is a harmonization of orientations. All species of animals are affected by how they stand with reference to all the scales of things to which they might be oriented, from their historical place in the swarming of cosmic gasses, the gravity of their planet, the metabolic options of their local environment, and the contingent development of a new bug in their niche. But human beings more than any other species we know understand themselves in terms of how they orient themselves to the cosmic array of scales of orientation. We all have myths if not science about the grounding roots of the cosmos, about what elements of the environment make human life sustainable, about the fundamental cultural importance of singing and brewing beer, and about how our group has related to other groups. We all have understandings of how we can become disoriented in some crucial respect, and have to find orientation again through dancing, prayer, better science and technology, or the grand tour. We understand how orientation and disorientation affect both groups and individuals, and how much of personal maturation is the attainment of what counts as sophisticated orientation to the array of orientation scales in one's culture.

Religion has a lot to do with the harmonization of orientations to the many scales to which human orientation is appropriate. Some religions say that disorientation at certain scales is very serious and perhaps built in to the human condition. Disorientation of systematic sorts is the East Asian version of what the South Asians characterize as ignorance requiring enlightenment and West Asians characterize as sin requiring redemption.

The human cultural religious project of developing a harmonious orientation of orientations to the array of scales of processes and events to which we should be oriented is recursive like obligation. This is to say, the question of problematic orientation has something of this form: what is the proper or best human way to be oriented or to integrate one's orientations? The reference to the human way might be answered by identification with one's group, for instance, the American way; or with one's history, for instance, Western culture, or the accumulated cultures of people on spaceship Earth; or with a part of one's culture, for instance, the educated person's way; or in reference to physical circumstances, for instance, the desert way or arctic way; or in biological terms, for instance, the way appropriate to the genetically shaped forms of human life. After I have said all this, of course, we will want to define the achievement of orientation in reference to all these things that go into our definition. In so doing, we note that the project of orientation, of orientation of orientations, defines us as it defines the orienting activities and attitudes. Becoming oriented gives us a center, an accumulated nature honed by sensitivity to the myriad conditions to which we should be oriented. And because the process of orientation is recursive, we need to develop more and different parts of our natures in order to become better oriented, and so take up orientation to those things which we identify with ourselves and our responses. Human nature is partly, indeed largely, framed by our representations of what we should be, in all complexity, in order properly to be oriented to all that is relevant to our position. But note that I have slipped back into talking about "us" and "our position" as if we had settled that point.

OBLIGATIONS AND HUMAN CONDITIONS

My argument so far has two sides. One pursued the point that human beings, like all beings, have essential features, and the other tracked the point that they have conditional features. Human nature would have to be the harmony of both.

On the one side I have argued that what is essential to any cultured creature, including human beings, is that we lie under obligation. The obligations pertain not just to possibilities for human beings but to the whole field of possibilities, outcomes which we might affect. The field of possibilities includes a wide array of nature beyond those things considered as possible common conditions defining the human. The discussion of orientation reformulated the issues of relating to the field of possibilities so that the diversity of scales of obligation might be seen in greater complexity. Furthermore, lying under obligation is not just a defining trait of individuals but needs to be parsed out in terms of the varieties of shared action, institutional actions, and the like. Indeed, our partners in action, who thus share in defining responsibilities for action, might include nonhuman cultural agents who can enter into the cultural definitions of our own agency.

On the other side I have argued that the conditional features of human life do not constitute a unique and bounded set but are contingently connected with many factors that might change. Our biology, our habitat, our cultures, and our self-conceptions are contingent and are in fact changing. We might discover that they should change much more. However the boundaries are set, we are parts of biological, physical, cultural, and semiotic systems that have connections far beyond what we might conceive the human to be today.

Therefore, although we have essential obligations and contingent defining conditions, there is no discriminable essence for human nature, either descriptive or normative. Our bodies, the definition of membership in our community of shared normative obligation, our habitats, and our self-conceptions might change. What we are today may not be what we ought to be, and tomorrow we will be different, and ought to be. In many respects, therefore, the notion of the human as it involves boundaries with the nonhuman is fairly trivial. We share normative responsibilities with a wider community than the human commonly defined, and that common definition is based on conditions that are evolving. When it comes to our responsibility to "save the Earth," "we" might mean "us and the dolphins."

Though not an essence of human nature, there is something very like it, however. It is that, among the norms of identity are those that shape our obligations as a biological species with a history of habitats and cultural adaptations, a history of civilizational extensions beyond the needs of nature to the excellences made possible by culture, and an orientation to the problems of orientation on all scales we can discern. Noting our species characteristics, we can ask how we ought to relate to the ecological systems within which we live, for instance. Noting the conditions of possible habitats, we can ask how our cultures ought to be adapted, especially to the mutual engagement of nearly all the world's civilizations in our own lifetime. The more or less unified habitat of Planet Earth means our diverse cultures should be modified to get along together. Noting the vast expanse of the universe beyond primitive ken, we can ask what we should learn and do in order to understand and engage that cosmos. Noting the disparity of privilege in the diverse conditions of human groups, we can ask what minimal conditions of resources, wealth, power, dignity, and self-determination ought to be guaranteed for all people at the price of taxing or limiting people with abundance in those respects, all on the grounds of how human and other goods are best conceived in our complex time.

All this is to say that the normative identity of each one of us is partly defined by what is normative for the communities of human beings in historical connection. Orienting ourselves to being human, and in continuity with other human beings, is part of individual as well as cultural normative identity. Of course we are also oriented to other cultured animals, animals such as pets that share our cultures, someday aliens, and perhaps angels.[20] But we are not oriented to them as needing human goods, variously defined, or as having issues of human orientation to the array of orientation scales in the cosmos. Any beings who do conceive themselves as defined in part by how they orient themselves to the harmonizing of the array of orientation scales, and take their own definition to include biological and environmental continuity with us, and are joined with us in history and the self-conceptions in history, would have to be counted as "humans," whether invertebrate, silicone-based, or made of angel stuff. The closest thing to an essence of human nature is having the obligation to take responsibility for being part of the history in which we ourselves are engaged, and including that in one's orientation to the orientation points of reality.

NOTES

1. The generalization in my previous sentence exhibits a preoccupation of guilty white Western males. Being a Christian, I do not take the guilt seriously save where remediation is possible. Nevertheless, although Christians need not take guilt seriously in some sense because of Christian justification, in another sense guilt is among the things that define human identity, over time and in eternity, a theme of this paper. See the more complete discussion in my *Eternity and Time's Flow* (Albany: State University of New York Press, 1993), pt. 1.

2. See for instances Aristotle's *Metaphysics*. For a brilliant discussion of Aristotle's response to Plato, see Robert S. Brumbaugh, *Platonic Studies of Greek Philosophy: Form, Arts, Gadgets, and Hemlock* (Albany: State University of New York Press, 1989), pt. 3, especially chap. 10, "If Aristotle Had Become Head of the Academy. . . ."

3. Plato *Republic* 10.618c–619b.

4. For recent discussions of Plato on form see Robert S. Brumbaugh, *Plato on the One: The Hypotheses in the Parmenides* (New Haven, Conn.: Yale University Press, 1961); and Stanley Rosen, *The Question of Being: A Reversal of Heidegger* (New Haven, Conn.: Yale University Press, 1993).

5. The theory of things as harmonies of conditional and essential features is very important for my thinking and also for the argument of this essay. Because I am not going to defend it at length here, I should cite places where I have done so. The most metaphysical expression is in *God the Creator* (Albany: State University of New York Press, 1992; original ed., University of Chicago Press, 1968), chap. 2; the most cosmological is *Recovery of the Measure* (Albany: State University of New York Press, 1989), chap. 5; the most axiological, oriented to values and norms as the discussion here requires, is *Normative Cultures* (Albany: State University of New York Press, 1995), chaps. 2–3.

6. I have analyzed obligation at length in *The Puritan Smile* (Albany: State University of New York Press, 1987), chap. 3; *The Highroad around Modernism* (Albany: State University of New York Press, 1992), chap. 10; and *Normative Cultures*, chaps. 5–6.

7. For a systematic defense of realism with regard to values and the knowledge of value, see the three books in my *Axiology of Thinking*, namely,

Reconstruction of Thinking (Albany: State University of New York Press, 1981), *Recovery of the Measure,* and *Normative Cultures.*

8. Neville, *Highroad around Modernism,* chap. 10, and *Normative Cultures,* chap. 6.

9. These are analyzed at much greater length in Neville, *Normative Cultures,* chap. 5.

10. On deference, and its distinction from concerns for order, or rational order, see David Hall, *Eros and Irony* (Albany: State University of New York Press, 1982), chap. 4; and David Hall and Roger Ames, *Anticipating China* (Albany: State University of New York Press, 1995), chap. 3.

For a splendid example of the aesthetic elements in deference, see David Strong, *Crazy Mountains: Learning from Wilderness to Weigh Technology* (Albany: State University of New York Press, 1995).

11. See Immanuel Kant, *Critique of Judgment,* trans. James Creed Meredith (Oxford: Clarendon Press, 1952), "Analytic of the Beautiful" and "Analytic of the Sublime."

12. See Immanuel Kant, *Foundations of the Metaphysics of Morals,* sec. 2 in *Critique of Practical Reason and Other Writings in Moral Philosophy,* trans. and ed. Lewis White Beck (Chicago: University of Chicago Press, 1949), pp. 86ff.

13. See the remarkable book by William McNeill, *The Rise of the West: A History of the Human Community* (Chicago: University of Chicago Press, 1963, 1991), especially the essay in the 1991 reprinting, "The Rise of the West after Twenty-five Years."

14. The Confucian tradition in particular has emphasized advancing beyond bottom-line utilitarian human relations to the civilizational excellences of family love and life, friendship, public life, and accomplishments in the arts. The best ancient philosopher on this was Xunzi. See Edward Machle, *Nature and Heaven in the Xunzi* (Albany: State University of New York Press, 1993). I have discussed the matter at length in *Normative Cultures,* chap. 7.

15. This is one of the central points of Plato's philosophy, not the description of those excellences in definitions or essences.

16. See Charles Taylor, *Sources of the Self: The Making of the Modern Identity* (Cambridge: At the University Press, 1989).

17 . See Taylor's discussion of this, ibid.

18. See Machle, *Nature and Heaven in the Xunzi,* for a translation of Xunzi's treatise on nature (or Heaven) and a discussion of this point.

19. The beginning of the *Dao De Jing.*

20. I don't really believe in angels, understand, but I'm willing to be surprised.

PART II

The Human Struggle
to Be Humane

Human Intelligence
and Social Inequality

GLENN C. LOURY

I. *THE BELL CURVE* AS SCIENTIFIC DISCOURSE

A MEDITATION ON HUMAN NATURE and social inequality must necessarily entertain certain questions: What do we mean by *human
intelligence*? Whatever one means by *intelligence*, is it well measured
by Spearman's factor-analytic construct, *g* (the entity which is more
popularly known as IQ)? To what extent does a person's IQ determine
his or her social position? Is intelligence fixed by genetic factors? Are
there racial differences in intelligence of genetic origin? Can disparities of cognitive functioning be remedied by social policy?

In their widely discussed book, *The Bell Curve* (1994, Free
Press), Charles Murray and the late Richard Herrnstein take up these
questions. Their conclusions may be summarized as follows: There
has emerged in the twentieth century a "cognitive elite"—persons of
high social status whose main distinction is that they are extremely
smart. That is, the social rewards for intelligence have dramatically increased in recent decades. Moreover, differences among individual
Americans regarding certain behavioral difficulties—unemployment,
poverty, illegitimacy, crime—are determined to a significant degree by
differences in their intelligence. Thus, corresponding to the cognitive
elite there is a cognitive underclass—low-status persons whose main
distinction is that they are, in Herrnstein and Murray's words, "extremely dull." Further, racial and ethnic groups differ, on the average,
in intellectual abilities. This fact largely accounts for racial and ethnic
inequality in this country, and some considerable part of the racial intelligence disparity is genetic in origin. Finally, these truths about cognitive disparity constitute a stubborn reality unlikely to be ameliorated

through social policy. Well-intentioned egalitarian efforts could easily make things worse. Yet, if we face all the hard facts, manage "not (to) run screaming from the room," and act wisely upon what we know, then we can construct a political order in which everyone can find "a valued place."

Publication of this book set off an intense, often angry, public controversy over the role of intelligence in accounting for social and economic inequality in American society. The product of nearly ten man-years of labor by two prominent social scientists, with some eight hundred pages of text, appendices, notes, and references, the book announces to all the world, *"We are doing some serious science here!"* Yet, at the same time the authors obviously intended that their work reach a nontechnical audience. In this they have succeeded mightily. Indeed, *The Bell Curve* is a tour de force of expository social science writing. Complicated ideas are conveyed through folksy illustrations which, though often oversimplified, nevertheless make it possible for lay readers to grasp the essence of difficult and subtle notions. Each chapter begins with a one- or two-page summary, making the thrust of the book's argument accessible to any reader willing to spend a half hour flipping its pages.

What then, you may ask, is all the fuss about? Two analysts take on important technical questions bearing on a crucial aspect of our society, in a work of sustained social science analysis, backed by an impressive array of data. They exhibit a broad knowledge of the relevant literatures, present their findings with full documentation, and nevertheless manage to make themselves comprehensible to a popular audience. Have they not done a service? Is not the hysterical denunciation of these authors and their work but one more dreary instance of the effort of politically marginal forces to censor a legitimate public discussion which threatens to erode support for their favored policy initiatives?

My answer to these questions is an emphatic "no." For along the way the authors engage in speculation about social calamities of the future, and in lamentations about lost virtues of the past. They theorize about the political implications of "cognitive segregation" and "genetic partitioning"—what they assert to be the growing division of American society into hereditary classes defined by mental ability. They conclude, on the basis of a study of intelligence, that we move to restigmatize out-of-wedlock births; that we cut welfare payments to the bone; that we totally abandon the practice of affirmative action; that we restructure employment training assistance to the poor, given their mental limitations; that the criminal codes be simplified; that we be mindful of the effect on social stability in future decades of the "dysgenic trends" associated with the lower fertility rates of the smart, as compared to the not-so-smart. They even construct a "middle class values index"—a measure of the extent to which a person's marital, childbearing, and civic behavior accords with social standards—and then purport to account for variation in the attainment of "middle-class values" among Americans citizens on the basis of differences in their IQ scores.

While political speculations and cultural lamentations such as those offered in this work can be found in many other quarters, here they are purportedly legitimated as scientific findings. I will argue that this is a deeply problematic misappropriation of the authority of science.

Chapter 13, on racial differences in intelligence, begins by chiding the reader for having turned first to the middle of the book, like a teenager searching through Nabakov's *Lolita* for the good parts. Though Murray has repeatedly complained, *"The Bell Curve* is not about race," the first treatment of the book in a national venue was a special issue of *The New Republic* entitled "Race and IQ," to which he contributed an adaptation of chapter 13. Thus the findings on race were evidently intended to get major public attention. At numerous points in the text the authors warn that their conclusions, which might appear to justify illiberal or even racist policies, should not be interpreted in that way. Thus, they urge that their attribution of some substantial part of the black-white IQ difference to genetic factors should not encourage among whites any belief in black inferiority. Nor, they say, should their finding that the poor, the unemployed, the criminal—those with low scores on a "middle-class values index"—are that way mainly because they are a dim-witted lot (and not because they lack opportunity or moral instruction) necessarily undermine the social commitment to expand opportunities for the disadvantaged. Yet these self-consciously prophylactic statements are tacit acknowledgment of the unavoidably political character of their exercise.

My claim is that, in effect, *The Bell Curve* represents a kind of advocacy—not for partisan political ends, but rather in an effort to establish as compelling a particular vision about human nature and social inequality, a set of metaphors and basic empirical generalizations. If this claim is accepted, then how are its arguments to be judged, and by whom? It is a remarkable and alarming fact that the authors' success in this endeavor of advocacy may be, at least to some significant degree, independent of the scientific validity of their claims.

A recent Conservative Book Club ad for *The Bell Curve* reads in part as follows:

> Is Charles Murray now the most dangerous conservative? The *New York Times* is worried. Why? Because Murray and the late Richard Herrnstein prove something threatening to Politically Correct Liberalism: Intelligence—not environment, poverty, or education—is at the root of our worst social problems.

Of course, they "prove"—that is, establish beyond doubt as a scientific truth—no such thing. But many Americans believe they do; moreover, some of these people regard the claims of academic experts to the contrary as evidence in *favor of* the Herrnstein-Murray thesis.

Murray himself has brazenly exploited this public credulity. Two years after its publication, he has yet to answer the growing number of expert critiques of the technical arguments in *The Bell Curve*. When I suggested to the president of the American Enterprise Institute, as a member of his academic advisory council, that Murray should be encouraged to meet these criticisms (perhaps at an AEI-sponsored conference) I was rebuffed with the observation that Murray "is tired of *The Bell Curve* controversy, and wants to move on." Murray has even ducked an opportunity to defend his work in an academic setting, canceling a scheduled appearance at a University of Chicago workshop where James Heckman, one of the world's leading econometricians, was to appear. Murray wrote to the conference organizer: "I am canceling out of the session. . . . My experience of the last few months leads me to this position. . . . I will be glad to collaborate one-on-one with anyone who is doing work on issues related to TBC. . . . I will be glad to give out data, conduct special analyses, or comment on other analyses. [But] I will no longer deal with academics in groups." Yet, within weeks of the Chicago seminar, Murray appeared at Harvard's Kennedy School of Government to debate his ideas with a nonspecialist, and under a strictly regulated format.

Thus Charles Murray has avoided facing expert critics of his "scientific findings" in a forum allowing the kind of extended exchanges characteristic of colloquy among academic peers. Yet, in the May 1995 *Commentary*, one finds him asserting, in *ad hominem* fashion, that criticism of the science of *The Bell Curve* tells us more about the critics than about the validity of the book's argument. Quoting Murray: "The Left has invested everything in a few core beliefs about society as the cause of problems, government as the solution, and the manipulability of the environment for reaching the goal of equality. For the Left . . . *The Bell Curve's* message *cannot* be true. . . ." He goes on to speculate (in the manner of those Freudians who see every denial of the master's theories as evidence of psychosis) that the main impact of his book will be to expose the inadequacies of contemporary liberal social science:

> The attacks on *(The Bell Curve)* have often read like an unintentional confirmation of our view of the "cognitive elite" as a new caste, complete with high priests, dogmas, heresies, and apostates. They have revealed the extent to which the social science that deals in public policy has in the latter part of the twentieth century become self-censored and riddled with taboos—in a word, corrupt. Only the most profound, anguished, and divisive reexamination can change that situation.

For someone who has, in fact, not responded to some devastating scientific criticisms of his work, this is an evidently disingenuous posture.

It is worth reflecting for a moment on what makes this argument by Murray—apparently so self-serving—nevertheless credible with so many people, the editors of *Commentary*, for example. The fact is that real taboos *have* operated within the social sciences, and to an even larger extent among popular writers who discuss social policy and social science findings. An egalitarian bias is detectable, as a historical matter, in the disciplines of sociology, psychology, and (to a lesser extent) economics. Certain hypotheses have been presumptively disfavored. Some research has been frowned upon, regardless of the validity of its findings. This has been especially so when sensitive questions bearing on the issue of race have arisen. In the early, popular criticism of *The Bell Curve,* the political enemies of Herrnstein and Murray overstepped, attacking the authors' motives, calling them "racists," accusing them of using tainted sources, and generally lamenting the damage to politically progressive causes which this "dangerous" book is likely to do. In response to such criticism, some readers may have reasoned: "If so many of the usual liberal suspects are so upset about this book, it must have some validity to it."

It is arguable that "political correctness" in the social sciences has led to the relative neglect of cognitive ability as an explanatory factor in the study of social inequality. The authors of *The Bell Curve* have, as a result, been able to position themselves as the breakers of a barrier against the discussion of these issues. The irony is that this has insulated them from accountability to the expert communities whose very authority they so freely invoke in their advocacy. Yet the problem with *The Bell Curve* is not that it is *politically* incorrect, but simply that many of its assertions are either incorrect, or are not established by its arguments. In fact, despite the wide-ranging and often technical character of the issues taken up in *The Bell Curve,* its ambitions to making original scientific contributions are extraordinarily modest. The fifty-seven pages of references cited include virtually no previously published work by the authors which adduces evidence or develops theory relevant to the claims of their book. What original statistical analysis they present in the text is extremely pedestrian and econometrically naive, as a number of expert reviewers have noted. Murray has publicly admitted that the simple regressions he reports do not identify causal relationships among the variables he studies. Yet the text contains assertions which only make sense if causality, running from individual IQ to some social outcome, has been established. ("If you have a choice, it's better to be born smart than to be born rich," is a typical formulation.)

Upon examination, one can see that the main rhetorical posture in *The Bell Curve* is one of reportage. The authors take the position of truth tellers, informing the intelligent lay public about facts already (purportedly) established by *science,* but which many scientists are unwilling to discuss in public. The book therefore benefits from the separation of popular and scientific discourses, and the low tolerance for complex technical argument among even the most well-educated lay readers.

But the reportage is selective and incomplete. To give but one example, on pages 78–79 one encounters a discussion of how IQ correlates with job performance, even in menial jobs. The restaurant busboy is offered as an illustration:

> A dozen things are happening at once. The busboy is suddenly faced with queuing problems, with setting priorities. A really

good busboy gets the key station cleared in the nick of time, remembering that a table of new orders near that particular station is going to be coming out of the kitchen; when he goes to the kitchen, he gets a fresh water pitcher *and* a condiment tray to save an extra trip. . . . The point is one that should draw broad agreement from readers who have held menial jobs. . . . Given the other necessary qualities of diligence and good spirits, intelligence helps. The really good busboy is engaged in using *g* when he is solving the problems of his job; and the more *g* he has, the more quickly he comes up with the solutions and can call on them when appropriate.

This passage reads like a self-parody, but the authors mean it! The passage illustrates the methods of persuasion employed throughout the book. The discourse is not itself scientific; the "science" has been done already in the finding of a [weak] correlation between *g* and job performance (though not specifically for busboys), and this after having excluded any other explanatory variable; no evidence is presented in this vast book on what *g* adds to an explanation of job performance once education, experience, and temperament are taken into account. The quoted passage is really all about *interpretation*— determining what the purported scientific findings mean. Is it plausible to anyone that the best conceivable predictor of who will be a good *busboy* is performance on an IQ test? Does anyone find it convincing that a diligent, disciplined person *cannot be taught* the tricks of the busboy trade, even if he is a bit dull? Yet these are the broader meanings which sneak in the back door if one uncritically accepts the allegorical interpretation which the authors so artfully advance here. This is many things; but it is not science.

II. *THE BELL CURVE* AS MORAL DISCOURSE

I want now to set aside the issue of whether or not Herrnstein and Murray are doing science, and focus on some broader implications of their morality tale. For reading *The Bell Curve* caused me to reflect on the limited utility in the management of human affairs of that academic endeavor generously termed social science. Analyses of this kind are inherently incapable of addressing in a satisfactory manner the most fundamental social problems. The authors undertake to pronounce upon what is possible for human beings to do while failing to consider that which most makes us human. They begin by seeking the causes of behavior, and end by reducing the human subject to a mechanism whose horizon is fixed by some combination of genetic endowment and social law. Yet we, even the "dullest" of us, are so much more than that.

If social scientists are to give advice about such matters as the appropriate methods for dealing with social inequality, then we must reckon with the human soul. We must look beyond our deterministic behavioral models, and add a humanistic dimension. Now, as an economist I am a card-carrying member of the social scientists' cabal, so the point I'm making here has far-reaching personal implications. But the stakes in discussions of this kind are quite high. The question on the table, central to our nation's future, is this: Can we sensibly aspire to a more complete social integration than has yet been achieved of those who now languish at the bottom of American society?

Of course, Herrnstein and Murray are not entirely direct on this point. They stress, plausibly enough, that we must be realistic in formulating policy, taking due account of the unequal distribution of intellectual aptitudes in the population, recognizing that limitations of mental ability constrain which policies are likely to make a difference, and how much of a difference they can make. But implicit in their argument is the political judgment that we shall have to get used to there being a substantial minority of our fellows who, due to their low intelligence, may fail to perform adequately in their roles as workers, parents, or citizens. I think this is quite wrong. Social science ultimately leads them astray on the political and moral fundamentals.

For example, in chapters on parenting, crime, and citizenship, they document that performance in these areas is correlated in their samples with cognitive ability. Though they stress that IQ is not destiny, they also stress that it is often a more important "cause" of personal achievement than factors which liberal social scientists typically invoke, like family background and economic opportunity. Liberal analysts have offered false hope by suggesting that with improved economic opportunity one can induce underclass youths to live within the law. Some citizens simply lack the wits to manage their affairs so as to avoid criminal violence, be responsive to their children, and exercise the franchise, Herrnstein and Murray argue. If we want our "duller" citizens to obey our laws, we must change the laws (for example, by restoring simple rules and certain, severe punishments), not the citizens. Thus: "people of limited intelligence can lead moral lives in a society that is run on the basis of 'Thou shalt not steal.' They find it much harder to lead moral lives in a society that is run on the basis of 'Thou shalt not steal unless there is a really good reason to.'"

Now, there is a case to be made for making criminals anticipate certain and swift punishment as the consequence of their crimes, and for adhering to traditional notions about right and wrong as exemplified in the commandment "Thou shalt not steal." But there is no reason that I can see to rest such a case on the presumed mental limitations of a sizable number of citizens. Rather, there are political arguments for such policy prescriptions as these which are, to my mind, both more compelling and more likely to succeed in the public arena than the generalizations about human capacities which Herrnstein and Murray claim to have established with their data.

The claim, implicitly advanced in this book, to having achieved a *scientific* understanding of the *moral* performance of the citizenry adequate to provide a foundation for social policy is, to say the very least, breathtakingly audacious. Access to morality is not contingent on mental ability. God is not finished with us when he deals us our genetic hand. We human beings are spiritual creatures; we have souls; we have free will. Of course, we are constrained in various ways by biological and environmental realities. But with effort we can make ourselves morally fit members of our political communities. We can become decent citizens and loving parents by exploiting fully our material and spiritual inheritance, despite the constraints. And we demand from our political leaders an expansive vision which recognizes and celebrates our human potential. Great leaders instinctively know this. But these spiritual considerations are hard for social scientists to grasp.

Nevertheless, the appropriation of the spiritual resources of human beings is key to the maintenance of social stability and progress. It is the ultimate foundation upon which rests any hope we can have that the social malaise of the underclass will be overcome. This is why I insist that the mechanistic determinism of science is, in the end, inadequate to the task of social prescription. Political science has no account of why people vote; psychology has yet to identify the material basis of religious exhilaration; economics can only say that people give to charities because it makes them feel good to do so. No analyst predicted that the people of Eastern Europe would, in Vaclav Havel's memorable phrase, rise to achieve "a sense of transcendence over the world of existence." With the understanding of causality in social science so limited, and the importance of matters of the spirit so palpable, one might expect a bit more humble circumspection from these analysts, as they presume to pronounce upon what is, and is not, possible for human beings to accomplish.

Herrnstein and Murray are in a moral and political cul-de-sac. The difficulty is most clearly illustrated by the fierce debate over racial differences in intelligence which *The Bell Curve* has spawned. Now, let me stipulate that there are measurable differences, on the average, in the cognitive functioning of the members of various population subgroups; that in the case of black and white Americans this difference is substantial; and that group differences in cognitive functioning of this extent must be part of the explanation for racial differences in educational and economic achievements.

Nevertheless, the suggestion that we accommodate ourselves to the inevitability of this difference in mental performance between the races in America is an immoral response to today's tragic reality, one that is not dictated by any finding of science. It is, in effect, an invitation to abandon the hope of achieving racial reconciliation within our national community. Herrnstein and Murray argue that, to achieve such reconciliation, it is essential for people to begin to talk openly of racial differences in intelligence, a matter already being discussed behind closed doors. But why? The fact is that one cannot engage in such a discourse without simultaneously signaling other moral and political messages degrading to the humanity of blacks.

Declaring a stark and intractable gap between the intellectual abilities of black and white Americans is a political act. It inevitably signals something about the intrinsic value of persons in the respective groups, and about the fundamental obligations we have to one another, as fellow citizens of a common republic, to redress the stark inequalities evident all about us. The record of black American economic and educational achievement in the post–civil rights era has been ambiguous—great success mixed with shocking failure. Though many explanations for the failure have been advanced, the account which attributes it to limited mental abilities among blacks is singular in its suggestion that we must learn to live with current racial disparities.

It is true that for too long the loudest voices of African-American authenticity bluffed their way past this ambiguous record by cajoling and chastising those who expressed disappointment or dismay. For decades racial activists have offered discrimination by whites as the excuse for every black disability, treating evidence of limited black achievement as an automatic indictment of the American social order. These racialists are hoist on their own petard by the arguments and data in *The Bell Curve*. Having taught us to examine each individual life first through a racial lens, the racialists must now confront the specter of a racial intelligence accountancy which suggests a rather different explanation for the ambiguous achievements of blacks in the last generation.

So the question in the minds of blacks as well as whites is whether blacks are capable of gaining equal status, given equality of opportunity. It is a peculiar mind which fails to fathom how poisonous a question this is for our democracy. Let me state unequivocally my belief that blacks are, indeed, so capable. Still, any assertion of equal black capacity is a hypothesis, not a fact. The fact is that blacks have something to prove, to ourselves and to what W. E. B. DuBois once characterized as "a world that looks on in amused contempt and pity."

The apostle Paul wrote to the Corinthians many centuries ago: "No temptation has seized you except what is common to man; but God is faithful, He will not allow you to be tempted beyond your ability, but when you are tempted He will provide a way out so that you can bear it" (1 Cor. 10:13). The Greek word for *temptation* can also be translated as "trial" or "test." If, indeed, black Americans must bear up under the weight of a great trial, then God remains faithful.

As one who has been urging black Americans to recognize, accept, and rise to this challenge, I find it spectacularly unhelpful to be told, "Success is unlikely given your average mental equipment but never mind, because cognitive ability is not the only currency for measuring human worth." This, in so many words, is precisely what Herrnstein and Murray say. In an expository magazine article published on the release of *The Bell Curve*, they even celebrate a vision of humanity divided into "clans"—various nationality or racial groups which impute to themselves superiority over other clans by virtue of possessing some desirable trait to a greater degree than do other "clans." Thus, the Irish are poets, the Russians have soul, black Americans are great athletes, etc. Each group, they say, draws its sense of self-esteem from the success it enjoys within its own sphere. Intelligence isn't everything, after all!

But this vision is arrant nonsense. At a point when the authors should be stressing individualism as the antidote to the racist sentiments which their objective analyses might feed, we find them instead engaging in the crudest of racial generalization. Let me speak plainly. Blacks are in no need of a defense of our humanity in the face of Herrnstein and Murray's evidence that there is an average difference between racial groups in performance on intelligence tests. Least of all do we need to invoke "It's a black thing; you wouldn't understand"—declaring ourselves separate in some essential way, members of a different sphere in which even blacks can be superior to all other "clans." I have always supposed that the inherent equality of human beings was an ethical axiom, not contingent on any psychological finding. Indeed, it has always seemed to me that learning to see ourselves as individuals first and foremost is the surest way to protect against the pernicious chauvinism that leads a black to feel himself superior in view of the demographic composition of the National Basketball Association, or a Jew to sneer at the goyim in light of the religious affiliations of recent Nobel physicists.

One cannot help wondering what would lead Herrnstein and Murray to their condescending apologia. I shudder at the prospect that theirs could be the animating vision of a governing conservative coalition in this country. But I take comfort in the hope that, should conservatives be unwise enough to embrace this vision, then the American people will be decent enough to reject it.

III. RACIAL JUSTICE WHEN STATUS ATTAINMENT IS MEDIATED BY SOCIAL ORGANIZATION

I want now to call attention to the way in which social structures mediate between the natural endowments of persons, on the one hand, and their achievement of social status, on the other. Indirectly, this is yet another line of criticism of *The Bell Curve*.

Suppose hypothetically that earnings are attached to jobs and the supply of jobs is fixed. Then the distribution of earnings—that is, the amount of inequality in the society—is also fixed, and it is independent of individuals' characteristics. In such a world, IQ may determine the outcome of the competition for this fixed supply of jobs, and yet it will also be the case that changing individuals' IQs would not alter the number of people at the bottom or the top of the hierarchy. That is, the *distribution of income* would not depend on IQ, even though *a given individual's income* would.

The economist Mark Sattinger illustrates this point with his allegory of the "dog bone economy." Imagine that there are one hundred dogs of varying physical characteristics, and a dump truck containing one hundred bones of varying desirability to the dogs. Suppose that a physically superior dog—one with more *s*, we could say—is always able to take away the bone of a physically inferior dog. Hence, at the end of the day the dogs with the most *s* will have the most desirable bones. As an empirical matter there will be a strong positive correlation between the physical traits of a dog and that dog's "income." Indeed, an external observer—some econometrician, say—might be led to think he has discovered an important causal link between "dog poverty" and *s*. He might lament the "dysgenic trends" associated with the growing number of dogs in the population with low levels of *s*. And yet, in this dog bone economy, the extent of poverty could in no way be mitigated by measures which focused on the distribution of the physical attributes of the dogs.

This allegory makes a point, but it also strains credulity. We do not think that the supply of jobs is fixed in our economy, or that the rewards for personal development are set, somehow, without reference to the productive qualities of the population. But neither are these rewards wholly determined at the level of the individual. Let me expand on this simple point. Certain aspects of the process by which individuals develop their productive capacities are fixed by custom, convention, and social norms, and are not responsive to market forces, or reflective of the intrinsic worth of individuals. It is an elemental social fact that people make associational choices—about whom to befriend, whom to marry, where to live, with whom to enter into joint business ventures and professional associations, to which schools to send their children, and often (to the extent they can exert influence on this decision) who the prospective mates of their children will be. Societies are not simply amalgamations of individuals pursuing exogenously given goals. All societies exhibit significant social segmentation; various groups of individuals and families are tied together in various ways, as a result of their historically derived commonalities of language, ethnicity, religion, culture, class, geography. Networks of social affiliation among families and individuals, while most often not the consequence of calculated economic decisions, nevertheless exert a profound influence upon resource allocation, especially those resources important to the development of the productive capacities of human beings.

Think of human development as a production process where the output, an adult worker of some degree of skill, is "produced" by inputs of education, parenting skills, acculturation, nutrition, socialization, and so forth. Though some of these inputs are acquired through markets to which all agents at least have access (though they may lack the requisite financial resources), many relevant inputs are not obtained via formal economic transactions at all. Instead they are available to the developing person only as the by-product of noneconomic activities. Parenting services, for example, are not available for purchase on the market, but accrue as the consequence of the social relations obtaining between a mother and father. The allocation of parenting service among the prospective workers in any generation is the indirect consequence of the social activities of members of the preceding generation.

Though this may seem an odd way to think about human development, this view underscores the critical roles played by inalienable, nonmarketed, social and cultural resources in the process of human development, and thus in the creation of economic inequality. The relevance of such factors is beyond doubt. *Whom* you know affects *what* you come to know, and what you can do with what you know. The importance of networks, contacts, social background, family connections, informal associations of all kinds has been amply documented by students of social stratification. Through such network ties flow important information about economic opportunities. All of these social processes associated with naturally occurring relationships among persons, which also promote the acquisition of traits valued in the market place, constitute what I mean by *social capital*. I want now to suggest that in a world where social capital is unequally distributed between the races because of racial discrimination in the past, the color-blind notion as a normative principle of social justice is inadequate.

The idea is to note that a principle of public action can hardly claim general validity if, by adhering to it, it becomes impossible to correct the consequences of its violation. Such a principle would be inconsistent in an essential way were this so, for then a transitory departure from the principle would have permanent deleterious effects. On the basis of the foregoing observations, it seems clear that the principle of race neutrality may be inconsistent in just this way. Historical departure from equal opportunity in economic transactions, together with ongoing social segmentation along racial lines, generally means that, in the absence of further departures from race neutrality, the implications of the initial violation will be permanent inequality between racial groups. *Because the creation of a skilled workforce is a social process, the meritocratic ideal—that in a free society individuals should be allowed to rise to the level justified by their competence— is in conflict with the simple observation that no one travels that road alone.*

Inequality in the endowments of social capital in their communities of origin generally implies inequality in the outcomes that otherwise equally competent persons can achieve. Therefore, absent a radical and draconian intervention in the private lives of individuals intended to neutralize the effects of unequal endowments of social capital, absolute equality of opportunity, where an individual's life chances depend only on innate abilities, cannot be achieved. (This point, and its political implications, have been stressed by James Fishkin in *Justice, Equal Opportunity and the Family*.) However, it is also true that, if government restricts itself to race-neutral action in the face of a racially discriminatory history, then the current members of the disadvantaged racial group may face significantly less auspicious prospects than those whose social capital resources have not been diminished over the generations by the unfair treatment of their ancestors.

It should be emphasized that social segregation—in residential communities, religious affiliations, friendship networks, fraternal organizations, marital relations, and the host of other important associations to which people are attracted—has implications not just for the extent of inequality, but also for the efficiency with which resources are allocated. There is a strong presumption that the outcome will generally not be efficient, and can be improved upon by government intervention. Membership in the various networks that form the structure of our social life is not allocated according to market principles. The fact that the benefits from a given individual joining a certain group may exceed the costs does not assure that the inclusion will take place, since there may be no mechanism for expressing the

"willingness to pay," or for carrying out the requisite monetary trans-
fers. For example, a very able child born to very poor parents might
benefit greatly from the social capital associated with living in a
middle-class community, and receiving the "parenting resources" of a
better educated, wealthier couple. Yet there is no way that this child,
or the child's parents, could command these resources by promising
to compensate those providing them with the gains, in terms of the
child's increased future income, that the provision of those resources
would make possible. Similarly, an adolescent with interest and ap-
titude in academic matters, but with peers who have disdain for
intellectual pursuits, may not be able to gain access at any price to association with another group of peers whose values would be more
complementary with his or her interests and aptitudes.

This point is particularly salient in the context of a discussion of
racial inequality. Of course a variety of means have been attempted
to break down barriers to social participation—integration of education and housing primary among them. But these efforts, by their
quite limited success, only underscore how deeply ingrained is the
practice of discrimination in social affiliation. For this reason I have
come to believe that government intervention aimed specifically at
counteracting the effects of historical disadvantage, and taking as
given existing patterns of affiliation, will be required. This may mean,
for example, less of an emphasis on desegregation, and more stress
on targeted efforts to improve the schools, neighborhoods, and families where poor black children are concentrated. All three factors—
that they are poor, that they are black, and that they live in areas
of concentrated poverty—are important in this assessment. Dealing
with our current problem of racial inequality may require preferen-
tially greater expenditures by public institutions which serve large
numbers of poor black people. The general point is that such color-
conscious disbursement of public funds should be permitted, where
deemed prudent, because we cannot expect laissez faire to produce
equality of opportunity among social groups when these groups
have experienced differential treatment in the past, and when among
the channels through which parents pass on status to their children
are included social networks which form partly along group and class-
exclusive lines. To do anything about this, the government may well
need to take racial group identities into account when formulating its
policy.

One possible implication of this reasoning is the conclusion that one can embrace principles of liberal individualism, and yet nevertheless believe that racial inequality should constitute an independent concern, over and above any concern about inequality in general. One can argue that the race-neutrality ideal, while worthy in principle, ought not preclude targeted public action intended to reverse specific effects of past racial discrimination in our society. To be blind to color, given our history and our social structure, may well mean that one must be blind to justice as well. In any case, approaching the problem of racial inequality in terms of the purportedly inherent incapacities of blacks completely overlooks social influences of the sort just analyzed.

Fall/Fault in Human Nature/Nurture?

RAY L. HART

> For in fact what is man in nature? A Nothing in comparison
> with the Infinite, an All in comparison with the Nothing, a
> mean between nothing and everything. Since he is infi-
> nitely removed from comprehending the extremes, the end
> of things and their beginning are hopelessly hidden from
> him in an impenetrable secret; he is equally incapable of
> seeing the Nothing from which he was made, and the Infi-
> nite in which he is swallowed up. . . . Who will follow these
> marvelous processes?
>
> Pascal, *Pensées*

> It is a tremendous act of violence to begin anything. I am
> not able to *begin*. I simply skip what should be the begin-
> ning. Nothing is so powerful as silence. It would never
> have been broken, if we had not, each of us, been born
> into the midst of talk.
>
> Rainer Maria Rilke, *Where Silence Reigns*

AS DELIVERED BY A VIRTUALLY unbroken theological tradition in the
Christian west, fault and fall are humanly intractable, inaccessible to
revision, and so are intimately connected with Creation itself. The
character of that intimacy has been hotly disputed and is something
of which we must speak, if but indirectly. If fault and fall are indeed
humanly intractable, are they not aboriginally embedded in the very
structure of creation? That they are so embedded is the essential
claim of all gnosticisms, which yielded a Manichaean cosmos and humankind, a view scarcely limited to late antiquity and that seems to
fire this twentieth, most monstrous, century. It is no accident that the
notion of *creatio ex nihilo* arose in the second century of the common
era in part if not in the main to contest the metaphysical coincidence
of creation and fall/fault. Not only in the modern secular world but as

well in Christendom in all times and places, the Manichaean option has been rampant. That says the *creatio ex nihilo* has not been thought through, has not been augmented in relation to fall and fault. Such a thinking would rehabilitate a hoary distinction between eternal and temporal creation,[1] and within the latter would discriminate afresh *creatio origine* and *creatio continua*. Above all, such a thinking would accord the *nihil* its due, both the nothing *from which* and *toward which* we are created, what may be called the "duplex nihil" house of human being. Such a thinking would end the conspiracy of silence about nonbeing (or nothingness) no less regnant in the mainline onto-theological tradition in Christendom than in the passion of perennial philosophy, in Gadamer's phrase, to "render nonbeing harmless."

A final word about the difficulty of beginning. The subject is fall/fault, not creation, but since the former is not unrelated to the latter in the tradition of my examination, beginning on fall/fault entails thought that one has begun reflection on that Beginning. The subject is fall/fault, not being and nothingness, but if the *nihil* in *creatio ex nihilo* is endemic to fall/fault, thought must have begun on being and nothingness. Like Rilke, I must skip the beginning on these weighty matters and insert myself in discourse already underway in respect of them. What I have to say is a proleptive abstract from a long-range project, one that will issue in a two-volume study. That much larger work is only partially thought through and is largely unwritten.[2] My remarks on fall/fault are therefore somewhat like a Borgesian review of a book not only unread but unwritten.

There is no simple standpoint from which to surprise the human phenomenon in its totality. One's reflection is engaged by that totality in its complexity from the beginning or not at all. But that totality is in Marcel's sense a "mystery," an intractable fact inaccessible to revision, one that sources at once the greatness and the baseness of humankind. As such it instantiates Kierkegaard's passion of reason to think what cannot be thought; or, as I should prefer to put the matter, the passion to think a limit not itself the product of thought. What gives itself to be thought in this hiatus is reflexively the very pathos of reason.

A reflective anthropology whether philosophical or theological aspires to describe and explain what is made or "given," *and* what persons can and do make; what is up for human disposition and what is not. Just as the subject-person thinking a subject matter is now one, now diffused, so the stipulated subject matter is now one, now double when the subject matter is "human nature." Even when single, the matter has a double face. That is why my title is neither just "fall" nor just "fault" but fall/fault. Fault and fall are the fundamental distinctions to be made within the totality of the human phenomenon, and between them lies the *aporia,* the metaxy, of which I have spoken. The hiatus is more the dark center between two penumbral fields. The reason of the philosophical/theological mind, like that of the astrophysicist's, is light-trained (alas without the benefits of radio telescopy) upon dark bodies verging upon a Dark Hole.[3]

At length and at last, let us turn then to our two "f" words. First "fault," then the real four-letter "f" word, "fall." At this late date, "fault" and "fall" probably cannot be dissociated entirely from their Christian overtones. Although I am a philosophical theologian principally in the Christian traditions, I claim the reflective anthropology under development here to be intelligible and indeed defensible without special theological appeals.

Fault. In the more purely Romance languages one will hear the connections of fault with "fail." In all uses of fault one hears the resonance of lack, of defect. In the moral sense, fault betokens culpable or blameworthy lack, failing, wrongdoing. As I shall use it here fault bespeaks in the first instance not the moral but the structural sense, that of defect, as evident principally in geology. Fault is crack, breach, rupture. In electricity talk it is the point of defect in a circuit which prevents the flow of current; in hunting it is a break in scent that throws the dogs off track; in tennis it is an error of service, a failure of service to the proper court. In geology fault is the zone of fracture in the plane of plates. Fault is not actual earthquake but its subterranean possibility.

What referent does the metaphor *fault* mark in the human person? It is the acute self-consciousness of ontological instability. Much Western metaphysical ingenuity has been lavished upon attending the Richter Scale of Being by graphing the rise and fall of tremors in a human reality that inhabits displacement.

In what does the ontological instability of the human person consist? In starkest and plainest terms, the human person does not coincide with herself. She is a one-in-two, a two-in one. Our becoming being, our being becoming is noncoincident. Since there must be at least two or more things to coincide or not coincide, what does not coincide with what? Here the classical distinctions come into play both in description and in explanation of the ontological instability of the human reality. The perennial candidates are all familiar: essence and existence, form and matter, substance and accident, identity and difference, presence and absence, and so forth. In any slice-specimen of what I am I find that I both am and am not what I am. My kind of being is a being becoming, and becoming being, that both is and is not in that remarkable way whereby "I" am not lost but refound and refounded in swirling genesis. My form and matter, my essence and existence, are not wholly internally related but rather, to a degree I cannot anticipate or even learn, externally related. My body-matter expands and contracts in the course of birth, growth, and decay and so is vulnerable to different formations. The form of my existence is not laid up in some Charter except as some dark limit to exceed or subvert which would take me out of humanity; it rather is significantly vulnerable to cultural influence, and to my own decisions. Add the prominence of *freedom* as the core of externality in relations, and you have the heart of ontological instability in the human person. This is especially so if one "completes" the picture, as we will when we turn to "fall," by the complications of freedom itself in what I have called simply "the human reality."

It says the same thing by elaboration to say that the fault line in human reality runs between the indicative and the imperative. In any given state of affairs I am one thing, but I intuitively sense that I should be other or more. I am the kind of being who knows himself not to be exhausted in what is at hand, who knows that I am not only *from* a state of affairs but also that I am vocated *toward*, that in any moment I am suspended between *from* and *toward*. What I am is not reducible to what is *made*; my being is not exhaustively and without remainder a *product*. Although I am biologically and culturally "made," I am ever under summons to "make something" of what is made, and am the center of a contest between being made and self-making. Martin Buber put the matter succinctly: "'I am given over for disposal' and know at the same time that 'it depends on myself.'"[4] If I know this extensionally about every human person, thus of "human nature," I must not forget it when I come intensively into the presence of another human person. Every individual human person, as contrasted, say, with a rock or a moose, has a singularity and unsubstitutability of being. The disparity between human nature and *this* person, Mary, is qualitatively different from the disparity between mooseness and *this* moose. In the case of the human person, the old rule in logic about the inverse relation between extension and intension (the more I have of human nature, the less I have of Mary; the more I have of Mary, the less I have of human nature *überhaupt*) takes on ontological weight. What is precious about Mary I would not know merely from her extensional range, but only from her lived intensification of that range in her own story. While using the language of "summons" or "vocation," these remarks do not privilege a specifically religious or Christian reading of human ontological instability. They are consonant with diverse Western metaphysical schema, above all with Plato's fivefold ontological scheme in the *Philebus*. There Plato said that among the plural ultimate factors necessary to account for the being of anything whatever, one is its *telos*, end, or goal. This *telos* is the Good which, in the *Timeaeus*, he says is "beyond being in dignity and power." We do not know the being of a thing until we know what it is *for* or *toward*. To be sure, for Plato the Good was somehow external to the other ultimate factors, including the soul, as their "lure" or summons.

Let us look at this matter of the ontological instability of the human person in a way that is demonstrated in William James's *Varieties of Religious Experience*. In his inspection of the human soul he finds in all such varieties something characteristic not only of his infamous "sick-minded" soul but of all souls. He calls this sentiment an "uneasiness" that, "reduced to its simplest terms, is a sense that there is *something wrong about us* as we naturally stand."[5] For him no living sentiment can be kept alive by a merely metaphysical or theological scruple. We know a living universal sentiment not in its root so much as in its fruit. This fruit of uneasiness signals that we are not what we belong to, and that what we most deeply long for signals what we belong to; that what we long for produces effects in another reality, namely, us, and that "that which produces effects within another reality must be termed a reality itself."[6]

The faulted person is fallible, is "failable" in respect of being, even though she exists as absolutely as any other merely existent thing. What does the human person most deeply yearn for, long for? One might answer "infallibility," but that answer is useless because whatever infallible being might be it would not be human being, in whom freedom means minimally the latitude of possible failure. The human person yearns for the finishing of her unfinished selfhood, for the completed coincidence of her self with herself. She longs to belong to a stability of being that does not annul the conditions of her fallibility but fulfills them through acceding to a claim upon her existence that is neither just heteronomous nor just autonomous but the coincidence of both.

What do immemorial affections of the human heart disclose about the deepest yearning for locative and durative stability? I think we find at least two aspirations that move counter to each other—and the cumulative effect of their countering is to establish fallibility even more firmly in the affections. I will speak of the two as a "downward" and an "upward" aspiration.

By "downward" aspiration I refer to the human affection for the *inanimate*, an emotion that arguably is a vestigial affective residue of "phylogeny recapitulates ontogeny." I do not mean to slight the animate substratum of human being—one has only to remember the role that totem animals have played in the affections of religious cultures over time and place, the principal secular residue of which among us "civilized" ones is our "pets," our dogs and cats. But nothing in the merely animate world can quite compare with the residual human admiration for the inanimate. Above all else in this respect is the immemorial human fascination with *stone*. A stone *qua* stone cannot fail to be what it is; wherever and whenever it is it fully is all that it is. In the reverie of stability whether of locus or duration, the affections will be drawn to stone. Let the affections loose in eternity and they will fix on stone as its locus in time. Let the mind overhear genesis at rest in completion, through what Bergson called acts of "intellectual auscultation," and one hears the speech of stone. In stone form and matter seem perfectly coincident, the one offering amplitude to the other. No one has understood the human reality, says E. M. Cioran, who does not envy a rock. From this vantage the history of religions is the story of the hermeneutics of stone. Where the instability of human reality peaks, there stand to counter it the Herms, the cairns, the pyramids, the Acropolises, the temples, the skyscrapers. Wander into the outbacks of the affections, often associated with geographical remoteness—the American prairies or deserts, rural Korea, the vastnesses of Siberia—and you will find stones placed on top of each other, artifacts of human aspiration toward and through the inanimate. Of course, as with everything that human instability touches, we do not let stones be but press them into the service of our own aspiration, their being into the service of our becoming being, our not-being of what we have become. How much human life has been spent (in the title of a grand little book by Annie Dillard) *Teaching a Stone to Talk*?[7] Architecture and sculpture arose from and perdure in this instruction. Think of the masters at teaching stone to speak: Michelangelo, Rodin, Brancusi. Think of the stones that mark graves, that duratively and locatively mark the final instability of the human being that fails not only imperative essence but finally indicative existence as well, that underneath the stone disintegrates into elements that will finally sediment and start again the cycle eventuating in stone. All things that persist and recur, thought the Greeks, are divine. It would be empirically based and not merely jocular to say that who has a sense for the divine simplicity of coincidence has rocks in his soul, if not in his head.

A proclivity of the affections for downward aspiration to the inanimate, notably stone, is matched by a counter upward aspiration toward an intensification of the animate. This upward aspiration is the *anagoge* of the human condition, the "leading up" of human fallibility. If an excess of human instability can and immemorially does lead downward to a stability seated in an excess of stability, as in the passions for inanimate stone, a like excess of instability can and immemorially does lead to a counter-passion for stability at the apex of the intensification of the animate. That apex marks the exacerbation of the imperative and is the very *anagoge* of the contest between what we are and what we ought to be. *That* we are and *that* we ought to be otherwise, we know well enough. *What* we are and *what* we ought to be, if human history offers any clue, is known by contrast. Our very *ordinariness*—whether of baseness or nobility—is situated by contrast. Every human culture has its heroes, heroines, sages, saints, those exemplars of the *anagoge* of the human condition, those who at once position us in baseness and lure us toward nobility. The ordinary Greek warrior does not know the baseness of his ordinariness until, after the battle, the poet at the symposial banquet sings the nobility of the victor king into realization as hero. Each such *exemplatum* of humankind is not so much an archetype as it is a "breakthrough," a new excess of the imperative. Such is the nobility of the hero or sage as to be characterized by no single metaphor—a giant tree at the center of the human condition, a sun whereby there is human day, a moon in cosmic darkness, their stone images bedecked in luminous precious stones, themselves the residuum of eternity in time. The saints are eternity's insomniacs in time. They arouse in us not only a sense of what fallible humankind is fallen from, but vertigo before what we fall short of.

Aspiring to the upward limits of the imperative, this soaring from the contrarieties of existence, is a kind of natural grace. With the expanding knowledge of both inanimate and animate nature that the modern sciences have brought, we are less confident than earlier ages about breaks in the *scala perfectionis*—less sure where the animate bottoms and where it peaks. We know only that in us *self-consciousness* of contestation marks our days and nights, and that both downward and upward aspirations are not to be explained exhaustively and without remainder by vestigial instinct. What would we not give to know whether dolphins and porpoises have heroes and heroines, sages and saints—and, above all, angels? We know that *we* have them; they are a human fact about human reality in all cultures and times, however embellished by a cumulative mythical imagination.

It is no accident that in the Middle Ages the *anagogical* crowned all other maneuvers of hermeneutics; the anagogical held superiority over both the literal and the allegorical senses for construing meaning for the human person. The apex of upward aspiration was not the saint—whether in Christianity, Islam, or Judaism—but rather was angels. Angels—unlike the saints and other holy ones who sought to transcend human fallibility but in the end could not—angels, in an absolute *ascesis* of existential contestation, were pure essences, the triumph of the stability of the imperative. As such, angels have lost all individuation, are pure essences faced toward eternal creation, and as such are the "guardian angels" of aspiring souls in time. To be sure, angels were visible as such only in the power of what medievals called a supernatural grace. To the natural eye they were but stars, bodies in the heavens reflecting here dimly and there brightly the light of eternity in the darkness of time's night.

I have said that upward aspiration for us, in our qualified *scala perfectionis*, and thus even without the apex of angels, is a kind of natural grace. As such it is not a straight line of ascent but a kind of undulation drawn by the combined force of yearning and an embodiment that is beyond our achievement hitherto, and probably ever. Upward aspiration is proleptic relief from the paroxysms of a temporally habituated individuation. We are solicited by and invited into a life not yet our own, but not absolutely discontinuous with it either, else we could not feel our baseness in relation to it. In the life of the other person in the higher plane—historical or mythical—we see the antinomies of our own existence subdued in that triumph of the imperative in a stability beyond our grasp but aspiringly within reach. Not quite the Sublime, it limns the Sublime, is the human saintly simulacrum of the Sublime.

If the saint, hero, or sage is incapable of the *perduring* rapture of ascending stability—whether of moral achievement or "enlightenment"—that is because she is not free of the rupture and displacement of *negation* and *negativity*. The more we penetrate the *mythos* and gain access to the biography of the saint or heroine, the more we know this to be the case. Negation dogs the heels of ascent because the rise is by reason of *ascesis*. In the saint we can peer but fleetingly into a negation that has lost its sting, that has lost its stench of irreparable loss. What every saint/hero discovers about herself—as do we in our aspiration—is that she is flawed. That contestation and negation remain in the saintly exemplar and in our aspiration toward her signals that the abyss of human being is never left far behind. We cannot imagine a stone *qua* stone hanging over an abyss, which is perhaps why we envy it. But neither can we imagine a stone, however fleetingly, in a seizure of ecstasy. So we are back to two primordial counter-aspirations. Religions always and everywhere may be read as efforts to make sense of them: traditional or "oral" religions with their stones and totem animals; Catholic and Orthodox Christianity with their saints and icons; Greek religion with its cultic heroes and heroines; Protestant Christianity, Judaism, and Islam with their unremitting iconoclasms, the collision of the two aspirations in a raid on all idolatries.

Let us recapitulate where we have been. Fallibility is the structure of the possible human mode of being/becoming, a structure faulted. It belongs to the made character of her being/becoming that she is to make something better, truer, more beautiful. Her being/becoming is unfinished. Fault is as incorrigibly there as what lies to either side, a state of affairs and a not-yet state of affairs that obliges. We have considered immemorial aspirations to either side. But we are still in the realm of ontological *possibility*. How is faulted humankind *actualized*? To take up this question is to move to the other side of the slash, fall/fault, from fault to fall. In doing so, it will be useful to call up an old surrogate for *possibility*, namely, *potency*. No possibility can be actualized without power. Fault itself in humankind pertains to power, although not in strict analogy with geological fault. In a geological fault line, the line will distribute and displace power, but the power itself resides in the shifting subterranean plates. It is an old metaphysical argument about where power vests in the becoming of all this is. For Plato the power to actualize what becomes is not Limit (the Forms), not the Unlimited, not even their mixture, but rather is, in different senses, the Soul and the Good. I have already said that the remnant of Platonism through the Neoplatonists is the conflation of these powers into that of human soul, a soul that, by reason of its partition from the All-Soul, is a faulted actualizing power. From faulted possibility to fallen actuality, this is the trajectory now of our attention.

Fall. Fault and fall are not the same although they refer to the same reality, and are related as possibility is to actualization. All metaphors have their faults, especially the metaphor *fault* in the geological sense. As I just now suggested, the power of an actual earthquake is wholly internal to its possibility. In the natural course of things, no externality has power over the actualization of an earthquake: one plate can only go over or under the other, and power is distributed to both sides. But in the human person it is otherwise. If by reason of structural "fault" we are one-in-two, it is by reason of *will* that we are two-in-one, although will itself, by reason of its "fall," is a one-in-two. The person's will is the power of externally relating her determinate possibilities as act, as this or that, as actual concrete life. This will, the unitary *dynamis* of actualization, is however ambivalent. The very act of willing engages a doubleness, a trace of the two in the one: I cannot ask "Will I?" without asking "Nill I?"

To search for the root of "the fall" is like seeking the origin of bursting unaccountably into tears, is like seeking the tap root of a branching insomnia. The organon of fall, the will, is no structure nor is it a component of structure, and so does not function as form, essence, or matter in human reality. Fault as sketched above can at best tell us only about the structural complication of human reality, of "human nature" in its extensive ontological range. But extensive human nature is not intensive human biography. Human history is about events, largely events in which persons have been complicit, persons differentiated by their wills as the actualization of the *principium individuationis*. Fault is no one's history, is no one's intensive earthquake existence, but rather is one's determinate structural possibility. Fall is not and cannot be a structure, hence is not embedded in creation. Fall's compossibility is indeed potentiated in the structure of fault—which *is* embedded in creation. We may say that fault belongs to *creatio origine*, fall to *creatio continua*, in which latter the human creature is complicit.

If some minimal theology has entered these remarks, that is not by accident. As Arendt has written in her magisterial *The Life of the Mind*, "the faculty of the Will was unknown to Greek antiquity,"[8] although (which she does not say) *some* variant of the Fall was. Not until the first century of the common era is the force field of the will and its freedom "discovered," immediately in Christianity—although derivatively from the Hebraic emphasis upon the will of God. Thus began the philosophically frenzied effort to "save the appearances" of both willing and thinking, of the *volo* and the *cogito*. Which shall be accommodated to which, Athens to Jerusalem (thinking to will), or Jerusalem to Athens (will to thinking)? Does will infect thought, or thought will? Or are they parallel, noninteracting tracks in the doubleness of the human reality? Above all, how does this force field overlay the ontological schemas of classical antiquity, wherein power of actualization was distributed ambiguously between Soul and the Good (Plato), or less ambiguously and more directly in Greek and Roman religion to fate (*Ananke, Moira*)? Freedom, once discovered, is the most intoxicating of "ideas." And we should not forget that this "discovery" largely coincided with its Christian (and derivatively Judaic) explanatory framework, that of the *creatio ex nihilo*. According to this explanatory account, indeterminate Godhead is rendered determinate Creator, calling forth from "nothing" the determinate human creature who, as image of God, preserves a residuum of indeterminancy over which she is to preside (of course, within conditions themselves determinate—those of "fault").

Although he has had a few heirs in this respect, it was only Paul the Apostle on the Christian side of the conjunction who was willing to think the *volo* apart from the Greek *cogito*. In the burst of freedom and its organon, with their concentration upon the inner human life, most of the Fathers established themselves in the conjunction of their interest with classical philosophy. Their interest was less in freedom as a postulate of ethics or any convention of laws, as modern moralists would have it, more in free volition (as Bergson put it) as an "immediate datum of consciousness." As such, acts of willing seem free of *necessity*, the darling of so much Greek and Roman thought, much more free than thinking which, properly executed, is subject to such necessities as that of noncontradiction. Our awareness of freedom is made acute by the recognition that of the possible things we could have done we could have left undone what we actually did. This is the blessing of a free will and at the same time the curse of thought reflecting on a life convoluted by actual choices that have come to count. The curse of the blessing is evident in Paul's lament—"that which I would I do not and that which I would not that I do"[9]—the scrambling of will in its exercise of freedom. Every exercise of will in the actualization of possibility, for which the human subject is responsible, restricts her range of possibilities for subsequent actualization. We see the stark difference between Greek necessity and responsible free will in Clytemnestra and Lady Macbeth. Both are complicit in the death of their husbands, but Clytemnestra is calm and remorseless, fate having run its course, whereas for Lady Macbeth not all the perfumes of Araby can remove the stench of blood from her hands.

The very organon of freedom, the will, not free and not free by its own exercise—can it be that the very power by which we actualize the possibilities of humankind serves to depotentiate, or repotentiate, the range of those possibilities? Does the very exercise of its freedom render the will less free, or, more precisely, differently free? It is the exploration of such questions that is like seeking the unaccountable origin of tears, of insomnia. Our tears and our insomnia must have *something* to do with us and our doing, else why is it *we* who weep and are sleepless?

In pursuit of such questions *the* thinker of the will at the conjunction of Christian and classical motifs *ne plus ultra* was Augustine. The Augustine to whom I refer is not the later, older Augustine, the one of what could be called doctrinal closures, but rather the Augustine recently converted from the cult of the Manichees to a profound blend of Neoplatonism and Christianity, the one still dumbfounded by what he had become. I mean the Augustine of the *Confessions*. The *Confessions* are a project of "acknowledgment." What Augustine wanted to know above all else was why and how he had become to himself a wasteland, to know his own complicity in wastrelness. Through acknowledgment he would own up to his ownmost. In this he continues the old Socratic insight: acknowledging that I don't know is essential to knowing. "I know that I don't know" was a stunning recognition no less for Augustine than for Socrates. The affirmed knowing must have a different standing than that of the negative. For Augustine the affirmed knowing ("I know") vests not in a dim recollection of a mythological preexistent state in which the Forms were directly apprehended, but in the presence of One by whom one is *known*. He is persuaded he can make no progress out of the "I don't know"—that is, come to know what he does not know, namely, himself—until he, the subject of the affirmed "I know," is himself known, until he knows himself as known, for the precise reason that his not-knowing infects his knowing. This says that his knowing/not-knowing throughout his life hitherto was marked by self-aggrandizement, a lessening of not-knowing in favor of his knowing. There is then in his acknowledgment a cry for a limit to self-deception, a cry to know *what* he does not know, what is ascribable only to himself. That is why his acknowledgment is made in the context of prayer, in which there is but one petition: let me know myself even as I am known—beyond the deceptions I practice upon myself, the deceptions I and my friends practice upon each other. A certain sacrifice of self-aggrandizing willfulness is necessary if the actualizations of will are to be recognized and reckoned with. One cannot come to one's ownmost without owning up to manipulations that cover up one's ownmost, the known knower.

Beyond these considerations, one may note without expansion two other presuppositions of Augustine's acknowledgments that signal his divergence from the classical tradition with which he is otherwise so congruent. First, he rejects out of hand what had previously held him in thrall in his addiction to the Manichees, the explanation of his wastrel existence that located the source of aberrant will in a cosmic source outside himself, and thus with *fate*. Second were his revolutionary meditations on *time* in the *Confessions*. For Augustine time is no longer the handmaiden of fate with its recurrences but rather is the arena of human freedom and its abuse. The past, what happened, is no longer cumulative fate, the unredeemable burden on my back. The past, my past, cannot be reversed or altered, that is true. It is a "made" not to be unmade, but it was a made in which my making was complicit. It is finished, but it is also crucially unfinished because I am not finished with it. To that extent, the past is unfinished, because I am unfinished. The past has a certain openness, that of what I am to make of it, what I am to make of the making I made. My past is not finished until every potentiality established in it is exhausted in one actualization or another, in which actualization my own freedom is not free of claim. This says, among other things, that time is redeemable, depending upon the "time present of things past."

While these presuppositions attend his meditations, they are not immediately propaedeutic to a full-blown theory of human nature. In his *Confessions* Augustine is concerned with his intensive story. A certain incident in his adolescence, his complicity with boyhood chums in the theft of some pears, nags his memory, is something with which he is not finished. It remains there in his personal mass like a grain of sand in an oyster shell, an irritant attracting layer on layer of subtle accretion. If one could reverse the process of genesis, get back to the aboriginal irritant, one would have come upon a pearl of great price. At one level, the incident hardly warrants adult reflection: "But are you [the incident] anything at all, so that I could analyze the case with you?"[10] After all, "boys will be boys," and who did not attest his adolescence by pranks and mischief? It's all a part of growing up, even if in adulthood such incidents are to be outgrown. But there's the hitch, the rub. In the pear theft incident Augustine sees something not so much outgrown as ingrown, a disposition that was not born in this incident but which riveted itself to his consciousness. The event of the theft of pears seems to be paradigmatic of the very eventfulness of his life.

So Augustine thinks that the will has delivered him into a wasteland, and he goes in quest of that first willing which set him on the course he has taken. He has eschewed every source of actualizing power outside himself, and that because he senses himself altogether responsible for that course. But he is unable to recover any incident, including the pear theft, embodying his will as the first efficient cause of wastrelness. At the farthest tether of memory each incident seemed already to display a tendency to confirm a disposition in him. He saw that a profligate wastrelness invited incidents of a certain sort, which only served to establish him more and more in a wasteland, so that while he could not find in himself a wastrel *nature*, his incidental wastrel life was never without decisional *nurture*. Of the paradigmatic event itself Augustine asks, Why did I do it, since I could have left it undone? Surely there must be a reason I did it? Was it premeditated, something I had long planned? No. Was I hungry? No. Was I poor and in life-threatening need? No. Did I do it because I was swept up in a crowd frenzy? Yes and No. I could have said: you guys go ahead if you wanna, but I'm not gonna, and the truth is I wanted to and derived a certain pleasure from doing the deed. The only reason Augustine could give himself was that he *could* do it and he *wanted* to do it. But *thinking* Augustine knows that just because one *can* do something and *wants* to do something is neither a necessary nor a sufficient reason for doing it. One cannot deny, at least Augustine could not, that there is an exhilaration in "taking liberties," of doing just "what I want." But all taking of liberties merely in the service of what I want is at the cost of freedom. It is not that taking liberties because I want to makes me less free and responsible, but such "taking" cumulatively restricts the subsequent range of possibilities over which my will may freely preside. Ask any drug or alcohol addict. Ask yourself. Ask yourself as a student: so you don't want to study, and blow it off, and blow it off, and pretty soon what you wanted to do didn't get you where you wanted to be. What, who, will deliver me from what I *want*? Taking leave of Augustine, we may say that at bottom we have come upon the residuum of indeterminacy in all desire or want, venting itself in "taking liberties," an exercise of will without regard to determinate possibility, an exercise that ironically serves only to render possibility ever more determinate.

If the remarks on Augustine help us understand the will as one-in-two, it remains to unpack a claim made at the beginning of this section on "fall," that the will is at the same time a two-in-one by reason of being ambivalent. In exegeting this ambivalence I shall adopt Hannah Arendt's felicitous phrase, the phenomenon of "the counter will" that accompanies every arousal of will itself.[11] I suspect all are tempted to think any one of us could have fashioned a more perfect creature than we in fact are, a person fully coincident with herself. But could we, as we are, be such a person? Rather, could we design a fully coincident person whose actualizing power was *voluntary*? Augustine noted a curious thing about the will: I will to raise my arm and (in a healthy body) my arm rises. But let the will address a command to itself, or receive a command, and something quite different happens: the emergence of a "counter will." The earliest developmental commands we can recover are also primordially constitutive of the person. The earliest commands of our parents were arousals of the will. We were asked voluntarily to do or not to do. Whether the command was "you shall" or "you shall not," either sets up through the arousal of will its counter, its possible negation. To either I respond out of aroused will—Will I? Nill I?—and do so, as we say, willy nilly. If in our earliest development there was a preponderance of "you shall nots," that owes perhaps to laying a logic of thinking upon what may loosely be called a logic of willing. As many a logician has pointed out, the affirmative can yield only itself whereas the negative can yield itself and the affirmative, the negation of negation being affirmative.[12] Everyone knows more or less that the Hebrew scriptures are suffused with "You shall not," and that the first command to the first persons in the Genesis myth was "You shall not eat of the fruit," the very condition of the arousal of will, just as the Christian Gospels are suffused with "You have heard it said that you shall not, but I say you shall. . . ." Either command in the "logic" of the will, whether *to* the will or *by* the will, will arouse its "counter." It is in the very character of its willing that the will inhabits the *metaxy,* that it "falls" *between* Will I? and Nill I?, between counter wills, although every actualization must be one or the other. As such, ambivalent will is not in human nature as fault is, but it is my "second nature," freely nurtured for good or ill, in a decisional intensive history.

There is yet another metaxy of the will to comment on. As a stand-alone word, *fall* carries with it the connotation of gravity, and indeed we might say that *the Fall* is the specific gravity of *fault.* In the sense of weighted descent, fall was a favored word of pre-Christian Neoplatonists to characterize all partitive, privative existents, everything that has fallen away from the One and thus is manifold, everything that is a two without a one. In *our* ordinary usage the meaning of "fall" is largely controlled by qualifying prepositions and adverbs. Fall in—in love is one thing, in rank is another. Fall out—a disagreement, or out of rank? It fell out—it happened. The fallout—the consequence of what happened. To fall for—to be infatuated, to be deceived, to be suckered? Taking the fall for—sacrificing oneself for—and so on; one's voice "falls away. . . ."

Prior to will's taking of center stage in the human person, "fall" was all but exclusively "fall from." Virtually every human culture has had its paradise, its dream time of the race, an actualization in a time not our time, from which our every actualization in our time is a declension. With the emergence in Western thinking consciousness of linear, purposeful time, directly connected with the centrality of will in the person, there arose in addition to the primordial dream time that of the eschatological end time, in religion assuming various forms of messianism, in secular equivalents such varieties as Kant's

Kingdom of Ends, Hegel's temporalizations of Absolute Spirit, Marx's classless utopia. The self's willing/counterwilling is situated in the space-time between a mythical actualization lost or fallen from and a mythical actualization not gained, fallen toward but fallen short of. This metaxy is the trace or "second nature" of that metaxy re-marked earlier in connection with fault, between downward and up-ward aspiration.

I close with a homely example concerning scholars and their Work of scholarship and thinking. To use some language from two contemporary French indwellers of sundry wondrous metaxies, Ed-mond Jabés and Maurice Blanchot, each of us is engaged in a life-Work that depends for episodic and temporary closure upon the Book each is writing. But the Work and the Book never quite coincide. Willy nilly, neither is an adequate carrier for the other.

On the one hand, there is the lost Book, the Book that is the clo-sure of the Work. Jabés is preeminently the thinker of the lost Book, the Book in which my name is anonymously inscribed, to read which would coincide with my writing of the Book. This is not a matter of age, not a sentiment of the aged. Who has not felt when he has crafted the sentence that justifies a life that he has read it from a constituted text? Could he but find all the other lost sentences that go with it! He is a lucky one who gets a paragraph from the lost Book. The result of our Work at thinking and studying is at best a sighting now and then of the palimpsest text of the lost Book, to which we add our erasures and deformations. What we publish is yet another palimpsest, a further distancing, a further falling away from the Book.

On the other hand and at the same time, the Work is not alone nostalgia for the Book lost in a time not my time, but expenditure to-ward the Book not present because not now or ever written. You may think, you who are starting out, that the palpitations of the "not yet" or of the "falling short" beat more rapidly in the young than in the old; you have only to wait to be disabused. We start and end as much in falling toward and falling short as we do in falling from. In terms of William James's famous distinction, one is between the written but lost and unfound Book of the "sick-minded" and the unfound be-cause unwritten Book of the "healthy-minded." Given the optimism that marked modernity, and the hold of time-consciousness upon late and postmodernity, it is remarkable that so few have made good on the option of "healthy-mindedness," whether in philosophy or the arts. Who gives herself over to "the agony of composition" without even the faintest guide from the lost Book will find her willing/counterwilling so overdetermined by *desire* that the Book fallen short of is dirempted by the Work: witness the consummate Work of Nietzsche whose unwritten Book is released into the "final rest" of clinical madness. Such a one cries out with Franz Rosenzweig: "I wish I were a symphony by Beethoven, or something else that has been completely written." Consider the transcendingly great Goethe, arguably the greatest of modern healthy-minded souls, whose love of time and the earth was the very model for Nietzsche: his Faust would happily hand over his eternal soul to Mephistopheles could he but present one moment to which Faust could say *verweile doch*, "tarry, it is enough." Toward the end of a long life Goethe persisted in refusing to file grievance against existence, saying "I will say nothing against the course of my existence." The selfsame Goethe in the following sentence says: "But it has been nothing but pain and burden, and I can affirm that during the whole of my seventy-five years, I have not had four weeks of genuine well-being. It is but the perpetual rolling of a rock that must be raised up again forever."[13]

I too would not file grievance against (faulted) human nature extensively, nor against its nurtured (fallen) "second nature" intensively, but rather, as here, look at both as steadily as I can. Steadily, yes, but not unflinchingly. For it/they look back, and it is I who blink.

NOTES

1. See my essay, "God and Creature in the Eternity and Time of Non-Being (or Nothing): Afterthinking Meister Eckhart," in a *festschrift* honoring Robert P. Scharlemann to appear shortly.

2. A small foretaste can be gained from the essay cited in the previous footnote, and in two of my essays in *Voici Maitre Eckhart,* ed. Emilie Zum Brunn (Grenoble: Jerome Millon, 1994), "La negativite dans l'ordre du divine," pp. 187–208, and "Pensées d'apres Eckhart," pp. 473–78.

3. This remark will be sufficient to identify me as some kind of Platonist *contra* Aristotle: such understanding as we have is not foremost in things but from the mind's searchlight. And that, *pace* nineteenth-century German readings of Plato, is precisely *not* Idealism.

4. Martin Buber, *I and Thou*, trans. Ronald Gregor Smith (New York: Charles Scribner's Sons, 1958), p. 96.

5. William James, *Varieties of Religious Experience: A Study in Human Nature* (New York: Viking Penguin Books, 1982), p. 508.

6. Ibid., p. 516.

7. Annie Dillard, *Teaching a Stone to Talk: Expeditions and Encounters* (New York: Harper & Row, 1982). See also two other of her earlier books, *Holy the Firm* (New York: Harper & Row, 1977); and *Pilgrim at Tinker Creek* (New York: Harper's Magazine Press, 1974).

8. Hannah Arendt, *The Life of the Mind*, vol. 2, *Willing* (New York: Harcourt Brace Jovanovich, 1978), p. 5.

9. Rom. 7:19.

10. Augustine *Confessions* 2.6.

11. Arendt discusses "the counter will" in her discussions of Paul the Apostle, Epictetus, Augustine, Nietzsche, and Heidegger in *The Life of the Mind,* passim.

12. These matters are worried at some length in my article, "To Be *and* Not Be: *Sit Autem Sermo (Logos) Vester, Est, Est, Non, Non," Journal of the American Academy of Religion* 53, no. 1: 14–18.

13. This passage is quoted in James, *Varieties of Religious Experience,* p. 137, without locating it in Goethe's corpus. I am morally certain it is from *Wahrheit und Dichtung,* but my dog-eared copy of that work reposes in my library in Montana and so is unavailable at this writing.

The Place of the Human in Nature: Paradigms of Ecological Thinking, East and West

GRAHAM PARKES

> For a fundamental investigation of human existence, the human-centered point of view . . . has to be broken through . . . to a horizon that embraces the other forms of existence and types of species within the world.
>
> Nishitani Keiji[1]

THE IMPETUS BEHIND MY bringing nature *per se* into a series of lectures on the topic of human nature is a concern with the dire state in which the global environment currently finds itself. I shall be discussing the place of human nature in nature more than human nature *simpliciter*, since I believe that a major factor in our having reduced nature to such a state is a prevalent conception of the human being's relations to the natural world. The fact that we talk, in English, of "nature" and of "human nature" might suggest that the latter is to be understood within the larger context of the natural world as a whole; but this way of understanding it has generally *not* been the way that philosophical and religious views of the human nature relationship have taken in the West. These views have been subject to criticism for several decades now, with the Christian tradition bearing the brunt, and with occasional unfavorable comparisons with Eastern ways of thinking. In what follows I shall consider several East Asian ways that seem conducive to more salutary attitudes toward the environment—as well as parallels with some side-currents of thinking in the Western tradition. Since environmental problems now affect the world as a whole, the philosophical ideas behind prospective solutions will have to avoid being parochial and rather aim for a global reach. A comparison of Eastern and Western approaches is therefore worthwhile, even though limitations of space preclude more than a sketch of the relevant features of each philosophy to be considered.[2]

Beginning with the Orphic tradition, which predates Socrates and Plato, there has been a tendency to understand the human soul as being of an essentially different nature from the natural world; or—to put it the other way round—to understand the body, which would seem to be the most natural aspect of human being or the locus of the most powerful manifestation of nature in human existence, as being a merely contingent and inessential aspect of our true being. This line of thinking extends from Plato's *Phaedo*, through Descartes and his disciples, to issue in a major strain of Christian thinking about the human-nature relation in this country today.[3] From the scientific point of view, it seems fair to say that the present ecological predicament is strongly conditioned by a worldview based on Cartesian philosophy and Newtonian science which has made possible, with some help from capitalism, the technological domination of the earth. Intrinsic to this worldview is the *separateness* of humans from natural phenomena, as well as our putative superiority to them, which combine to sanction a condescending attitude toward nature as "other" and inferior, and ultimately suited for domination and exploitation by humans.

One finds in the Asian traditions by contrast a variety of worldviews for which nature is the locus of ultimate reality, a direct manifestation of the divine, or a sacred source of wisdom. Where such worldviews prevail, it seems reasonable to expect that people will tend to restrain themselves from ruthlessly exploiting or inflicting gratuitous damage on the natural world. The dismal environmental track records of countries like China and Japan in the modern period have nothing to do with their being the homes of philosophies like Daoism and Zen Buddhism, since the relevant philosophical ideas lost their influence with the majority of the respective populations long ago.

But if we consider the Western tradition more closely, we find a current of thinking that has been opposed to the mainstream all along. Beginning with the Pre-Socratic thinkers, it reappears to some extent with the Stoics and again in the Italian Renaissance, attains full flow with Goethe and the *Naturphilosophen* in Germany, and eventually results in figures like Emerson and Thoreau in this country and Nietzsche on the other side of the Atlantic. To the extent that such Western ideas about nature turn out to be in harmony with the ecologically salutary East Asian understandings to be outlined first, there are good grounds for hoping that future discussion of environmental problems may attain a more truly global tone and scope.

I. CHINESE DAOISM

The Confucian philosophy that predominated during the early period of classical Chinese thought acknowledged the place of the human in nature by regarding the human world as inseparably connected with, and dependent on, the realms of heaven and earth. Nevertheless, from the standpoint of Daoist thought which came after, the Confucians were too narrowly focused on human society and ignored the larger matrix of the natural world.

The philosophy of nature contained in the two great classics of early Daoism, the *Laozi* and *Zhuangzi,* which date from the fourth or third century B.C.E., is a paradigm of ecological thinking. The end of the twenty-fifth chapter of the *Laozi* reads as follows:

> The human emulates earth,
> earth emulates heaven.
> heaven emulates *dao,*
> *dao* emulates what is natural [*ziran*].[4]

The human being is here encouraged to emulate, or "take its law [*fa*] from," the powers of heaven and earth, *tian di*. Earth and heaven constitute the world of nature, often called simply *tian,* as forces greater than but continuous with the human. These are not forces of another order of being, such as inhabit a Platonic intelligible realm or the Heaven of a transcendent deity, but are fully immanent within the natural world. Although earlier generations had understood *tian* as a quasi-personal deity to be worshiped and propitiated, for the Daoists it is rather a field of forces that are without concern for the beings (including human beings) that arise and perish within its horizons. The fifth chapter of the *Laozi* begins with the lines, "Heaven and earth are not humane: the ten thousand things are straw dogs to them." (Straw dogs are discarded when they have served their ritual purpose.) The powers of earth and heaven nevertheless display an order or pattern in their workings, such that human beings are encouraged to take their law from them.

Perhaps on the basis of a sense that the greater part of the human body is composed of water, the Daoists recommend emulating the behavior of that element especially:

> Best to be like water,
> Which benefits the ten thousand things

And does not contend.
It pools where humans disdain to dwell,
Close to *dao*.

(*Laozi* 8)

The idea is that if we pattern our behavior and thinking after the various features of water—its fluidity, a readiness to change course when confronted by obstacles, its ability to conform immediately to changing conditions, a perseverance that enables it over the long term to shape even landscapes of rock, and so forth—our lives will flourish more richly than if we take more confrontational or defeatist courses.

To return to the lines from chapter 25: *dao* would be the patterning of the totality of heaven and earth as it unfolds over time. So while it may transcend the life of any particular focus within that field of forces, *dao* is immanent within the natural and cultural history of the cosmos as a whole.[5] Thus following the Way is not a matter of going beyond this world but rather of making one's way *within* it in a manner patterned after *lian dao,* the way of nature. When it is said that *"dao* emulates what is natural," the term *ziran,* which could be translated "self-so-ing," refers to what is natural in the sense of spontaneous unfolding. The final trope of these lines, where *dao* is said to emulate not something else but its own spontaneity, also serves to short-circuit any tendency toward transcendence and hold our energies and attention within the realm of the natural.

The Daoists acknowledge of course that the human is a cultural as well as a natural being, and the *Zhuangzi* explicitly takes up the question of nature and culture, in the form of the distinction between heaven and the human, as one of life's most difficult problems. Chapter 6 begins with the supposition that "to know what is Heaven's doing and what is man's is the utmost in knowledge."[6] The distinction is of practical importance since in current debates about the environment the term *natural* is often used normatively, when it is claimed, for example, that human beings will flourish better if their lives are lived more toward the natural than the artificial end of the spectrum. One can acknowledge that "nature" is always to some extent a social construct, or that it is impossible to apprehend the natural world without the imposition of some kind of human projection onto it, and still argue that the epithet *natural* denotes something that conduces to a more sane and healthy life. It seems natural, for example, for humans to seek shelter in caves, and further—on the model of animals that build nests, hives, or dens—to construct houses to live in. But we might want to say of a life that is lived in hermetically sealed, air-conditioned apartments, cars, and office buildings, such that one rarely comes into contact with a molecule of unprocessed air, water, or earth, that it is a somewhat unnatural existence. The issue would then be to distinguish those forms or features of civilization that detract from naturalness, to the point where human flourishing is impaired, from those that are compatible with such flourishing. At the end of the *Zhuangzi's* discussion of this distinction, the "true human" is said to be able to act as a member of "Heaven's party" and of "man's party" at the same time: "Someone in whom neither Heaven nor man is victor over the other, this is what is meant by the True Man" (p. 85).

While in Daoism all things are understood as being configurations of the basic energy known as *qi (ch'i)*, each kind of thing has its own distinctive way of being and its own "power" *(de)* to act and/or react in the world, and so does each individual existent. The Daoists thus acknowledge that living beings live by virtue of the deaths of other beings, by destroying and incorporating other living things; yet there is also a sense of limits to such destruction, which humans alone transgress. Zhuangzi recognizes that human beings are distinguished from other beings by their dual potential, on the one hand, for obscuring and subverting the energies that come from *tian* through making conceptual distinctions between self and other, right and wrong, and so forth; and, on the other hand, for cultivating or training their own "power" as well as the *de* of other creatures.

The way of being that optimally issues from the proper cultivation of one's power and which corresponds to the spontaneity of *ziran*, is *wu wei*, which is often translated as "inaction" but means something more like "nondisruptive activity." Thanks to the broader range of perspectives available to human beings, it is possible for us to act in fuller awareness of the total situation than other creatures can—and thus to act in harmony with, or counter to the flow of, the greater forces of the cosmos. Zhuangzi's philosophy is thus by no means quietistic, nor does he advocate merely "going limp" or "going with the flow": it is rather a matter of a fully aware *"flowing* with the flow." While part of this flow is constituted by social practices, the much larger part is the natural world that is the matrix for all human activity—and which is on that account worthy of respect and consideration.

II. JAPANESE BUDDHISM

When Buddhism was transplanted from India to China, some thinkers there began to ask whether the Mahâyâna Buddhist extension of the promise of buddhahood to "all sentient beings" failed to go far enough. A long-running debate got underway in China during the eighth century, in which thinkers in the Tian-tai school argued that the logic of Mahâyâna universalism required that the distinction between sentient and nonsentient be abandoned, and that Buddha-nature be ascribed not only to plants, trees, and earth, but even to particles of dust.[7] (The contrast with the Christian tradition is striking, where Aristotle's musings on the vegetal soul were soon forgotten, and arguments over the reaches of salvation were restricted to the question of whether animals have souls.)

When Buddhist ideas from China began to arrive in Japan, they entered an ethos conditioned by the indigenous religion of Shinto, according to which the natural world and human beings are equally offspring of the divine. In Shinto the whole world is understood to be inhabited by *shin (kami)*, or divine spirits. These are not only spirits of the ancestors but any phenomena that occasion awe or reverence: wind, thunder, lightning, rain, the sun, mountains, rivers, trees, and rocks. Such an atmosphere was naturally receptive to the idea that the earth and plants participate in Buddha-nature. The first Japanese thinker to elaborate the idea of the Buddhahood of all phenomena and make it central to his thought was Kûkai (744–835).

Behind the discussions in Kûkai's works of the awakened nature of vegetation and earth are two major features of his philosophy: his identification of the cosmos with the Dharmakaya (*hosshin*), or "reality embodiment," of the cosmic Buddha Dainichi Nyorai (Mahâvairocana), and his idea that the Dharmakaya expounds the true dharma (*hosshin seppô*).[8] Buddhism before Kûkai had regarded the Dharmakaya as the Absolute, so it was a radical innovation for him to identify it with the physical cosmos. He does, however, equivocate on occasion, as in the following passage: "The existence of the Buddha [Dainichi Nyorai] is the existences of sentient beings and vice versa. They are not identical but are nevertheless identical; they are not different but are nevertheless different" (p. 93). It is interesting to note a similar equivocation in the philosophy of a close contemporary of Kûkai's in the West, John Scotus Erigena. Erigena's major treatise is on nature—the *Periphuseon,* or *De Divisione Naturae,* from the year 865—and he argues there that the natural world is God "as seen by Himself" (704c). His understanding of the relation between God and the natural world is informed throughout by a tension between his Catholic faith and his devotion to Greek philosophy, as exemplified in the tension in Neoplatonic theology generally between God's emanation throughout creation *(processio Dei per omnia)* and His remaining in Himself *(mansius in se ipso).*

The idea of *hosshin seppô* means that the physical cosmos, as the embodiment of Dainichi Nyorai, teaches the truth of Buddhism through all phenomena, and through *speech* as one of the three "mysteries." The element of mystery, or intimacy, comes in because Dainichi's teaching is strictly, as Kûkai often emphasizes, "for his own enjoyment." It is only in a loose sense, then, that the cosmos "speaks" to us—for properly speaking Dainichi does not expound the teachings for our benefit. But by chanting certain syllables *(mantras)* the practitioner is able to enter into the intimacy of Dainichi's speech and thereby experience direct participation in the Dharmakaya.

Since visualization plays an important role in the meditation practices advocated by Kûkai, the sacred nature of the world is accessible also to the sense of sight. As well as hearing the cosmos as a sermon, Kûkai sees, or reads, the natural world as scripture. As he writes in one of his poems:

Being painted by brushes of mountains, by ink of oceans,
Heaven and earth are the bindings of a sutra revealing the truth. (p. 91)

There are remarkable parallels here between Kûkai and the seventeenth-century German thinker Jakob Böhme. Not only is the natural world of paramount soteriological importance for them both, but their suggested ways of realizing this, by meditation on images and sounds, are interestingly comparable. In reverting to the root syllables of the Sanskrit in which the mystical aspects of early Buddhism were embodied, Kûkai employs them as sounds as well as visual images. Böhme is equally concerned with mystic syllables, in his native German as well as in the Latin and Hebrew of the alchemical and Kaballistic traditions. And just as for Kûkai nature is Dainichi Nyorai expounding the teachings for his own enjoyment, so for Böhme the natural world is the "corporeal being" of the Godhead in its joyous self-revelation.[9]

The philosophy of Dōgen (1200–1253) shares many common roots with Kūkai's thought, and his understanding of the natural world is similar. Parallel to Kūkai's identification of the Dharmakaya with the phenomenal world is Dōgen's bold assertion of the nonduality of Buddha nature and the world of impermanence generally. He famously rereads the line from the *Nirvana Sutra*, "All sentient beings without exception have Buddha nature," as "All is sentient being, all beings are Buddha-nature."[10] Dōgen thus argues that all beings are sentient beings, and as such *are* Buddha-nature—rather than "possessing" or "manifesting" or "symbolizing" it. Again, however, the usual logical categories are inadequate for expressing this relationship: just as Kūkai equivocates in identifying the Dharmakaya with all things, so Dōgen says of all things and Buddha-nature: "Though not identical, they are not different; though not different, they are not one; though not one, they are not many."[11] Again as with Kūkai, it takes considerable effort to see the relationship properly: Dōgen regrets that most people can perceive only "the superficial aspects of sound and color" and are unable to experience "Buddha's shape, form, and voice in landscape."[12]

Perhaps in order to avoid the absolutist connotations of the traditional idea of the Dharmakaya, Dōgen substitutes for Kūkai's *hosshin seppô* the notion of *mujô-seppô*, which emphasizes that even *insentient* beings expound the true teachings. And just as the speech of Dainichi Nyorai is not immediately intelligible to us humans, so for Dōgen the ways "insentient beings expound the true teachings" will be comprehensible only after some effort on our part.[13] Only from the anthropocentric perspective would one expect natural phenomena to expound the true teachings in human language.

While the practice followed in Dōgen's Sôtô Zen is less exotic than in Kūkai's Shingon, the aim of both is the integration of one's activity with the macrocosm. Whereas Kūkai's practice grants access to the intimacy of Dainichi's conversing with himself for his own enjoyment, Dōgen tells his students:

> When you endeavor in right practice, the voices and figures of streams and the sounds and shapes of mountains, together with you, bounteously deliver eighty-four-thousand gathas. Just as you are unsparing in surrendering fame and wealth and the body-mind, so are the brooks and mountains. ("Keiseisanshoku")

If we devote our full attention to them, mountains and streams can, simply by being themselves, teach us naturally about the nature of existence in general.

Kûkai's idea that heaven and earth are the bindings of a sutra painted by brushes of mountains and ink of oceans is also echoed by Dôgen, who counters an overemphasis on study of literal scriptures in certain forms of Buddhism by maintaining that sutras are not just texts containing written words and letters.

> What we mean by the sutras is the entire cosmos itself . . . the words and letters of beasts . . . or those of hundreds of grasses and thousands of trees. . . . The sutras are the entire universe, mountains and rivers and the great earth, plants and trees.[14]

As in Kûkai, natural phenomena are a source of wisdom and illumination, as long as we learn how to "read" them. It is clear that anyone who successfully practices such a philosophy will be inclined to treat the natural world with reverence and to refrain from inflicting gratuitous damage on it.

The ecologically salutary ideas outlined above have not prevented a tremendous degradation of Japan's natural environment since the country's modernization. This is because Buddhism has not been a powerful force in the culture in the modern period, and because people have been largely oblivious to the naturalist features of the indigenous religion of Shinto. But we do find a legacy of Buddhist thinking about nature in contemporary Japanese philosophy, and especially in the work of Nishitani Keiji (1900–1990).

Nishitani is well known for his discussions of nihilism, but his insights concerning the connections between this phenomenon and the disruption of human relations with the natural world have not, as far as I know, received any attention. In the third chapter of his major work, *Religion and Nothingness,* he points out two related tendencies that have come to the fore in the modern period. On the one hand, with the advent of the machine, human life has become progressively mechanized and depersonalized, and culture has become dominated by "an abstract intellect seeking scientific rationality"; correspondingly, nature has undergone a progressive "denaturalization" through being reduced to abstractions. On the other hand, "man now behaves as if he stood entirely outside of the laws of nature" and thus finds himself "in a mode of being of the subject that has adapted itself to a life of raw and impetuous desire, of naked vitality." The upshot of this "perversion of man's original relation to nature" and his becoming "a subject in pursuit of its desires" is *nihilism*—albeit "a nihilism that has yet to reach self-awareness."[15]

In the forty years since he wrote this, the tendencies Nishitani pointed to have been exacerbated to the extreme. In the industrialized countries the products of technology have brought about, for much of the population, an alienation from the natural world that is unprecedented in human history. At the same time the rampant growth of consumerism, driven in part by this alienation, attests to the vast number of people who understand themselves primarily as subjects in relentless pursuit of their desires. This high pitch of materialism in turn increases the alienation, at the same time as it wreaks devastation on the natural environment. Nishitani's association of the disrelation to nature with nihilism seems most prescient, and progress on environmental issues would surely improve if people could "see through" consumerism as a symptom of an underlying nihilism that needs to be confronted as the major pathogenic factor.

One of the key ideas in *Religion and Nothingness* is a development of the central Buddhist idea of "codependent arising" *(pratitya-samutpâda),* which asserts mutually conditioning relations among all things, such that they are "empty" of "self-nature" or "essence." Nishitani goes on to characterize "the field of emptiness" as "a field of force."

> All things that are in the world are linked together, one way or the other. Not a single thing comes into being without some relationship to every other thing. . . . [This lets us] conceive of a *force* by virtue of which all things are gathered together and brought into relationship with one another, a force which, since ancient times, has gone by the name of "nature" *(physis).*[16]

The idea that the world of nature consists in the mutual dependence and interrelationship among natural phenomena has also been central to the development of Western ecological science.

In discussing the possibility of our experiencing things as they are in themselves, rather than merely as they appear to us, Nishitani borrows the examples of pine and bamboo from the famous lines of the haiku poet Bashô:

> From the pine tree
> learn of the pine tree,
> and from the bamboo
> of the bamboo.

He glosses these lines by saying:

> [Bashô] means for us to enter the mode of being where the pine
> tree is the pine tree itself, and the bamboo is the bamboo itself,
> and from there to look at the pine tree and the bamboo. . . to
> attune ourselves to the selfness of the pine tree and the selfness
> of the bamboo. . . . . It is on the field of emptiness that this be-
> comes possible.

If we are able to "enter the mode of being" of pine or bamboo, we
will no longer be projecting the *lumen naturale* of reason onto them,
but will rather be seeing them in their *own* natural light. This would
be what the Daoists call "opening things up to the light of Heaven
[tian]" rather than viewing them from the merely human perspective
(*Zhuangzi* 2). Whereas environmental ethics in the West wonders
about the possible bases in human existence for obligations toward
natural phenomena, Nishitani says of this "reverting to the 'center'
of the thing itself" that the obligation comes from the natural phenomena themselves: "Even a single stone or blade of grass demands as
much from us."[17]

In the same vein he talks of the "dharmic naturalness" (*hôni
jinen*) of things, where the *hô* is a translation of *fa* and *dharma,* and
jinen is the Buddhist reading of the characters denoting the Daoist
ziran ("self-so-ing"). In modern Japanese these same characters are
read *shizen*, which corresponds to *nature* in the sense of the natural
world. In their "dharmic naturalness" things "express themselves,"
and Nishitani uses language reminiscent of Kûkai's and Dôgen's when
he characterizes this self-expression as "things preaching the dharma."
Just as those thinkers acknowledged a necessity for a profound shift in
perspective if we are to be able to hear or understand such preaching,
so for Nishitani we have to transcend the anthropocentric standpoint
if we are going to become truly ourselves: "Man, to be truly himself,
has to rid himself of the merely 'human' or 'man-centered' mode of
being. He has to turn toward the field of will to power and there to

overcome himself ecstatically."[18] The mention of Nietzsche's will to power in this context is apposite, since a major thrust of his philosophy is toward a "renaturalization" of the human through a reduction of anthropocentrism.

III. AMERICAN TRANSCENDENTALISM

Resonances with the views of nature discussed above can be found in Western traditions of thought. In North America one might naturally look to the philosophies of various Indian tribes, many of which gave rise to admirable ecological practices. But there are also important resources in the less indigenous tradition of Transcendentalism, and especially in the thinking of Emerson and Thoreau. While Emerson's philosophy remained for the most part under the sway of the Platonic and Neoplatonic traditions, influences from German *Naturphilosophie* (from Goethe in particular), as well as from his readings in Asian texts, gave some of his thinking about nature a more immanental and less anthropocentric cast.

Philosophy of nature in the Christian tradition tended to lose sight of Aristotle's discussions of the vegetal soul, especially after Descartes, who denied soul to the animal as well as the vegetal realms. But in the vein of late-Romantic thinking about the soul of plants and the vegetal aspects of the human psyche, Emerson reaffirms the connections. In the first chapter of his first book, *Nature* (1836), he writes:

> The greatest delight which the fields and woods minister, is the suggestion of an occult relation between man and the vegetable. I am not alone and unacknowledged. They nod to me, and I to them. The waving of the boughs in the storm, is new to me and old. It takes me by surprise, and yet is not unknown.[19]

This passage exemplifies the power of Emerson's language to transform our experience. This feeling of communion with trees, which lies at the basis of so much mythology and ancient religion, is not something accessible only to the Wordsworthian child or the so-called "primitive"—but also to the intellectually mature adult. And people who might hesitate to hear the news from a Zen Buddhist priest or a Native American shaman will surely be more comfortable when it flows from the pen of a respectable Unitarian literatus.

We also find in Emerson an idea reminiscent of the Buddhist notion that all things expound the true teachings:

> All things with which we deal, preach to us. What is a farm but a mute gospel? The chaff and the wheat, weeds and plants, blight, rain, insects, sun,—it is a sacred emblem from the first furrow of spring to the last stack which the snow of winter overtakes in the fields. (p. 29)

Again, a view that sees the natural world as sacred scripture, and for which "the moral influence of nature upon every individual is that amount of truth that it illustrates to him," is likely to promote an attitude of reverential respect for natural phenomena. Emerson's talk of "a sacred emblem" alludes, however, at this early stage in his thinking, to the Christian idea that all creatures proclaim the glory of their Creator, which directs one's attention beyond the natural phenomena to the ultimate source; whereas the Japanese Buddhists regard the phenomena themselves as being the Buddha and the Dharma at the same time.

Emerson's attitude toward the natural world tends to vacillate between feelings of close relationship and alienation. By the time of the second series of *Essays* (1844—the year of Nietzsche's birth and of Emerson's acquisition of the property at Walden Pond, which Thoreau would occupy the following summer), a series of deaths in the family had made Emerson feel increasingly alienated. The essay "Experience" marks a turning point, a nadir of estrangement, where alienation appears universal, or at least pervades the animal realm.

> We fancy that we are strangers, and not so intimately domesticated in the planet as the wild man, and the wild beast and bird. But the exclusion reaches them also; reaches the climbing, flying, gliding, feathered and four-footed man. Fox and woodchuck, hawk and snipe, and bittern, when nearly seen, have no more root in the deep world than man, and are just such superficial tenants of the globe. (p. 480)

Emerson might well have included plants among the ranks of the rootless, insofar as *all* life is ephemeral, being subject to death, and no roots permanent. There is a remarkable resonance here with Zen Buddhist ideas on this topic. In an essay on *ikebana,* the art of arranging cut flowers, Nishitani argues that by cutting off the flowers' natural drive to live and propagate themselves, the artist reveals the basic nature of finite beings as ephemeral counterforces to death and noth-ingness.

> From the perspective of their basic nature, all things in the world are rootless blades of grass. Such grass, however, having put roots down into the ground, itself hides its fundamental rootlessness. Through having been cut from their roots, such things are made, for the first time, to thoroughly manifest their basic nature—their rootlessness.[20]

In Zen, however, full acceptance and affirmation of this rootlessness—which implicates our own—leads to enlightenment, to the realization that creative existence can flourish on the ground of the emptiness disclosed by absence of roots. For Nishitani, the human condition is revealed most fully in this kind of artistic intervention into natural process: "With [cutting of the roots] the emptiness that lies hidden in the depths of the plant is unveiled . . . [so that] emptiness is unveiled in the depths of all existence, and the eternal moment is realized" (p. 26). We shall see Emerson begin to approach such a view in his later writings.

The essay "Nature" contains some of Emerson's finest reflections on the natural world, even though the characteristic ambivalence per-sists. As in the earlier *Nature,* trees play an important initiatory role, this time helping to ground the soaring transcendentalist in the en-thusiastic author. After we pass through "the gates of the forest,"

> the incommunicable trees begin to persuade us to live with them, and quit our life of solemn trifles. . . . [There] we come to our own, and make friends with matter, which the ambitious chatter of the schools would persuade us to despise. We can never part with it; the mind loves its old home; as water to our thirst, so is the rock, the ground, to our eyes, our hands, and feet. (pp. 541–42)

Finally the mind has come home—down to earth; and it seems that talk of ascendant spirit has been left behind. At least insofar as "the day was not wholly profane, in which we have given heed to some natu-ral object," Emerson no longer invokes the God of Christian mono-theism but simply "the most ancient religion." He appears thereby to have arrived at a deeper appreciation of the sciences of the earth.

Geology has initiated us into the secularity of nature, and taught us to disuse our dame-school measures, and exchange our Mosaic and Ptolemaic schemes for her large style. We knew nothing rightly, for want of perspective. Now we learn what patient periods must round themselves before the rock is formed, then before the rock is broken, and the first lichen race has disintegrated the thinnest external plate into soil, and opened the door for the remote Flora, Fauna, Ceres, and Pomona, to come in. (p. 546)

The secularity of nature celebrated here has to do with great spans of time and need not exclude nature's being sacred: it reveals rather how restricted the Old Testament view of it is, and how anthropocentric were the views of most premodern cosmologies and astronomies. A more open and expansive mind is needed, one able to transcend exclusive preoccupation with the animate and so correspond to the "large style" of nature.

Emerson gradually came to place less emphasis on the human being's superiority to nature, and by the time of the essay "Wealth" (1860) there are signs that a less domineering and more receptive attitude has supervened.

The rule is not to dictate, nor to insist on carrying out each of your schemes by ignorant wilfulness, but to learn practically the secret spoken from all nature, that things themselves refuse to be mismanaged, and will show to the watchful their own law. . . . Nature has her own best mode of doing each thing, and she has somewhere told it plainly, if we will keep our ears and eyes open. (pp. 1007–8)

This is a paradigm case of following *tian dao,* the way of nature, by attending to the dharma expounded by all phenomena.

Emerson's younger friend Thoreau was even more adept than his mentor at responding to nature's "large style" by broadening his perspectives, perhaps in part because he read more widely in Indian, Chinese, and Persian philosophies, and his thinking was able to develop farther from the sway of the Platonic and Christian traditions. Though as cultured a man as his elder contemporary, Thoreau lived closer to nature and devoted more of his thinking and writing to the topic: "I feel that I draw nearest to understanding the great secret of my life in my closest intercourse with nature. . . . I suppose that what in other men is religion is in me love of nature."[21]

Although Thoreau's reading in Chinese thought appears to have focused on the Confucian classics, his profound reverence for nature reduces anthropocentrism close to the minimum that is characteristic of Daoist thought. A passage describing sailing down the Merrimack River echoes a major theme in the *Laozi:*

> All things seemed with us to flow. . . . The hardest material seemed to obey the same law with the most fluid, and so indeed in the long run it does. Trees were but rivers of sap and woody fibre, flowing from the atmosphere, and emptying into the earth by their trunks. . . . There were rivers of rock on the surface of the earth, and rivers of ore in its bowels, and our thoughts flowed and circulated, and this portion of time was the current hour.

Thoreau's experience with husbandry during his time at Walden Pond sounds like a perfect exercise in *wu wei*, in its responsiveness to the earth's natural tendencies to express itself. He describes his daily work there as "removing the weeds, putting fresh soil about the bean stems, and encouraging this weed which I had sown, making the yellow soil express its summer thought in bean leaves and blossoms . . . making the earth say beans instead of grass."[22]

Although his familiarity with Asian thought did not extend to Japan, Thoreau shares the Japanese Buddhists' appreciation of nature as a source of wisdom. In his account of the week he spent on the Concord and Merrimack Rivers, he writes: "The skies are constantly turning a new page to view. The wind sets the types on this blue ground, and the inquiring may always read a new truth there." And while he was an avid reader of literature (he took his Homer with him to Walden Pond), Thoreau warns that if we concentrate too much on reading "particular written languages, which are themselves but dialects and provincial, we are in danger of forgetting the language which all things and events speak without metaphor, which alone is copious and standard."[23]

Just as the Japanese thinkers undermined the distinction between sentient and nonsentient in their ascription of Buddha-nature to such natural phenomena as rocks and rivers, so Thoreau likes to shift the focus away from organic life toward the so-called "inanimate" realm. A well known passage from *Walden* reads:

There is nothing inorganic. . . . The earth is not a mere fragment of dead history . . . but living poetry like the leaves of a tree, which precede flowers and fruit—not a fossil earth, but a living earth; compared with whose great central life all animal and vegetable life is merely parasitic.[24]

Thoreau's emphasis on the vitality of the mineral realm serves to mitigate the effects not only of anthropocentrism but also of biocentrism, in a way that anticipates contemporary "ecocentric" thinking.

We find a similar appreciation of the inorganic world in Nietzsche's philosophy of nature, and there is conversely a strong Dionysian element in Thoreau's thinking.[25] He writes of the way a mortal can become "immortal with her immortality," on occasions when nature "claims kindredship with us, and some globule from her veins steals up into our own." He also anticipates Nietzsche's call for the "renaturalization" of the human when he says, "Men nowhere, east or west, live yet a *natural* life, round which the vine clings. . . . [Man] needs not only to be spiritualized, but *naturalized,* on the soil of earth."[26]

Although Thoreau became an accomplished naturalist, he never allowed scientific observations to eclipse his profound sense of *participation* in the natural world. This excerpt from his journal sums up his attitude well:

To insure health, a man's relation to Nature must come very near to a personal one; he must be conscious of a friendliness in her. . . . I cannot conceive of any life which deserves the name, unless there is a certain tender relation to Nature. . . . Unless Nature sympathizes with and speaks to us, as it were, the most fertile and blooming regions are barren and dreary. (23 January 1858)

Compare these lines from a public lecture by Nietzsche, delivered fifteen years later:

If you want to lead a young person onto the right path of education and culture, be careful not to disturb his naively trustful and personally immediate relationship with nature: forest and cliff, storm and vulture, the single flower, the butterfly, the meadow and the mountainside must speak to him in their own tongues; at the same time he must recognize himself in them.[27]

IV. STAYING LOYAL TO THE EARTH

The enormous impact Emerson had on Nietzsche, who discovered the sage of Concord's essays when he was seventeen, can hardly be overestimated. Insofar as they shared a love of Goethe's writings, Nietzsche was prepared to be influenced by Emerson's ideas on nature in particular; and had he been acquainted with Thoreau's works, he would have discovered in their author an even closer "brother soul" than he found in Emerson.[28] Emblematic of Nietzsche's attitude, which is radically opposed to Platonic metaphysics and Christian otherworldliness, is this exhortation from his mouthpiece, Zarathustra: "I swear to you, my brothers, *stay loyal to the earth* and do not believe those who speak to you of otherworldly hopes! . . . The most dreadful thing is now to sin against the earth."[29] Having explicated the relevance of Nietzsche's ideas for ecology elsewhere, I shall focus here on the implications of one of his central notions: that of "the world as will to power."

Nietzsche was acquainted early on with Emerson's ideas about will and power. In *Nature* Emerson wrote that "the exercise of the Will or the lesson of power is taught in every event," and by the time of the essay by that name he had come to espouse a corresponding monism: "From the beginning to the end of the universe, [nature] has but one stuff. . . . Compound it how she will, star, sand, fire, water, tree, man, it is still one stuff, and betrays the same properties."[30] Compounded in various particulars, however, this one stuff naturally tends to conflict with itself (as described in an earlier passage, from "The Method of Nature"): "There is something social and intrusive in the nature of all things; they seek to penetrate and overpower, each the nature of every other creature, and itself alone in all modes and throughout space and spirit to prevail and possess" (p. 126).

While these ideas prefigure Nietzsche's notion of will to power, Emerson's later qualification to the effect that the whole somehow reconciles conflicting elements will mark a point of divergence. In "Uses of Great Men," he writes:

> For nature wishes every thing to remain itself; and whilst every individual strives to grow and exclude and to exclude and grow, to the extremities of the universe, and to impose the law of its being on every other creature, Nature steadily aims to protect each against every other. (p. 628)

Nietzsche is reticent about positing a protective agency in this context, since it would be reminiscent of divine providence. When Zarathustra proclaims that he has "redeemed all things from their bondage under purpose," he reflects Nietzsche's wish to liberate natural phenomena from the constraints of any universal teleology, including the projection of a scientific view of progress, in order to let them be—or, rather, come and go—in what he calls "the innocence of becoming."[31] This affirmative attitude respects what the Chinese Daoists celebrate as *ziran,* or Japanese Zen practitioners as *jinen/shizen:* spontaneous unfolding in accordance with one's particular nature.

In the context of Emerson's ideas about the protective order of nature, it is interesting that Nishitani draws attention to a remarkable passage in Rousseau's *Emile* in which the Savoyard vicar, in professing his faith, talks about the order of nature in terms that may well have influenced Emerson. In discussing "the intimate correspondence by which the beings that compose [the universe] lend each other mutual assistance," the vicar says:

> [Nature] was not satisfied with establishing order. It took certain measures so that nothing could disturb that order. There is not a being in the universe that cannot in some respect be regarded as the common center around which all the others are ordered, in such a way that they are all reciprocally ends and means relative to one another.[32]

The idea of the interrelatedness of all things is central to the thought of eternal recurrence as expounded in *Thus Spoke Zarathustra,* though Nietzsche would ascribe any ordering of those interrelations to the power of the things themselves.

Following Emerson, "Life is a search after power; and this is an element with which the world is so saturated,—there is no chink or crevice in which it is not lodged," Nietzsche's Zarathustra undertakes a thorough investigation of life and announces the result: "Where I found the living, there I found will to power."[33] Most readers have overlooked the ecological features of Nietzsche's thinking, thanks to a tendency to understand will to power as the desire to exercise brute force, and to infer that Nietzsche would endorse human domination of nature. But will to power is fundamentally *interpretation,* such that its highest form—"the most spiritual will to power"—is philosophy.[34] Thus when Nietzsche goes beyond even the biocentric standpoint in this way (from "life as will to power" to "the world as will to power"), he ends up with a kind of panpsychism ("all existence [as] essentially *interpreting* existence") similar to that found in Daoism, and which has also been aptly described by Nishitani as a Dionysian, pantheistic affirmation of the totality of becoming.[35]

A major implication of Nietzsche's central idea, the thought of eternal recurrence, is that all natural phenomena, just as they are, in the innocence of becoming, are to be affirmed—such that the totality, which from the nihilistic standpoint looks like a vicious circle, turns out, after all, to be divine. The difficult thing, after nature has been appropriately "de-divinized," is to avoid falling back into "divinizing this monster of an unknown world again in the old way." But it is clear that for Nietzsche there are circumstances in which the world *presents itself,* naturally, as divine. And it is from such a Dionysian, trans-anthropocentric standpoint that he delivers his sharpest—and sadly prophetic—criticism of the arrogance of the modern stance toward the natural world: "Our whole attitude towards nature today is *hubris,* our raping of nature by means of machines and the inconsiderately employed inventions of technology and engineering."[36]

Here, then, is the source of the modern ecological crisis. While the thinkers I have discussed have somewhat differing views on the place of the human in nature, all would agree that the rape of nature results from modern *hubris*, the prideful conviction that humankind is inherently superior to other beings in the natural world. The common sense from these ecological thinkers in both East and West is of nature as a realm to be respected as a source of wisdom—if not also revered as sacred. If such a modest sense of the place of the human in nature could be established again, destruction of the natural environment would diminish accordingly and the species flourish all the better.

NOTES

1. Keiji Nishitani, *Religion and Nothingness*, trans. Jan Van Bragt (Berkeley: University of California Press, 1982), p. 172.

2. I have dealt with these topics separately in previous essays, referred to below, but this is the first time these figures have been brought together for a more general comparison.

3. Harold Bloom, *The American Religion: The Emergence of the Post-Christian Nation* (New York: Simon & Schuster, 1992), chaps. 1 and 2.

4. *Lao Tzu: Tao Te Ching,* trans. Stephen Addiss and Stanley Lombardo (Indianapolis: Hackett, 1993). Subsequent citations will be based on this translation, sometimes slightly modified (as in this case).

5. The idea of regarding *dao* and *de* as being on a continuum between field and focus, which squares nicely with the uses of the terms in both the *Laozi* and *Zhuangzi,* comes from an essay by Roger Ames, "Nietzsche's 'Will to Power' and Chinese 'Virtuality' (*De*): A Comparative Study," in *Nietzsche and Asian Thought,* ed. Graham Parkes (Chicago: University of Chicago Press, 1991), pp. 130–50.

6. A. C. Graham, *Chuang Tzu: The Inner Chapters* (London: George Allen & Unwin, 1981), p. 84. I have discussed the remarkable parallels between Zhuangzi and Nietzsche on this topic in "Human/Nature in Nietzsche and Taoism," in *Nature in Asian Traditions of Thought: Essays in Environmental Philosophy,* ed. J. Baird Callicott and Roger T. Ames (Albany: State University of New York Press, 1989), pp. 79–98.

7. For an illuminating account of this development, see William R. LaFleur, "Saigyô and the Buddhist Value of Nature," in *Nature in Asian Traditions of Thought,* ed. Callicott and Ames, pp. 183–209. I have discussed the relevance of medieval Japanese Buddhist ideas to environmental philosophy in "Voices of Mountains, Trees, and Rivers: Kûkai, Dôgen, and a Deeper Ecology," in *Buddhism and Ecology,* ed. Mary Evelyn Tucker (Cambridge, Mass.: Harvard University Press, 1997).

8. On the buddhahood of vegetation and the cosmos as Dharmakaya, see *Kûkai: Major Works,* trans. Yoshito S. Hakeda (New York: Columbia University Press, 1972), pp. 254–55 and 229, and LaFleur, "Saigyô and the Buddhist Value of Nature," p. 186. (Subsequent references to Kûkai will be to the page numbers of Hakeda's translation.) For an explication of the idea of the Dharmakaya's expounding the dharma, see Thomas P. Kasulis, "Reality as Embodiment: An Analysis of Kûkai's *Sokushinjôbutsu* and *Hosshin Seppô,*" in *Religious Reflections on the Human Body,* ed. Jane Marie Law (Bloomington: Indiana University Press, 1995), pp. 166–85.

9. "We show you the revelation of the Godhead through nature . . . how the Unground or Godhead reveals itself with this eternal generation, for God is spirit . . . and nature is his corporeal being, as eternal nature. . . . For God did not give birth to creation in order thereby to become more perfect, but rather for his own self-revelation and so for the greatest joy and magnificence" (Böhme *De Signatura Rerum* 3.1, 3.7, 16.2).

10. Dôgen Zenji, *Shôbôgenzô,* "Busshô" (Buddha-nature). Subsequent references to Dôgen will be made simply by the title of the relevant chapter/fascicle of his major work, *Shôbôgenzô* (in vol. 1 of *Dôgen zenji zenshû,* ed. Ôkubo Dôshû [Tokyo: 1969–70]). For the most part I have followed the translations by Hee-Jin Kim in his excellent study, *Dôgen Kigen—Mystical Realist* (Tucson: Association of Asian Studies, 1975).

11. Dôgen, "Zenki" (Total working).

12. Dôgen, "Keiseisanshoku" (Sounds of streams and shapes of mountains).

13. Dôgen, "Mujô-seppô" (Nonsentient beings expound the Dharma)

14. Dôgen, "Jishô zammai" (The samâdhi of self-enlightenment); cited in Kim, *Dôgen Kigen,* p. 97.

15. Nishitani, *Religion and Nothingness,* pp. 85, 85–86, 88.

16. Ibid., pp. 150, 149.

17. Ibid., pp. 128, 140.

18. Ibid., pp. 194–95, 232.

19. *Ralph Waldo Emerson: Essays and Lectures,* ed. Joel Porte (New York: Library of America, 1983), p. 11. (Subsequent references will be to the page numbers of this edition.)

20. Keiji Nishitani, "The Japanese Art of Arranged Flowers," trans. Jeff Shore, in *World Philosophy: A Text with Readings,* ed. Robert C. Solomon and Kathleen M. Higgins (New York: McGraw Hill, 1995), p. 25 (translation slightly modified).

21. Thoreau, from a draft of *A Week on the Concord and Merrimack Rivers* (1849), cited in Robert D. Richardson, Jr., *Henry Thoreau: A Life of the Mind* (Berkeley: University of California Press, 1986), p. 159. (This biography conveys a wonderful sense of Thoreau's philosophy of nature.)

22. Thoreau, *A Week on the Concord and Merrimack Rivers,* "Thursday," in *Henry David Thoreau* (New York: Library of America, 1985), pp. 269–70; *Walden,* "The Bean-Field," p. 447. (Subsequent references will be to this edition.)

23. Thoreau, *A Week on the Concord and Merrimack Rivers,* "Friday," p. 292; *Walden,* "Sounds," p. 411.

24. Thoreau, *Walden,* "Spring," p. 568.

25. For more on Nietzsche's concern with the mineral realm, see section 7 of my essay "Staying Loyal to the Earth: Nietzsche as an Ecological Thinker," in *Nietzsche and the Future of the Human,* ed. John Lippitt (London: Macmillan, 1997).

26. Thoreau, *A Week on the Concord and Merrimack Rivers,* "Friday," pp. 306, 307. Compare Nietzsche's characterization of the task that should follow the withdrawal of traditional divinizing and humanizing projections onto the natural world: "When shall we be able to start to *naturalize* ourselves with pure, new-found, newly redeemed nature!" (*The Joyful Science,* aphorism 109).

27. Nietzsche, *On the Future of Our Educational Institutions,* fourth lecture, in *Friedrich Nietzsche: Samtliche Werke,* Kritische Studienausgabe (Berlin: de Gruyter, 1980), 1:715–16.

28. For a comparison of Emerson's ideas about nature with Nietzsche's, see my essay, "Floods of Life around Granite of Fate: Emerson and

Nietzsche as Thinkers of Nature," in *ESQ: A Journal of the American Renaissance* 41 (1997). Like Thoreau, Nietzsche developed a profound love for the natural world in his youth, which lasted throughout his career. Although he never became the naturalist that Thoreau was, Nietzsche always did his best thinking in natural settings and his philosophy of nature has similarly salutary implications for ecology.

29. Nietzsche, *Thus Spoke Zarathustra,* "Zarathustra's Prologue," sec. 3.

30. Emerson, *Nature,* "Discipline," p. 28; "Nature," p. 547. Nietzsche later found another important mentor, Schopenhauer, characterizing will as the "innermost being of the whole of nature" *(The World as Will and Representation,* vol. 1, sec. 21; see also 1:22 and 1:23).

31. Nietzsche, *Thus Spoke Zarathustra,* pt. 3, chap. 4 ("Before Sunrise").

32. Jean-Jacques Rousseau, *Emile: or On Education,* trans. Allan Bloom (New York: Basic Books, 1979), pp. 275–76; Keiji Nishitani, "Shizen ni tsuite" (On nature), in *Nishitani Keiji Chôsakushû,* vol. 14, p. 108.

33. Emerson, "Power," p. 971; Nietzsche, *Thus Spoke Zarathustra,* 2.12.

34. Nietzsche, *The Joyful Science,* aphorism 374, where he asks rhetorically "whether all existence [is not] essentially *interpreting* existence," and *Beyond Good and Evil,* aphorisms 9 and (for the world as will to power) 36. For more on will to power as interpretation, see the section "Drives Archaically Imagining" in chapter 8 of my *Composing the Soul: Reaches of Nietzsche's Psychology* (Chicago: University of Chicago Press, 1994) .

35. See the references to Dionysian pantheism in Keiji Nishitani, *The Self-Overcoming of Nihilism,* trans. Graham Parkes with Setsuko Aihara (Albany: State University of New York Press, 1990), esp. pp. 64–66.

36. Nietzsche, *Beyond Good and Evil,* aphorism 56; *The Joyful Science,* aphorism 374; *Toward the Genealogy of Morality,* essay 3, sec. 9.

Humanity as Embodied Love:
Exploring Filial Piety
in a Global Ethical Perspective

TU WEI-MING

FILIAL PIETY (*xiao*) IS the least appreciated and most vehemently attacked Confucian virtue in modern Chinese intellectual history. In a comparative cultural perspective, the main reason that most articulate twentieth-century Chinese intellectuals rejected filial piety was its perceived incompatibility with individualism and Western learning. Since individualism, which emphasizes dignity, autonomy, and independence of the person, was widely accepted as a defining characteristic of modern consciousness, filial piety was condemned as antimodern, traditionalistic, feudal, and reactionary. Assaults on filial piety have been fierce in tone and extensive in volume since the May Fourth Movement of 1919. However, filial piety as a core ethic has been continuously practiced, taught, and appreciated in behavior, attitude, and belief throughout cultural China. While the contemporary intellectual community may have lost its bearings in formulating a sophisticated philosophical argument for filial piety, it remains a moral impulse, a cherished value in the Chinese habits of the heart. This essay intends to explore the Confucian spiritual resources that have made filial piety a cardinal virtue in East Asia.

In the Confucian tradition human flourishing entails a series of concentric circles encompassing the self, family, community, society, nation, world, and cosmos. Since the self is conceived as a center of relationships rather than an isolated individual, we can envision Confucian self-realization in terms of a gradual expansion of self-consciousness to embrace an ever-extending network of human relatedness. The cultivation of the self provides a basis for cooperation in the family. The regulation of familial relationships enhances com-

172

munal participation which, in turn, facilitates social solidarity. As national security is rooted in social well-being, peace in the world is built on the governance of states. Since Confucian humanism is neither secular nor anthropocentric, it seeks harmony with nature and mutuality with Heaven. The two basic ideas governing Confucian ethics are being true to oneself (loyalty) and considerate toward others (reciprocity). The Confucian symphonic structure of the human community has a natural rhythm. People are differentiated according to degrees of affinity with others; as the emotional intensity extends toward the outer realm, so does one's moral obligation. But while the responsibility to care for one's own family, clan, kin, neighborhood, village, county, society, nation, world, and cosmos is differentiated into varying degrees of intensity, we are interconnected in an ever-expanding network of relationships involving all dimensions of human existence.

Filial piety, as "embodied love," is both a principle of differentiation and a principle of communication. As a principle of differentiation, it takes the relationship between parent and child as its point of departure. In this sense, the Confucian ethic demands that caring for one's parents takes precedence over social responsibility and political loyalty. As a principle of communication, however, the Confucian ethic demands that we transcend not only selfish interests but also the private concerns of our families, communities, societies, nations, and species. For we are and ought to be filial children of Heaven and Earth. This idea of filial piety is socially efficacious and ecologically sound. It can serve as a powerful critique of several modern ideologies, including excessive individualism, aggressive ethnocentrism, chauvinistic nationalism, religious exclusivism, and self-destructive anthropocentrism.

The most powerful and influential ideology the world has ever witnessed is perhaps the Enlightenment mentality of the modern West. The spheres of interest that characterize our emerging "global community," notably science and technology, market economy, democratic polity, mass communication, multinational cooperation, and research universities, are institutional manifestations of this mentality. The values we cherish as universal human aspirations such as material progress, rationality, liberty, equality, personal dignity, privacy, due process of law, and human rights are the ideational expressions of this mentality. The underlying life orientation is a quest for universality, a departure from the rootedness of the human condition. Filial piety, embedded in the Confucian concern for the sacredness of primordial ties, may seem to be diametrically opposed to this approach. Understandably, the ascendancy of the Enlightenment mentality signaled the decline of Confucian morality centered on filial piety in East Asia.

The denunciation of filial piety as illiberal, unequal, hierarchical, ritualistic, and duty-bound made it the *bête noire* of the feudal past in the minds of the May Fourth intellectuals. To them, being liberated from the constraints of filial attachment was a precondition for personal freedom and a clear indication of independent-mindedness. This rejection of parental authority, especially the tyrannical power of the father, features prominently in contemporary Chinese literature, notably in the novels of Ba Jin and the essays of Lu Xun. In retrospect, it seems that a consensus emerged among articulate modern Chinese intellectuals that the particularism of filial piety needed to be replaced by the universalism of the individual. Even the most brilliant defenders of the Confucian tradition, such as Xiong Shili, excluded filial piety from their discussions on moral metaphysics. Indeed, he repudiated Mencius' discourse on filial piety as parochial, nepotistic, and narrow-minded.

The assaults on filial piety necessarily discredited the family as a social institution. Sun Yat-sen, for example, in his call for national solidarity blamed nepotism as the basic impediment in developing a modern conception of citizenship. Although he was noted for his sympathy toward a reconstruction of Confucian ethics, he was highly critical of parochialism, nepotism, and narrow-mindedness in Confucian political culture. He strongly advocated impartiality as a standard for the transvaluation of particularistic Confucian values and encouraged the movement from filial piety to loyalty or from familism to nationalism. If we follow Sun's line of thinking, the emergence of the global village suggests that we should move beyond nationalism rather than retreat back to nepotism.

However, I intend to argue that while historically Confucian particularism, as exemplified by filial piety, has been rejected by Enlightenment universalism, philosophically the cultural resources of the Confucian tradition, with emphasis on "embodied humanity," can deepen and broaden the Enlightenment project with a view toward the future. This argument is predicated on the belief that the Enlightenment mentality is in crisis. It can only endure in the global community if its universalism becomes grounded in the concrete human condition. A clear indication of the Enlightenment predicament is the unworkability of its aggressive anthropocentrism. Bacon's idea that "knowledge is power" may have prompted the Faustian drive of the modern West to explore, conquer, and control nature in the early phases of industrialization. Yet, as we realize that our natural resources are limited, the need to understand nature and to harmonize our lifestyle with what it can provide becomes obvious. Similarly, as unbridled romantic optimism about progress and development wanes, we must learn to appreciate and practice sustainable growth. The global ethic that can guide us toward the twenty-first century must take the viability of the human species as its point of departure. It is imperative that we go beyond anthropocentrism so that we can fully appreciate the cosmic context in which we live.

What we need is a new vision of humanity which transcends anthropocentrism and locates the meaning of being human not only in an anthropological but also in a cosmological sense. The human arrogance that we can indefinitely increase our capacity to transform nature into raw energy for human consumption is no longer tenable. The prophetic voice of the good earth is heard throughout the world. If we want to remain a viable species, we must learn to respect nature and cherish the precious minerals, plants, water, and air that it provides for us. We may imagine many different worlds and speculate on the possibilities of living on other planets, but we have come to the realization that the evolutionary process that has made the earth hospitable to human existence is neither reversible nor repeatable. The danger of secular humanism lies not in its blind faith in human ingenuity but in its reckless degradation of nature. We must recognize the sanctity of the earth as a cardinal principle in this new vision of humanity.

Once we accept our rootedness in the earth as an irreducible reality in the human condition, we begin to appreciate who we are in our ordinary daily practical living. As we learn from comparative civilizational studies that concrete historical human beings survived by working with nature in an ever-expanding network of relationships, we can no longer unproblematically subscribe to the abstract universalism inherent in the Enlightenment assertion that we are self-interested, rational, rights-carrying, autonomous individuals. To be sure, the ideas of self-interest, instrumental rationality, rights consciousness, a sense of autonomy, and the doctrine of individualism are defining characteristics of the modern mindset. It is inconceivable that they can be relegated to the background in a contemporary discourse on the global ethic. We are so seasoned in this apparently universalizable value system that any significant departure from it smacks of a parochial retreat to particularism. Yet none of these ideas in itself addresses the human predicament: How can we remain viable as a species?

If we take the concrete living human being as the basis for our reflection, we must substantially revise the Enlightenment perception of the person. Common well-being, sympathy, duty consciousness, interdependency, and community are salient features of who we are and how we live in ordinary daily practical living. I am simultaneously a son, father, older and younger brother, nephew, uncle, colleague, teacher, student, patron, client, and friend. My self-interest is never purely and simply "mine," for it involves an ever-expanding network of relationships which realistically encompass the well-being of all those with whom I enter into communication. It is not at all possible for me to calculate the best possible way to maximize my profit without a sympathetic understanding of those around me. To ensure that my rights are properly protected, I must encourage the cultivation of duty consciousness because the demand for rights does not in itself engender a respect for the rights of others. My sense of autonomy depends on a reciprocal acknowledgment of my existence by those around me; without a tacit appreciation of the value of privacy among my associates, I cannot truly enjoy my positive experience of independence. Indeed, being part of the community of the like-minded is a precondition for me to enjoy the dignity of the individual.

In light of this discussion, the Enlightenment project can be enlarged and enriched by cultural resources springing from the Confucian tradition. If our diagnostic reading of the Enlightenment mentality is basically correct, the need to transcend anthropocentrism implies not only seeking harmony with nature and, by implication, mutuality with Heaven, but also establishing an inclusive sense of community. Indeed, fraternity, one of the three pronounced values of the French Revolution, did not feature prominently in the intellectual discussions of subsequent generations of modern Western thinkers. The preoccupation with the political rights of the individual vis-à-vis the state and self-interest in the marketplace tilted the Enlightenment discourse toward an individualist form of instrumental rationality. Understandably, the American sociologist Talcott Parsons defined modernity in terms of three inseparable dimensions: market economy, democratic polity, and individualism.

The Confucian emphasis on filial piety is predicated on a vision of humanity which is radically different from the Enlightenment conception of human beings. However, paradoxically, its concrete particularism is precisely the philosophical grounding that the Enlightenment project needs to overcome the crisis its abstract universalism has engendered. In light of the spirit of our time, the predicament of the Enlightenment mentality is twofold: (1) its secularity makes it too anthropocentric to allow the full flourishing of humanity; and (2) its instrumental rationality makes it too focused on self-interest to develop an integrated vision of being human.

Humanity as "embodied love" underlies all dimensions of our existence: self, community, nature, and Heaven. We are grateful for all those anthropocosmic forces that make our life livable and meaningful. We are here not merely as seekers of self-interest but also as contributors to the common good; our rationality is defined not only by its instrumental value but also by its communicative and transformative values. Our demands for inalienable rights are motivated by our willingness to assume responsibility for the well-being of the global community. We are autonomous and independent because we voluntarily and actively take part in an ever-expanding network of human-relatedness; and our personal dignity, while rooted in our individuality, is inseparable from our continuous participation in social intercourse.

"Embodied love" expresses itself not in abstract universalism but in lived concreteness. It moves and grows naturally from the core of closest family members to the periphery that eventually embraces humanity as a whole. The practice of "embodied love" never ceases to move and grow. Since its ultimate manifestation is the unity of humanity and Heaven, it must transcend anthropocentrism to embody nature and Heaven as well. Filial piety so conceived is always in a dynamic and dialectic interplay between immanence and transcendence. It is rooted in the self but it goes beyond self-centeredness; in the family but beyond nepotism; in the community but beyond parochialism; in ethnicity but beyond ethnocentrism; in the nation but beyond chauvinistic nationalism; in the world but beyond anthropocentrism. The thesis that envisions filial piety as an authentic manifestation of "embodied love" is Confucian thanksgiving.

The Chinese expression *ganen* (moved by a sense of gratitude) is the functional equivalent of the English idea of thanksgiving. The character *en* requires elucidation. A person whose kindness has alleviated my hardship defined in the physical, mental, and spiritual sense has *en* toward me. As a result, I am indebted to him or her as my *enren* (a person of *en*). Such a designation is rarely used lightheartedly. It signifies true indebtedness in interpersonal relationships such as benefactor, patron, mentor, sponsor, and donor.

Since, in the Confucian perspective, thanksgiving is often shared by the community, we are grateful to those to whom we owe our subsistence, development, education, well-being, life, and existence. The Chinese folk belief in "Heaven, Earth, Ruler, Parents, and Teachers" is an exemplification of *ganen* as a profoundly religious sense of gratitude. We are grateful not only to the people to whom we owe a great measure of *en* but to the cosmic forces that provide the ontological foundation for our existence, our self-realization, and our human flourishing.

The Confucians, motivated by a strong moral impulse for self-cultivation, add an ethical dimension to the discourse on gratitude, namely *baode* (repay kindness). This idea significantly broadens the scope of thanksgiving to include events in our ordinary existence. We are not only grateful to those who are instrumental in making our life possible, livable, and meaningful, but also to those who, in numerous ways, bring happiness and richness to our daily practical living. Since the Confucians cherish the hope that the ultimate meaning of life is realizable through the ordinary existence of daily practical living, the so-called "secular world" here and now is imbued with deep spiritual value. We can characterize the Confucian life orientation as regarding "the secular as sacred" (Herbert Fingarette) or, more appropriately, as creatively transforming our world of economics and politics into a fiduciary community, a community based on respect, trust, and mutuality.

The cultivation of fiduciary community is predicated on a measured and nuanced application of the idea of "repaying kindness." In the Confucian *Analects*, when a student evokes the Taoist principle of "repaying malice with kindness," Confucius retorts, "How are we to repay kindness?" His recommendation, then, is "Repay malice with uprightness (justice); repay kindness with kindness." Whether or not "repaying malice with kindness" symbolizes a higher morality, reciprocity pervades the Confucian ethos of respect, trust, and mutuality. Zhu Xi (Chu Hsi, 1130–1200) advocated a form of life seasoned in the spirit of reverence. The implicit deference in this spirit is not merely to those who are in power and authority. Reverence as a state of mind implies a grateful attitude toward community, nature, and Heaven.

Our body, for example, is a gift of our parents; we ought to take good care of it not only for our own sake but also to express our thankfulness to our parents and ancestors. Yet this sense of gratitude extends beyond the narrow confines of our biological reality, which, according to Chinese religious sensitivity, is intimately and densely intertwined with a ceaseless bloodline involving all the ancestors in our genealogical stream and embraces humanity as a whole. Thus the seventeenth-century Confucian thinker Wang Gen straightforwardly remarked that if human beings came into being through reproduction (*xingshen*), then our parents are Heaven and Earth to us; if human beings came into being through evolution (*huasheng*), then Heaven and Earth are parents to us. In either case, since we are indebted to them for our existence, it is only proper that we honor them with our respect. Similarly, we maintain a sense of fidelity to our community— family, kinship, neighborhood, society, nation, and the world— because our ordinary human experience constantly reminds us that we are not isolated individuals but centers of relationships.

As centers of relationships, we are embedded in our sociality. We are grateful for the primordial ties that make us a concrete living person. Our ethnicity, gender, language, land, class, and faith are constitutive elements of what we really are. They form a particular constellation and shape us into specific mold. Surely, each one of us is constrained—indeed, fated—to be a unique person. In a comparative religious context, all our primordial ties are, to a certain degree, culturally constructed. Therefore, we, as reflective and conscientious ethico-religious agents, possess the freedom to transcend, deconstruct, and reconfigure some or all of them. In the Confucian perspective, however, they are the physical, mental, and spiritual resources for our self-realization as well.

Actually, the Confucian project of learning to be fully human is based on the moral practice of transforming our primordial ties into instruments of personal cultivation. The very fact that I cannot choose my parents, gender, place of birth, mother tongue, class background, and socialization in taste, preference, and value orientation is not necessarily a cause for lamentation. It can be a celebratory occasion if I learn to tap their rich repertoire for in-depth self-understanding. I am grateful to my parents, siblings, other relatives, friends, colleagues, associates, and acquaintances because they provide an inexhaustible supply of nutrients for my ultimate self-transformation.

Wang Yangming (1472–1529), through personal experience informed by Confucian religiosity, insisted that filial love for parents is so deeply rooted in human nature that it serves as a point of departure for our ultimate concern. The feeling of gratitude towards the givers of our life is the foundation upon which our moral strength is built. The Confucians are suspicious of the claim that one can love the world without first showing any affection towards one's closest kin. The feeling of commiseration, sympathy, empathy, or compassion flows like water from one's innermost spring of good will. It is inconceivable that one can generate true love for humanity if one's well of gratitude and thanksgiving is poisoned. Moreover, the deliberate attempt to build a cultural code (a ritual, a value system, a life orientation, and a civilized mode of conduct) on the biological reality of the parent-child relationship is, in the words of Thomas Berry, profoundly meaningful in ecological terms. In the Confucian tradition, filial piety as a virtue nurtures respect for the teacher, loyalty to nation, caring for the suffering of others, sympathy with the myriad things, and veneration for Heaven, Earth, sages, and worthies. Obviously, the true spirit of filial piety transcends not only selfishness and nepotism but also parochialism, ethnocentrism, chauvinistic culturalism, aggressive nationalism, and anthropocentrism.

This mode of analogical thinking, guided by the principle of reciprocity—"Do not do unto others what we would not want others to do unto us"—compels Confucians to perceive ultimate self-transformation as necessarily a communal act. Indeed, our selfhood as a dynamic and open process of creative transformation, rather than a static and closed system, encounters an ever-expanding network of human-relatedness. Even in our self-imposed moratorium for spiritual inwardness, we are never alone; discipleship, fellowship, friendship, comradeship, and brotherhood/sisterhood define who we are. Mutuality with community, harmony with nature, and continuous communication with Heaven are universal human aspirations. While they may appear to be unrealizable ethico-religious ideals in light of the precarious human condition that circumscribes us today, they are common sense. Indeed, our corporate critical self-awareness that our existence as a viable species is at stake makes it our moral imperative to translate these seemingly untenable values into a day-to-day grammar of action.

Ultimate self-transformation, as the Confucians conceive of it, is not only a communal act but also a response to Heaven. The eleventh-century Confucian thinker Zhang Zai, in his celebrated Western Inscription, professes that Heaven is our father and Earth is our mother; accordingly, we as mere creatures find an intimate niche in their midst. All people are our brothers and sisters and all things are our companions. Filial piety, in this connection, is not only ethical but also anthropocosmic. Human beings as filial children of the universe are obligated to serve as stewards of the cosmic order. We are of course embedded in the good earth, but even though we are earth-bound, we are not consigned to be just earthly. We can, as Cheng Hao, another eleventh-century Confucian thinker, put it, actually "embody Heaven, Earth, and the myriad things" in our humanity. The diversity inherent in our nature enables us to take an active part in the creative and transformative processes of Heaven and Earth and thus form a trinity with Heaven and Earth.

This calls for celebration and, more importantly, duty. Our common sense dictates that we recognize that we are not what we ought to be; for we are losing the basic skills for survival and sustainable growth. Given the persistent danger of nuclear annihilation, the increasingly unmanageable ecological crisis and poverty, unemployment, and social disintegration in our shrinking global village, we are painfully aware that our human habitat is extremely vulnerable and that our way of life has been brutally destructive towards our own community and nature. The gap between what potentially we can be as filial children of Heaven and Earth and what existentially we have become is widening. Nevertheless, we are grateful to nature and Heaven as well as to all of our primordial ties for our existence. We are particularly thankful, at this critical juncture of human self-reflexivity, for the authentic possibility of not only imagining but also working toward a truly global ethic of responsibility.

Why Good People Do Bad Things: Kierkegaard on Dread and Sin

LEROY S. ROUNER

IF THERE WERE A CONTEST for the most unpopular idea in the history of human thought, the Christian idea of original sin would win easily. Swami Vivekananda spoke not only for himself but for the whole tradition of Hindu religious philosophy when, at the 1893 Parliament of the World's Religions in Chicago, he thundered, "It is a sin to call men sinners!" Confucians are not angry at the idea; they just don't understand how anyone could really think that. Buddhists have their glorious hells, but no sinners, lacking–as they do–a self to do the sinning. Even John Calvin, who was as stern on this matter as anyone, referred to original sin's cognate conception of predestination as "this dreadful doctrine."

All this raises an interesting question about how well we really understand our human nature. John Herman Randall, the Columbia historian of philosophy, used to say that the real difference between Plato and Aristotle was that Aristotle believed that if enough people had thought something for a long enough period of time, then there probably was something in it; whereas Plato believed that if you had learned it at your mother's knee, or heard it from the man in the street, it was probably wrong.

On the question of human nature, I side with Plato. Much of our common wisdom on this topic strikes me as wrong. For example, the idea that, in situations of pressure or crisis, people will always act in their own self-interest has long been popular dogma, despite all the evidence of self-destructive behavior amassed by psychologists of every persuasion. And the staggering amount of evil which humankind perpetrates on itself is so vast, so perverse, so recalcitrant, and so predictable that there is every reason to believe that human nature itself has a dark side, curiously bent toward doing bad things. Indeed, Reinhold Niebuhr was once moved to comment, wryly, that original sin was the only empirically verifiable doctrine in the whole of Christian theology. This was a joke—a fact that escaped several theological commentators who should have known better—because original sin in Christian theology is a failure of relationship between ourselves and God, and God is not an empirical object. So original sin, as a theological doctrine, is part of the content of revelation.

Niebuhr later regretted that he had used the traditional phrase "original sin" in trying to describe humankind's moral and spiritual malaise, because its content is so difficult to communicate to the contemporary mind. Niebuhr's regret stemmed from the difficulty in breaking through the crude popular interpretation which identified the "original" sin as the disobedience of two historical figures, Adam and Eve, which had somehow created an evil gene which we have all inherited, through sexual generativity, from them.

Nevertheless, Niebuhr's comment about the empirical verifiability of original sin points to a paradox of modern life. We are surrounded by overwhelming evidence of the human propensity to do bad things while, at the same time, our most influential philosophers and sages reaffirm the inherent goodness of humankind. Niebuhr called this phenomenon "the easy conscience of modern man." John Dewey's philosophy was his major target in this regard, but it could have been almost any of his contemporaries since this positive view of human nature is deep-seated in the liberal tradition with which many of us identify ourselves. I believe, with Niebuhr, that it has done much to blind us to the reality of our situation. In politics and social policy, for example, the "easy conscience" of modernity argues that the explanation for evil in human relations results largely from external causes. Most of us are persuaded that America's inner cities have become moral cesspools because of poverty, broken homes, unemployment, and the like. This view assumes that the external condition of poverty in society creates an internal condition of immorality in individuals. But I know of no evidence that the poor of the world are notably more immoral than the rich. The economist Robert Samuelson recently noted that the economy of America's urban poor had actually improved somewhat during a period in which violent crime, drug abuse, and all kinds of other antisocial behavior had increased dramatically.

So, although I am a political liberal, the view which I have begun to sketch will seem inherently conservative. This is a dilemma which Niebuhr also faced. He once ran for Congress as a Socialist, but conservative Republicans liked him for his view that expensive social programs would not, in themselves, cure crime in the streets. For the conservatives that was an argument for scrapping those programs. For Niebuhr that was only reason not to hold out unrealistic hopes for them. The programs were important, he thought, because they could make our social situation a *little bit* better; and because human nature is indeed morally recalcitrant, self-seeking, sinful, a little bit is all we are ever going to get. As a chastened liberal he criticized both conservatives and unchastened liberals in their romantic search for, and belief in, complete solutions. The problem was that neither group took the sinfulness of human nature seriously. The unchastened liberals simply didn't believe it. The conservatives believed it, but only for the poor and the unsuccessful. Their belief was a corrupted form of Calvinism which saw poverty as empirical evidence for sin, and their own wealth as a sign of God's choosing them for blessing and salvation. So our topic has important social and political implications

It was Søren Kierkegaard's view that sin is a universal human phenomenon, resulting from our dread, or anxiety, in the face of freedom. Since space is limited I set aside the theological dimensions of the doctrine, in order to focus on Kierkegaard's philosophical psychology. So our question is not concerned with an interpretation of the Adam and Eve story, although Kierkegaard deals with the story at some length. Nor is our question about the relation of individual acts of immorality to some generic structural defect in human character. The question is rather, What is the process by which we make moral choices, and why does it never work out the way we want it to? My argument is that there is a profoundly important sense in which we never, ever, *quite* get it right. Saint Paul put it rather broadly in his famous cry of the heart when he said, "The good that I would do, I do not; and the evil that I would not do, that I do" (Rom. 7:19). This is not to say that no one ever does anything good. Happily, good deeds abound in our world. Nor is this an argument for the total depravity of humankind. It is an argument that we can do no pure good. Some may say, "But we all know nobody's perfect." True; but what this response runs roughshod over is a hidden secret of the human heart. That is that when we are most ourselves—when we toss fitfully at night, worrying about nothing in particular and everything in general, yearning for some release from insecurity and ambivalence—we realize that we are not happy about the fact that nobody's perfect. So this is also the argument that "purity of heart," as Kierkegaard called it, is what we all really want; and that the fact that nobody's perfect is a spiritual problem for everybody.

The relevant text is *The Concept of Dread*, which I will quote from as little as possible. It is not easy reading, partly because Kierkegaard's genius bubbles over in a flamboyant style of writing; and partly because that same genius has invented an imaginative terminology—phrases like "dreaming innocence"—which will seem alien and incomprehensible if we don't examine our own experience first, to see if our inner world is anything at all like the inner world Kierkegaard is describing.

So I suggest a thought-experiment to take us into Kierkegaard's analysis. There are two fundamental human experiences which he builds on, and which are important as common ground for the argument I am going to sketch. If these fundamental experiences seem alien or weird, then none of what follows will make any sense. So my argument is really an appeal to your own experience. What Kierkegaard says speaks to my experience. Does it speak to yours? Does it have something of our common humanity in it?

The first is the experience of self-knowledge, or self-awareness, or self-transcendence. Whether one defines the distinctive and determinative aspect of human nature as will—a view characteristic of ancient Jewish thought—or whether, with the Greeks, one finds it in rationality, both recognize the distinctively human capacity to know ourselves by standing off from, or rising above, ourselves; examining ourselves, making choices for ourselves. We experience this in the common phenomenon of talking to ourselves. In these times a self, or a dimension of self, or a part of myself, in that moment *transcends* myself, knows myself, instructs myself, exhorts myself. The simple distinction between myself and my dog is that I know myself to be a man, and she does not know herself to be a dog. Whether one defines humankind as the animal who laughs; or the animal who thinks; or the animal who goes to school; it is always this element of self-transcendence which makes that definition possible. So Kierkegaard is presupposing our awareness of ourselves as "self-transcending" in the experience of what it means to be truly human.

The second precondition for understanding Kierkegaard's analysis is an inner sense of unfulfillment; a yearning for we know not what; the sense that somehow, in the process of trying to be who we most truly are, something went askew. In the intimately vulnerable moment of our nocturnal tossings and turnings, when we are bedeviled by bad dreams, our anxieties are only slightly less palpable than our desperate hope that, as Julian of Norwich once said, in the end "all shall be well, and all manner of thing shall be well." We want the peace that passes all understanding; the peace beyond the ambivalence of our ordinary daily round and the terrors of our darkest dreams; the peace that means fulfillment for the longings of the heart.

With these two presuppositions in mind, we are ready to get into Kierkegaard's argument. He notes at the outset that there is no proof for sin, any more than there is a proof for freedom. "Sin presupposes itself, just as freedom does."[1] Two notions are critical here. One is the *infinity* of freedom, good, and evil. The second is the much vexed Kierkegaardian notion of "the leap," which has been associated, unhappily, with the idea of a blind, irrational, dogmatic expression of a petulant will to fling oneself into whatever fantasy, fanaticism, or dogmatic commitment one chooses. In fact, however, the notion of "the leap" is a technical term in Kierkegaard's philosophical psychology, comparable to what is called "intuitive grasp" by less exuberant philosophers. Anyone who has read Pascal on the famous "wager," or William James on the controversial "will to believe," will recognize Kierkegaard's "leap" as a form of intuitionism, a philosophical perspective which goes back at least as far as Plato's reflection on how we know the idea of the Good. Those of you familiar with Kierkegaard's philosophy need to be warned that he is not speaking here of the famous "leap of faith." *This* intuitive "leap" concerns the occasion in our experience when we discover that we are free, and when we suffer the exhilaration and dread of what he elsewhere refers to as "the education of infinite possibility."

When and how do we discover our freedom? Kierkegaard answers: in "the moment" or "the instant." Here he criticizes Hegel's view that "the characteristic of the immediate is to be annulled (*aufgehoben*)."[2] The idea of negation is crucial for Hegel's dialectical logic. The thesis is "annulled" or "negated" in favor of its "antithesis," which is, in turn, annulled or negated in favor of a synthesis. But because the idea of *immediacy* is intimately related to the ethical idea of *innocence* for Kierkegaard, he insists that innocence as a kind of immediacy is not to be annulled as "something which properly speaking does not exist," in the sense of things that come and go in our world of sometimes being and then not being. Immediacy as innocence, for Kierkegaard, is "annulled by a transcendency." But it is a quality which can very well endure—indeed, does endure. Remember that this is not speculative metaphysics; this is philosophical psychology. In terms of our experience, we know innocence only after we look at ourselves and discover that we have lost it. We don't experience innocence directly. We experience it only as something that we have lost. But the reality of that innocence stays with us, because of our knowledge that we have lost it.

Let us return, for a moment, to our first presupposition concerning Kierkegaard's argument—that to be human is to be self-transcendent. I said that the transcendent position of the self-which-transcends-itself is no place; and Kierkegaard points out that the "moment" of immediacy in which this self-transcendence happens is really no time. We will see in a minute why this is so; why the only way one can make this "moment" into a discernible "thing" is to spatialize it, and thus compromise one's conception of time. But, for now, the important points in this Kierkegaardian drama of decision making are these. First of all, the choice is made in an "instant" in which the self transcends itself; an "instant" which existentialist poets like Rilke were to call a "moment out of time."

Second, the choice presupposes a prior condition of innocence, before the choice was made, in which one was still a "good person," because one hadn't yet done any "bad things." In fact, one hadn't *done* anything at all.

The movement of self-transcendence is a "leap" for Kierkegaard, in opposition to Hegel's logic of "steps," because he regards this "move" as an intuitive grasp rather than a logical progression. And the leap of immediacy, which is the leap into freedom, is possible because the "instant" of immediacy is a point at which the temporal touches the eternal—which raises the question of a philosophy of time.

Kierkegaard begins his discussion of time by referring back to his view of human nature as consisting of both body and what he calls "soul," but we might more easily call "mind." But for mind and body to be integrated into a self there must be a third element which conjoins them. Kierkegaard calls this third element "spirit." All this he regards as an unproblematic statement of the conventional wisdom.

Remember our discussion of the self which transcends itself and think of the transcendent self as "spirit." But we are also a synthesis of the temporal and the eternal, and this is more problematic.

Kierkegaard begins with the notion of time as infinite succession, plausibly defined as past, present, and future. The problem with this division, however, is that it requires us to *spatialize* a moment in time. And that spatial widening out of a moment in order to be able to see it blocks the movement of time as infinite succession. Hence "the infinite succession is brought to a standstill."[3] But the "instant" or the "immediate" in time is a metaphor, and hence a vanishing point, a pure essence, a "no thing." His point is that this coming together of time and eternity is not a new synthesis, but an expression of the first synthesis in which spirit unites body and mind (or soul) into a self. "No sooner is the spirit posited than the instant is there."[4] And it is this coming together of time and eternity which makes possible "the temporal," where time is constantly intersecting eternity, and eternity constantly permeating time. In this "moment" the reality of past, present, and future is born.

"Innocence," says Kierkegaard, "is ignorance." In this state we are not yet determined by spirit, although spirit is present. But spirit is *dreaming in us*. As in the biblical myth of Adam and Eve, we are determined "soulishly," as he puts it, in immediate unity with our natural condition. In this state of "dreaming innocence," we are purely natural beings. We have not exercised our spirit. And we are not yet free. This is "a condition of peace and repose," but there is also present something which is really nothing; yet it is this nothing which begets dread in us.

Dread is a qualification of "dreaming" as opposed to wakefulness, where objects are posited as other than myself; and as opposed to sleep, where the distinction between self and other is suspended. The dread in "dreaming innocence" is not fear, because fear has an object. Nor is it guilt, since we have not yet done anything to be guilty of. Guilt is a condition of the human spirit, and spirit is not yet active, engaged, operative.

Kierkegaard is really talking psychology. He is trying to describe an internal experience which we all have. In this sense, his psychology of dread is an appeal to universal human experience. His categories are all ambiguous, or dialectical, but his argument is that we experience ourselves this way. There is also a curious but compelling reversal in his thought. He speaks of innocence as prior to guilt, because logically it is prior. But in the order of experience, we know we *were* innocent only after we have become guilty. So the condition of "dreaming innocence" is never a present moment, in which we can say, self-consciously, "Oh, now I am dreaming." Dreaming innocence is known only in its vanishing into guilt. It is only when it has been lost that we know fully what it was. And this is, indeed, our ordinary human experience.

How then can we speak of the dread encountered in dreaming innocence, the dread without an object, which has not yet become guilt? Where would we look for an example of a dread which is still in harmony with innocence and therefore not a burden—a dread which I am tempted to describe as "the unbearable lightness of being"? Kierkegaard turns to the experience of children:

> The dread which is posited in innocence is, in the first place, not guilt; in the second place, it is not a heavy burden, not a suffering which cannot be brought into harmony with the felicity of innocence. If we observe children, we find this dread more definitely indicated as a seeking after adventure, a thirst for the prodigious, the mysterious. The fact that there are children in whom this is not found proves nothing, for neither in the beast does it exist, and the less spirit, the less dread. This dread belongs to the child so essentially that it cannot do without it; even though it alarms him, it captivates him nevertheless by its sweet feeling of apprehension.[5]

In his concept of dread everything is ambiguous; everything is both logical and psychological; everything is participant in both time and eternity. But how does one move from dread's sweet feeling of innocent apprehension to the heavy burden of guilt? Some have argued that prohibition produces the fascination which leads to guilt, and that Adam sinned precisely because the fruit of the tree was forbidden. But for Kierkegaard this is very superficial. The dread we feel in dreaming innocence is dread of the possibility of freedom. Freedom confronts us with what Kierkegaard refers to elsewhere as "the education of infinite possibility." He puts it this way:

> Thus dread is the dizziness of freedom which occurs when the spirit would posit the syntheses, and freedom then gazes down

into its own possibility, grasping at finiteness to sustain itself. In this dizziness freedom succumbs. Further than this psychology cannot go and will not. That very instant everything is changed, and when freedom rises again it sees that it is guilty. Between these two instants lies the leap, which no science has explained or can explain. He who becomes guilty in dread becomes as ambiguously guilty as it is possible to be. Dread is a womanish debility in which freedom swoons. Psychologically speaking, the fall into sin always occurs in impotence. But dread is at the same time the most egoistic thing, and no concrete expression of freedom is so egoistic as is the possibility of every concretion. This again is the overwhelming experience which determines the individual's ambiguous relation, both sympathetic and antipathetic. In dread there is the egoistic infinity of possibility, which does not tempt like a definite choice, but alarms (*aengster*) and fascinates with its sweet anxiety (*Beaengstelse*).[6]

This "grasping at finiteness" is what Paul Tillich later called the transition from essence to existence, where the perfection of moral innocence is lost in the free exercise of finite choice. And sin is posited in this choice because spirit, in its dread of the infinite possibility of freedom, chooses "selfishly."

In the instant "before" a choice has been made, one is not yet a self, because one has not yet decided anything. We exist "soulishly" as a combination of body and mind which has not yet been integrated by spirit. One has transcended oneself, so that one knows that one has the freedom to choose, but as yet nothing has happened. And in that moment of transcendence which is a moment out of time, and in that place of perspective which is no place, one becomes aware of the infinite possibilities which freedom offers. One yearns to actualize one's potential as a self and become "enspirited." One wants to become a self by choosing one of the infinite possibilities which freedom poses for us. But one choice cuts us off from the infinite possibility of all the other choices. In this confrontation with "the education of infinite possibility," we experience the "sweet apprehension" of dread. But we must become "spirited" if we are to be complete selves. So we are condemned to freedom. And in "the dizziness of freedom" we "grasp at finiteness" to sustain ourselves. And because that "grasp" at a specific, finite possibility was done in the dizziness of freedom, and "in order to sustain ourselves," we are now an actualized self, no longer mere potential. We are spirited, and free; but we are also now guilty because we chose egoistically, in order to sustain ourselves. It was not an "act of love." It was an act of self-establishment and, at the same time, an act of self-preservation. So we are no longer innocent.

Kierkegaard's analysis is fundamentally a philosophical psychology which stands on its own. It does, however, echo a metaphysical tradition which goes back to Plato's "myth of the fall." That tradition regards the true self as a prehistorical, immortal essence which, in actualizing itself in the contingent world of existent things, "falls" from the realm of essence into the realm of existence. Paul Tillich has recently used much of Kierkegaard's psychological analysis to rework that metaphysical position. This raises problems for Tillich's philosophy of religion in that it makes the idea of creation identical with the idea of the fall, and thus obscures the question of individual moral responsibility. The advantage in Tillich's treatment, however, is that he is able to articulate—in a way that Kierkegaard's psychology cannot—the meaning of the second of those two foundational experiences with which we began, our "yearning for we know-not-what." Kierkegaard can explain why we feel inadequate in our moral life. Tillich explains where we derive our standard for judging that we are morally inadequate.

Tillich points out that this essential stage of humankind—before the choices which turned dreaming innocence into existential freedom—is not a once-upon-a-time situation, but the continuing condition of all human choices. And Tillich introduces an element which is not emphasized in Kierkegaard, and which is crucial for our purposes. That element is nostalgia for the prehistorical condition of dreaming innocence; the longing of the existing decider for that time before time when decisions had not yet been made, and when one may not yet have been a truly existent self, but when it was still possible to be pure in heart. What Kierkegaard calls the psychological state of "dreaming innocence" Tillich equates with the metaphysical state of humankind's "essential being." He points out that

> the state of essential being is not an actual stage of human development which can be known directly or indirectly. The essential nature of man is present in all stages of his development, although in existential distortion. In myth and dogma man's essential nature has been projected into the past as a history before history, symbolized as a golden age or paradise."[7]

And the presence of this essential being in humankind—as Plato's immortal soul, or Augustine's *imago dei,* or Sankara's *atman*—is not only the standard of perfection by which we judge our moral condition, but the reality we yearn to regain. The "essential self" in us yearns for freedom from the existential distortions of our contingent, historical situation. Our true "home," where our essential selves belong, is in this realm of essences, a place where we have never been. In his Christian adaptation of Platonism, Augustine made the best-known statement of this nostalgia in his *Confessions:* "Lord thou has made us for Thyself and our hearts are restless till they find their rest in Thee."[8]

This concept of an essential self takes us back to why I like the doctrine of original sin, even though Swami Vivekananda—and so many others—hated it. He hated it because he read it as besmirching the moral nobility of humankind. He is right, of course, that there is much nobility in humankind, but as the relentless media of our day shows us repeatedly in regard to our heroes and heroines, no one is as good as we thought they were.

I like the doctrine of original sin for several reasons. The first is simply that it is realistic. Our morality is always tainted with self-interest. Good people always do some bad things. But perhaps even more importantly, because it is realistic, it is also humane. I'm really not okay, and it is very burdensome to have to go around pretending that I am. Nothing lightens the heart and gives one hope for tomorrow like the confession of sins. But that takes us to theology, which is a topic for another time.

NOTES

1. Søren Kierkegaard, *The Concept of Dread*, trans. Walter Lowrie (Princeton: Princeton University Press, 1944), p. 100.

2. Ibid., p. 32.

3. Ibid., p. 77.

4. Ibid., p. 78.

5. Ibid., p. 38.

6. Ibid., p. 55.

7. Paul Tillich, *Systematic Theology*, 3 vols. (Chicago: University of Chicago Press, 1951–63), 1:33.

8. Augustine *Confessions* 1.1.

Lifeboat Ethics[1]

SISSELA BOK

INTRODUCTION

How HELPFUL IS THE commonplace use of the lifeboat metaphor to explore human nature and human choice? The metaphor is familiar to us all from countless stories and news reports about shipwreck survivors adrift on rafts and in lifeboats. Through myth, literature, and art we have had vicarious experience of people striving to survive on such a fragile craft, not only adrift but at the mercy of wind and sun and predators, out of contact with the outside world and bereft of the slightest power to affect their environment. Whether it be from press coverage such as that of the sinking of the Titanic or, more recently, of Vietnamese and other "boat people," from plays such as Shakespeare's *The Tempest*, from novels such as Joseph Conrad's *Lord Jim* or works of art such as Théodore Géricault's *Raft of the Medusa,* our images of castaways, boat people, and shipwreck survivors blend together to shape one of the most powerful metaphors for human beings exposed to the elements, away from societal protections, struggling to survive.

It is natural that this metaphor should lend itself to use as a thought-experiment for studying, in imagination, human nature *in extremis*—human responses to adversity under circumstances pared down to the barest essentials. At what point might these responses lose characteristics often associated with humanity, and perhaps take on characteristics sometimes called "bestial"? Many thinkers have made such distinctions between the human and the bestial, placing human beings above animals in the chain of beings. Others, on the contrary, have insisted, as did Erasmus, that violence and deceit on the scale practiced by humans and with the means at their disposal are of an entirely different order than what is possible to animals, and that to call the most vicious forms of human conduct "bestial" is merely to calumniate animals.[2]

By means of thought-experiments focusing on the lifeboat meta-phor, it is possible to vary the relevant circumstances systemati-cally, much as in a chemistry experiment or photo laboratory. You can vary, for example, the numbers of persons present on board the lifeboat, the length of time that their ordeal lasts, and the conditions on board. In this way, you can conjure up in imagination elements of greater or lesser hardship, adequate or vanishing rations of food and drink, enough living space or overcrowding, friendship or enmity among those present, and growing or diminishing hopes of rescue.

One aim of such thought-experiments is to sharpen perception—to try to approach and to fathom the experience of persons in such desperate predicaments. Another aim is to aid deliberation and debate about human nature and moral choice under such circumstances, by addressing more focused questions about how individuals trapped on a lifeboat might respond as conditions worsen and as their need for water, food, and shelter from the elements becomes more des-perate: What becomes of fellow-feeling, of what the ancients called *humanitas*, and of the respect for human rights when survival itself is threatened? Does a time come when even the best lose all remnants of traits that we think of as distinctively human?

Such questions have long been explored in the law, especially through cases involving shipwreck survivors accused of maltreating or killing their companions, even of resorting to cannibalism. By now, lifeboat cases have become commonplace in courses and textbooks in law and ethics. But while many view them as useful tools for sharpen-ing moral conflict and for isolating different factors affecting choice, others object to the trivializing approach to issues of survival that such cases can present. This critique is especially common when ques-tions are posed about which persons might have to be jettisoned for purposes of collective survival, and why—whether the sick and the el-derly, for instance, should be sacrificed before the young, or whether a famous scientist or a physician should have priority over persons seen as more dispensable. Such questions about lifeboat cases are some-times even mindlessly put to grade school children. At times, lifeboat cases are not so much trivializing or coarsening as simply ludicrous—cluttered with improbable details or festooned with clusters of inter-twined dilemmas quite impossible to disentangle.[3]

A different set of problems arises when, as in recent decades, the lifeboat metaphor is extended to humanity at large in such a way as to advocate policies with respect to population policy, international co-operation, immigration, poverty, and human rights. Such extrapolations of the lifeboat image to the global scale have been thought to support vastly different predictions for the future of humankind, given the unprecedented population growth of the past century. Warring cliches abound. To those who argue that "we are all in the same boat" or that we travel together on board "Spaceship Earth" or "Lifeboat Earth," others answer that the time has come to jettison some people from any collective lifeboat lest we all perish together.

In this essay, I shall consider some of the uses and misuses of the lifeboat metaphor as thought-experiment in both narrow and extended forms and ask about the moral issues they can illuminate, but sometimes also confuse. I shall begin with Alfred Hitchcock's film *Lifeboat*, and then take up four uses of an extended lifeboat metaphor with sharply different perspectives on the needs of humanity and on the global and domestic policies most likely to further these needs: two paintings of human beings on a lifeboat and two articles devoted to choice on board such vessels. The first painting was commissioned from the artist Mark Stutzman, by the World Future Society for its meeting in July 1996 in Washington D.C.;[4] the second is *The Raft of the Medusa* by the French nineteenth-century artist Géricault. The two articles are the biologist Garrett Hardin's "Lifeboat Ethics: The Case Against Helping the Poor"[5] and the philosopher Onora O'Neill's "Lifeboat Earth."[6]

HITCHCOCK'S *LIFEBOAT* (1944)

In evaluating the most extensive extrapolations from the lifeboat image, it is important to keep in mind the more limited lifeboat cases involving but a single craft and a small number of persons, adrift, exposed to the elements, and out of contact with the rest of the world. In such cases, two sorts of moral choice arise: how to treat fellow passengers on board a lifeboat and what to do when additional persons struggle to climb on board. Alfred Hitchcock's 1944 film *Lifeboat* invites viewers to a thought-experiment: what would happen when Americans and Britons found themselves on a lifeboat with a Nazi officer—one, to boot, responsible for sinking the ship on which they had been passengers?

As the film opens, we see a freighter that has been torpedoed by a German U-boat going down, inexorably. Debris floats by on the water—a *New Yorker* magazine, a Red Cross crate, a deck of cards, a helmet. Then a lifeboat comes into view. In it sits Tallulah Bankhead, as a world-famous socialite journalist, immaculately made up, every hair in place, utterly out of place. She has brought her mink coat and her typewriter, and points a film camera hither and yon, clearly expecting to be rescued at any moment but eager to record the events for her newspaper. Then others clamber on board: a woman, two men, a wounded man, and a steward from the freighter who is helping a young mother clutching her dead baby. Calls for help echo across the water; one more man comes aboard—played by Walter Sleazak—who causes consternation when it turns out he is wearing a German uniform. He acknowledges being from the U-boat, but, when asked if he is an officer, he claims to be merely a crew member.

The group divides over what to do with him. Throw him out of the lifeboat? Keep him on board but treat him as a prisoner of war? A bitter dispute breaks out. In the end, the group reluctantly agrees to save the German. At first, he appears to want to help them. He volunteers to operate on the wounded man's gangrenous leg, and rows the boat while singing to keep everyone's spirits up. But it turns out that all the while he is betraying them—by denying that he is the captain of the U-boat, by steering them toward a German supply ship, and by cheating them of food and drink. Finally, they learn that while they were sleeping, he has pushed the wounded man, delirious with thirst and dying with gangrene, into the ocean "for his own good." When they learn what he has done and find that he had hoarded water in a flask without sharing it with the wounded man, they grow enraged and turn on him, throwing him overboard even as they beat him furiously. But their conscience gnaws at them. As one of them puts it, even as they are close to being rescued by an Allied ship: "My only regret is that I joined a mob."

By the time rescue is near, another German, a young, wounded sailor, clambers aboard; and another dispute breaks out, especially after the German threatens them with a gun. It is quickly taken from him and tossed into the sea. He asks: "Aren't you going to kill me?" The answer is that he will be treated as a prisoner of war and his wounds will be cared for; it would be approaching the bestiality of the Nazis to throw him overboard. At least some of those on board had clearly learned from their experiences—their perception of what was at stake had grown broader and deeper; their ability to discuss available choices and to single out which ones were and were not legitimate had been sharpened.

Hitchcock's thought-experiment proved troubling for wartime audiences used to enemies portrayed as straightforwardly evil, sometimes as subhuman. The captain turns out to be selfish, greedy, and cruel, but not the devil incarnate and at times capable of appealing conviviality. He does not threaten the others so directly that they can invoke self-defense in killing him. The central moral problem Hitchcock poses is that of how, under such circumstances, the group should relate to the German. Apart from that question, the fear and insecurity and increasing discomfort are stark, but not so severe as to lead the rest of the passengers to contemplate assaults on one another. The food supply has been shrinking, but not to the point of starvation. The boat is small, but adequate for the few people on board. The outside world is distant, but its laws still matter to all in the group.

In this floating world, Hitchcock has brought out the universality of basic human needs—for food, water, and shelter, above all— and the equal vulnerability of each person to dangers from the environment and from anyone else on board. This condition, pared down within a small, precarious human society, is the fundamental equality among human beings of which Hume writes in *A Treatise of Human Nature,* and that John Rawls characterizes as "the objective conditions which make human cooperation both possible and necessary":

> Thus, many individuals coexist together at the same time on a definite geographical territory. These individuals are roughly similar in physical and mental powers; or at any rate, their capacities are comparable in that no one among them can dominate the rest. They are vulnerable to attack, and all are subject to having their plans blocked by the united force of others. Finally, there is the condition of moderate scarcity understood to cover a wide range of situations. Natural and other resources are not so abundant that schemes of cooperation become superfluous, nor are conditions so harsh that fruitful ventures must inevitably break down.[7]

In lifeboat cases such as those discussed above, however, each of the conditions mentioned by Rawls is precarious in the extreme. To be sure, human cooperation is necessary and also, to an extent, possible; but it may not suffice to ensure survival. The few "fruitful ventures" available may indeed break down. Those on board are more vulnerable than most to attack, not least from their fellow passengers. The condition of scarcity may be shifting from moderate to acute.

FOUR EXTENDED LIFEBOAT ANALOGIES

The four extrapolations from the lifeboat metaphor that I shall consider present very different perspectives on the possibility for human cooperation of which Rawls speaks. The first is a painting by a contemporary artist, Mark Stutzman, commissioned by the World Future Society for its July 1996 annual meeting. According to the description accompanying this painting, it is modeled on the famous nineteenth-century painting by Théodore Géricault, *The Raft of the Medusa,* and shows "the survivors of a shipwreck, clinging to a make-shift raft, at the moment when they spot their rescuers." Today, this description continues, "all of humanity survives on a tiny craft we call the earth and we must work together if we are to survive and prosper in the future."

The raft seems less seaworthy than the lifeboat in Hitchcock's film; a few more passengers and the raft will sink. Yet we are to understand that if the people on the life raft—symbolizing all the peoples on earth—don't cooperate, all of them will founder together, whereas, by working together, they have a chance not only to survive but to prosper and thrive. To this end, the painting shows us representatives of the different ethnic and religious groups, men and women, religious and secular, all cheerily working together beneath the United Nations flag (though close inspection reveals that the role of the two women aboard is minimal—one seems to cooperate in spirit only, and the other is holding a rope most tentatively).

This painting conveys the best of what human beings are sometimes capable of in a crisis: the solidarity, the mutual respect and care, the refusal to inflict injury, and the ability to work harmoniously. It shows individuals living up to the highest ethical standards even under conditions of adversity. They exemplify moral nobility, as opposed to the violation of every ethical standard that we witness in so many crises and conflicts today.

Alas, however, it is that omnipresent moral nobility that also lends the painting its air of unrealism, insofar as it is meant to represent the human condition on earth. We can't imagine too many lifeboat crises, much less life on earth more generally, in these glowing terms. The painting gives no hint of the common failures to live up to even the most basic ethical standards in many a crisis; nor does it give an inkling about the new problems that population growth will pose for the world of the future. So we can't tell how well their devotion to ethics and to cooperation will hold up under the strains imposed by a population going from nearly 6 billion today to 8, 10, possibly even 12 billion in the coming decades.

The raft is crowded; but the painting represents one moment of time, one period of crowding that the persons on board could not in fact live with for long. Their hope is of rescue onto another ship, then of being able to go ashore, where such crowding will no longer be a problem. But when we consider the analogy between the life raft and the fragile craft of earth that it is meant to represent, we must also think of the growth in numbers of persons who are to live out their lives here on earth, and who must share the existing resources, with no prospect of being rescued onto larger ships, much less of being given more spacious living quarters elsewhere.

Even as some entertain a hopeful view of the future, moreover, others have long taken a far more dismal view of the prospects for humanity: a view that predicts ethical collapse into strife and savagery, driven by ethnic, religious, and other antagonisms, by moral failures deeply rooted in human nature, and by sheer relentless escalation in the numbers of human beings on earth—a collapse that will be especially devastating in the poorest societies competing for increasingly scarce resources. To them, the original painting by Théodore Géricault on which the contemporary one was modeled is more likely to bring home a realistic perception of what befalls human beings under stress. Géricault's *The Raft of the Medusa*, which hangs in the Louvre Museum in Paris, offers a different perspective on what happens to human beings under stress when their survival is threatened.

The painting was based on a great public scandal in France, shortly after the fall of Napoleon.[8] In 1816, a frigate that was part of an expedition bound for Senegal ran aground in calm weather near Cape Barras, out of what was seen as sheer ineptitude. As the weather grew stormier, it became clear that the frigate would be lost. Since the

existing lifeboats could not carry all 365 persons on board, the decision was made to build a raft for all the rest, that would be pulled by
ropes attached to the lifeboats and towed to shore. But soon after the
boats and the raft were set into the water, those who were in the boats
cut the ropes meant to pull along the life raft, and set off on their own.
About 170 persons were thus abandoned on the raft, with no way of
moving toward the shore. Within a few days, first in the storm, then in
glaring sun, they fell to fighting over food and drink, then to killing
one another, and finally, not long thereafter, even to cannibalism.

The moment chosen by the artist, when a ship is sighted on the
horizon, occurs after many persons have already been thrown off the
raft, and when, among the small number remaining, some are dead,
others despairing, and only a few can muster the energy to signal the
ship. This ship, as it turned out, went by on the horizon only to return
to rescue the last survivors after still more days of waiting, despairing,
fighting, and cannibalism. Géricault chose not to portray the worst,
most degrading actions, but rather the human suffering resulting from
them. He conveys no hopeful, noble, cooperative grouping of humans,
but rather every shading from despair to hope, from bestiality to
nobility, from conflict to cooperation. The view of human nature that
infuses the painting reflects the ease with which ordinary moral standards collapse in circumstances of stress and great fear and scarcity.

Géricault could not have known about the population growth
and wars of our century, and it would be wrong to use his painting
to impute views to him about the future. But others have made comparisons between the conditions on board the Medusa and large parts
of the world. Robert Kaplan, in elaborating his thesis of "The Coming
Anarchy," in his book *The Ends of the Earth*, reports on the calamities
and human misery he encountered in the course of his travels, first in
western Africa, then in a number of developing nations.[9] In the first
section of his book, Kaplan claims that "viruses luxuriating in Africa
may constitute a basic risk to humanity," and quotes a letter from a
U.S. diplomat that he carried in his rucksack:

> The greatest threat to our value system comes from Africa. Can
> we continue to believe in universal principles as Africa declines
> to levels better described by Dante than by development econo-
> mists? Our domestic attitudes on race and ethnicity suffer as
> Africa becomes a continent-wide "Wreck of the Medusa."[10]

In his book *Civil Wars*, Hans Magnus Enzenberger, the German social critic, sees the disintegration of all social and humane values spreading like a virus in cities and warring societies the world over.[11] The wars and civil wars of our century will grow to infest the entire globe, he predicts. As the epidemic of violence spreads, he foresees that collective responses will be increasingly futile. The best that can be done, however inadequate, is to undertake whatever limited efforts at rebuilding may be possible at the local level.[12]

Similarly grim prognostications are also espoused by Garrett Hardin, the biologist, in an influential series of writings, beginning in the 1960s and culminating in his 1993 book *Living Within Limits*.[13] Using the lifeboat metaphor as "the basic metaphor within which we must work out our solutions," Hardin argues that humanity faces ecological and social catastrophe unless nations take forceful steps to reverse population growth.[14] It was Hardin who coined the phrase "lifeboat ethics" to stand for the moral choices, sometimes ruthless in the extreme, that he sees as necessary to avoid collective disaster. Metaphorically, he suggests, "each rich nation can be seen as a lifeboat full of comparatively rich people. In the ocean outside swim the poor of the world, who would like to get in, or at least to share some of the wealth. What should the lifeboat passengers do?"[15] Imagine, continues Hardin, that we are fifty people in a lifeboat, with at the most room for ten extra persons, and we see one hundred persons swimming in the water outside. In that case, we have several options:

> we may be tempted to try to live by the Christian ideal of being "our brother's keeper," or by the Marxist ideal of "to each according to his needs." Since the needs of all in the water are the same, and since they can all be seen as "our brothers," we could take them all into our boat, making a total of 150 in a boat designed for sixty. . . . The boat swamps, everyone drowns. Complete justice, complete catastrophe.

Talk of charity or human rights only worsens the condition of the poor, prolonging their suffering until they meet a desperate end, bringing the rich with them into ecological disaster. And to anyone who claims to feel guilty at abandoning others thus, Hardin offers what he calls a simple reply: "Get out and yield your place to others."[16]

Extrapolating from the lifeboat metaphor to humanity at large, Hardin concludes that it is better to allow starvation and disease to take their course in poorer countries and to slam shut the doors of immigration into richer lands, than to cause all of humanity to go under. Impulses to humanitarianism and concern for human rights should be resisted, he urges: they will turn out to be suicidal for the human species in the long run and therefore not even moral in their own right, once the interests of future generations are taken into account.

Since Hardin first advanced his draconian thesis of coercive population control on a vast scale, with rich nations hoarding their resources in the face of Third World starvation, those who dreamed of some safe lifeboat in which nations could insulate themselves from poverty, disease, environmental damage, and war have had a rude awakening. It has become clear that nations cannot easily insulate themselves from miseries abroad, and that it is in their collective self-interest to cooperate in combating threats that cross all boundaries, such as the AIDS epidemic or the thinning of Earth's ozone layer. If societies cannot collaborate thus, no nation will thrive as conflicts over increasingly scarce resources escalate. What is at issue is not altruism alone, therefore, but enlightened self-interest. Both call for developed nations to reduce their own overconsumption and to provide aid and support to developing nations in order to further collective goals.

Morally, moreover, it would be corrupting and brutalizing for citizens of richer societies to adopt Hardin's "lifeboat ethics." To be sure, immigration policies and humanitarian aid missions are now under stricter scrutiny in many of the world's richest nations, including ours. But few suggest dismantling them altogether. It would not only be extremely difficult from a practical point of view to fence out all immigrants and to prevent all provisions of humanitarian aid, the very effort would also tear communities apart. And domestic experience teaches us that there could be no guarantee that the brutal disregard for human dignity that Hardin advocates on the part of rich nations would end up being practiced only toward foreigners.[17]

One who challenges the ethical premises behind such a conception of "lifeboat ethics" is Onora O'Neill, in her 1977 article entitled "Lifeboat Earth."[18] From her perspective, the proper analogy with a lifeboat is one that encompasses all of humanity. The lifeboat contains all of us, with no separate lifeboats for rich societies. And all, she asserts, have at least one basic human right—the right not to be killed. Only in cases of unavoidable self-defense is it justifiable to kill.

When O'Neill extrapolates from the lifeboat with six survivors to that of the entire earth, she arrives at a conclusion with respect to what rich societies do that appears, at first sight, to be the reverse of Hardin's. As citizens of richer societies, we are morally responsible for the deaths of victims of famines that could have been avoided by means of different policies, to the extent that we support commercial and diplomatic policies that contribute to impoverishment and famine. O'Neill goes so far as to claim that we are responsible not merely for letting the victims of such policies die but for killing them: "For as the result of our actions in concert with others, some will die who might have survived had we either acted otherwise or had no causal influence."[19]

The trouble with such limitless imputations of responsibility for killing is that they become diluted and impossible to pinpoint. How is anyone to weigh the various consequences flowing, for instance, from the NAFTA agreement, with sufficient precision to calculate increased or decreased health or mortality statistics, and thus to pinpoint or absolve governments, corporations, or individuals from guilt? And how is one to impute such guilt differently, depending on the degree of endorsement different citizens of a rich nation may have given to a particular policy—not to mention their endorsement of policies with conflicting results on O'Neill's scale?

To diminish such collective responsibility for death and famine, O'Neill suggests that we owe it to potential victims and to ourselves to adopt more urgent policies of resource management and population control. Her emphasis is on postponing and minimizing famine, whereas Hardin's is on allowing it to strike, if need be, among poor peoples and in societies he considers improvident, in order to make life tolerable for those who will come later. But when O'Neill considers actual policies to avoid famines, and in particular population policies, she opens the door to Hardin's own suggestions, by claiming that such policies might range from the mild to the draconian. Among the latter might be cutting back on public health expenditures in high fertility areas "to prevent death rates from declining until birth rates do so" and even universal sterilization—policies that might be wrong in situations other than those she has considered, she adds, as well as politically impossible.

By the time O'Neill sketches out these policy suggestions in her article, she has left the lifeboat metaphor far behind. As with Hardin's analysis, it turns out that her own analysis bears but a tenuous relationship to the metaphor on which she attempts to build her case. But in both cases, the metaphor turns out to be an impediment, not an aid, to reflection about global problems. It invites overhasty conclusions about violations of basic moral prohibitions and injunctions, such as those concerning the provision of emergency care and killing; and it bypasses consideration of much that individuals, societies, and organizations can in fact do to deal with the present extraordinary challenges, apart from merely drifting out of control or adopting draconian policies. The lifeboat metaphor can have considerable evocative force; but this force only adds to the likelihood that misperceptions and faulty arguments will go unchallenged. And a seemingly minute error in calculation when extrapolating from actual lifeboat situations can become multiplied a millionfold, even a billionfold, when applied to the world's population. Yes, we can use the lifeboat analogy to remind ourselves of just how perilous life can be and of what we have in common with others; but to draw specific public policy conclusions from such a strained analogy invites challenges both empirical and moral.

In later works, O'Neill has explored the moral issues of human rights, population policy, and economic development in depth. In so doing, she has expressly rejected the effort to rely on extrapolations from lifeboat cases to global polices.[20] She suggests that such analogizing leaves out of account all that societies can do, and that a number have already done, to achieve a demographic transition to reduced fertility over time; likening the world's population to individuals caught on a lifeboat leaves out of account the possibility of human efforts: "Population growth cannot be predicted by projecting present rates of increase to produce the fantasy of a world weighed down by living, starving humans. . . . The earth is neither a finite pasture nor a lifeboat."[21]

CONCLUSION

We have, then, two works of art with implications for the future, and two more specifically extrapolated visions of lifeboat ethics. Each offers a vivid image of what may befall humanity. But basing policy choices on any one of them presents problems that stem, in part, precisely from the extrapolation itself, when undertaken with no concern for what is analogous and what is different in comparing the situation of human societies to that of persons adrift in a lifeboat. The crisis in a lifeboat takes place in extremely limited space and is of limited duration. Extreme caution must be exercised before comparing humanity to a group of persons thus constrained, who are adrift, moreover, and totally at the mercy of the elements, totally out of touch with society, totally unable to predict what will befall them even within days or hours, totally bereft of the slightest power to affect their environment.

By contrast, thought-experiments that remain within the narrower bounds of lifeboat cases that concern small numbers of persons on board genuine lifeboats are more likely than the vaster imaginings to be of help in examining human conduct *in extremis*. Thus Onora O'Neill offers careful elucidation, in her first article, of different scenarios aboard a lifeboat built for six persons, depending on whether it is well or poorly provisioned with water, food, and other supplies needed for survival. Others have used the lifeboat thought-experiment to consider questions of triage in wartime: who should receive priority, who might have to be abandoned, when time and resources do not permit helping all?

Such debates are important. But, as indicated above, they, too, can go astray. They can evolve into callous comparisons between persons who deserve and do not deserve to be rescued. Such calculations can foster blindness to the needs and hopes and full humanity of those whose lives are weighed in the balance, and thus shortchange a crucial step in moral response. They can focus so strongly on interpersonal comparisons and the differing claims involved that they fail to focus on the fullest, deepest perception—perception that must precede and inform moral debates if they are to do full justice to the human beings whose lives are at stake.

Metaphors, parables, and thought-experiments are indispensable to moral perception and deliberation. But depending on how they are used, they can deepen perception or render it more shallow, and aid in deliberation or short-circuit it. Films such as Hitchcock's and paintings and novels and plays can help ward off such shortchanging and make us see more deeply into all that a metaphor can convey. As Iris Murdoch put it, in *The Fire and the Sun*,

> A portrayal of moral reflection and moral change (degeneration, improvement) is the most important part of any system of ethics. The explanation of our flexibility in such matters as

seeing the worse as the better is more informatively (though of course less systematically) carried out by poets, playwrights, and novelists.[22]

And so I shall close with a quotation from Shakespeare's play *The Tempest*: a play in which individuals fearing for their lives, in storms and fair weather, adrift on the sea and cast up on an island, illuminate for us the fullest range of what human beings are capable of doing to and feeling for one another. It is from Act V, Scene 1, when the spirit Ariel recounts to Prospero, dressed in his magic robes, what has befallen the group, some of whom had earlier set him with his little daughter Miranda to perish, and upon whom he has now worked his magic so as to imprison them together:

Ariel: They cannot budge till your release. The King,
            His brother, and yours, abide all three distracted,
            And the remainder mourning over them,
            Brimful of sorrow and dismay; but chiefly
            Him that you termed, sir, "The good old Lord Gonzalo,"
            His tears run down his beard like winter's drops
            From caves of reeds. Your charm so strongly works 'em
            That if you beheld them, your affections
            Would become tender.
Prospero: Dost think so, spirit?
Ariel: Mine would, sir, were I human.
Prospero: And mine shall.
            Hast thou, which art but air, a touch, a feeling
            Of their afflictions, and shall not myself,
            One of their kind, that relish all as sharply
            Passion as they, be kindlier moved than thou art?

NOTES

1. Revised text of a lecture given at the April 17, 1996, meeting of the Boston University Institute for Philosophy and Religion. I am grateful for comments and suggestions from Derek Bok, Victoria Bok, and Katherine Platt.

2. I have discussed the views of Cicero, Erasmus, Machiavelli, and others on this score in *Common Values* (Columbia, Mo.: University of Missouri Press, 1995), chap. 4.

3. For a tongue-in-cheek presentation of such a case, see Jared Goldstein, "The Mother of All Case Studies," *Hastings Center Report* 26 (January–February 1996): 23–24, with commentary by Arthur L. Caplan, p. 24.

4. Mark Stutzman, painting modeled on Théodore Géricault's *Raft of the Medusa*, cover of *The Futurist* (September–October 1995). Commissioned by the World Future Society for its Eighth General Assembly, July 1996. Reproduced with permission from the World Future Society, 7910 Woodmont Avenue, Suite 450, Bethesda, Maryland 20814.

5. Garrett Hardin's article, "Lifeboat Ethics: The Case Against Helping the Poor," in *World Hunger and Moral Obligation*, ed. William Aiken and Hugh La Follette (Englewood Cliffs, N.J.: Prentice-Hall, 1977), pp. 11–21. See also his "Living on a Lifeboat," *BioScience* 24: 561–68.

6. Onora O'Neill, "Lifeboat Earth," in *World Hunger and Moral Obligation*, ed. Aiken and La Follette, pp. 148–64. See also her *Faces of Hunger* (London: Allen & Unwin, 1986).

7. John Rawls, *A Theory of Justice* (Cambridge, Mass.: Harvard University Press, 1971), pp. 126–27.

8. I draw, for the account of this incident, on Julian Barnes, "Shipwreck," chap. 5 of *A History of the World in 10½ Chapters* (New York: Vintage, 1989). See also Lorenz Eitner, *Géricault: His Life and Work* (Maryknoll, N.Y.: Orbis, 1982).

9. Robert D. Kaplan, *The Ends of the Earth* (New York: Random House, 1996).

10. Ibid., p. 4.

11. Hans Magnus Enzenberger, *Civil Wars* (New York: New Press, 1994), pp. 66–71.

12. For further discussion of Enzenberger's views, see my *Common Values*, chap. 1, from which parts of the above paragraphs are taken.

13. Hardin, works cited in note 5.

14. Hardin, "Living on a Lifeboat," p. 562.

15. Hardin, "Lifeboat Ethics," p. 12.

16. Ibid., p. 13.

17. The two previous paragraphs are taken, in part, from my essay "Population and Ethics Expanding the Moral Space," in *Population Policies Reconsidered*, ed. Gita Sen, Adrienne Gerrmain, and Lincoln Chen (Cambridge, Mass.: Harvard University Press, 1994), pp. 13–26.

18. O'Neill, "Lifeboat Earth."

19. Ibid., p. 161.

20. Onora O'Neill, *Constructions of Reason* (Cambridge: At the University Press, 1989); and *Faces of Hunger*.

21. O'Neill, *Faces of Hunger*, p. 18.

22. Iris Murdoch, *The Fire and the Sun* (Oxford: Clarendon Press, 1977), p. 81.

Author Index

Subject Index

APF